Engagement is Not a Unicorn (It's a Narwhal)

Mind-Changing Theory and Strategies That Will Create Real Engagement

Heather Lyon

ISBN: 978-1-970133-96-7

To my Lyon narwhals

Howard, Nolan, Lilia, and Oliver.

I am totally absorbed by all of you!

Praise for *Engagement is Not a Unicorn*

"This book defines what engagement in classrooms could be. It provides a clear understanding for why engaging and disengaging behaviors exist and offers actionable strategies and resources for teachers to bring students to the highest level of engagement. Any teacher, administrator, or parent would benefit from the insight and ideas this book provides." ~ *Nilam Yagielski, New York State Master Teacher, Professor, and Co-Founder of Access Math*

"Engagement, engagement, engagement…we hear that word all the time, but what does it really mean? How do I really make an impact on students in my district, in my school, or in my classroom? Not only will you learn practical strategies that will have an immediate impact on your educational world, but Dr. Heather Lyon will also take you on a personal journey to a new understanding around what 'real' engagement is. You will be a more engaged educator and a more engaged person as a result of reading *Engagement is Not a Unicorn, (It's a Narwhal)*." ~ *Cathy Gruber, Teacher and Executive Coach*

"Heather has done what few authors in the education space have done…she has taken a theoretical concept like learner engagement and has made it relevant and practical to teachers and leaders at all levels. Her humor, storytelling ability, and research-based frameworks make this a fun and relevant book. It belongs in the hands of every teacher, leader, parent, or anyone looking to move a team from disengaged to completely absorbed in the mission, vision, values, and goals of the group." ~ *Gabrielle Hewitt, Teacher and Education Consultant*

"As an educator and administrator, true engagement has always been elusive, scarce, and difficult to describe. Heather Lyon has provided both a language and a framework to have conversations about the very essence of teaching and learning. *Engagement is Not a Unicorn (It's a Narwhal)* is a must-read for every educator and anyone who does professional development." ~ *Melissa Laun, Teacher and Supervisor of Instructional Programs*

"*Engagement is Not a Unicorn (It's a Narwhal)* is a thoughtful perspective on the different levels of engagement. It seeks to identify methods that teachers can utilize to create engagement in their classroom, but also highlights that engagement can come in many forms. *Engagement is Not a Unicorn (It's a Narwhal)* recognizes the differences between the various levels of engagement that can be demonstrated by students in a classroom. It was an excellent look into the rationale as to how and why students are willing to learn." ~ *Daniel Wodarczak, Teacher, Technology Integrator, and Staff Developer*

About the Author

Heather Lyon is a former English teacher and has a Ph.D. in Educational Administration and an Ed.M. in Reading from the University at Buffalo. She is an Assistant Superintendent of Curriculum, Instruction, and Technology for Lewiston-Porter Central School District in Western New York. Heather has been a staff developer and held various administrative titles, but the professional title she likes best is learner. She is also a proud wife and mother who (struggles with) but values the importance of work/life balance—which is so critical in a profession like ours. Heather lives with her husband and three children, who make her smile and teach her the importance of kindness, respect, and patience.

Please follow Heather on Twitter @LyonsLetters and visit her website www.LyonsLetters.com.

Acknowledgments

It feels monumental to think about who would deserve my gratitude for their support and contributions related to this book because the list is long and I am afraid I will forget someone.

The ideas that grew in this book began when I was working at Enterprise with colleagues who turned into friends. That's people like you (alphabetically) Marisa Adams, Megan Battista, David Cantaffa, Jeannie Cassidy, Dana D'Angelo, Patricia Pitts, Caity Srour, Kelly Staley, and Andy Starr. Though we became scattered to the wind, I am so glad to have had the time we had together!

I was compelled to finally put pen to paper while working in the Kenmore-Town of Tonawanda Union Free School District. I can't say enough about how encouraged I was working there. Specifically, I want to thank the 2016 cohort of Instructional and Technology Support Specialists, A.K.A, "The Coaches" who were my first audience of The Engagement Framework — (alphabetically) Judy Anthony, Claire Bellia, Mary Bieger, Mary Lynn Bieron, Lisa Davidson, Kari Fiutak, Phil Jarosz, Kathy Rieser, and Sandy Terrance. Their reception made me feel like I was really on to something. Your ability to help teachers and students boost their engagement is awe-inspiring. Big thanks to other friends whom I met there like (alphabetically) Steve Bovino, John Brucato, Lisa Cross, Mike Huff, Dave King, Pat Kosis, Michael Lewis, Michael Muscarella, and Robin Zymroz, who made my time in KT one that I will always look back on as one of best chapters in my career.

Catherine M. Huber, whom I also met while in KT, is someone who deserves her own line. Here's the "Breaking News…" Who do I think about when I think about someone who is wise, funny, and inspirational? YOU!

I don't know how my path came to cross Paul Casseri's again, but I am so grateful it did. I am honored by his respect for my work and me. The same is true for the Lewiston-Porter Central School District Board of Education, community, faculty, staff, and administration. You welcomed me with open arms and embraced me with open hearts.

Thank you to my review team (alphabetically) of Jennifer Borgioli Binis, Martine Brown, Cathy Gruber, Gabrielle Hewitt, Melissa Laun, Diana Maskell, Angela Stockman, Daniel Wodarczak, and Nilam Yagielski who were unbelievably supportive while also pushing my thinking to make this book the best it could be. In truth, the words "thank you" are too small to express my gratitude. This book would not be what it is without your encouragement and feedback.

I am so grateful (not greatful) to you, Judy Arzt, for your eyes and edits!

Gail Farrell, you pushed my thinking and because of you, I realized that I could identify more than three different manifestations of non-compliance and absorption. Thank you for that. The book is better because of you.

Thanks to Ashley Best. You made my fantasy of being a potter real again. How I gained a friend out of the deal is beyond me, but I am so lucky to have an adult friend like you!

This book would not be in your hands without Sarah Thomas—author, Founder, and CEO of EduMatch. Thanks to you and the full EduMatch team who have made my life-long dream of publishing a book come true.

Everyone deserves to have a connection like I have with Melissa Laun. You are my person and your friendship is priceless. I am so fortunate to have someone in my life who both gets me and inspires me. Thank you for driving through life by my side—literally and figuratively.

To my parents, grandparents, siblings (XOXO), and in-laws for your belief that I can do this. You believed in me even when I had doubts. I stand on the shoulders of giants and in the arms of love.

I'm so thankful to my children, Nolan, Lilia, and Oliver, for rooting me on and being muses for my thinking. I promise to always be in your corner doing the same for you!

Finally, there is not a word for the unconditional love and gratitude I feel for my husband, Howard. You are my biggest fan. To say that I couldn't have done this without your support is not an exaggeration. Howard, I hope you see that the "brushstrokes in the corner" are yours. I love you.

Contents

Introduction

Narwhals Are Real

Unicorns are ubiquitous. They are also completely mythical. They never have and never will exist. Nevertheless, when I say the word unicorn, you can envision a beautiful, white horse with flowing locks of (maybe rainbow) hair bestowed with a gleaming horn in the center of the majestic forehead.

Yet, when I say the word narwhal, many people do not know what I'm talking about, and some who do don't think that they're real. Narwhals, for those who don't know, are a horned whale that looks like a dolphin and a unicorn had a baby (there is one pictured on the back cover of this book). Narwhals have recently increased in popularity. If you have ever seen the Will Farrell movie, *Elf*, it's the animal that Buddy talks to when he sets off to find his dad. In this movie, some people may find the narwhal is just as fantastical as a man who thinks he's an elf. Nevertheless, unlike unicorns, narwhals are real animals that exist, but are uncommon and unusual.

There was a point in time when I was writing this book that I began to wonder if the highest form of engagement (what I call absorption) was an educational unicorn. Something everyone knew about but didn't actually exist in real life. In other words, I wondered if absorption in schools was mythical—a beautiful idea that anyone would desire to see in real life, but imaginary. That's not to say that absorption doesn't happen outside of school because I know it does. However, when I ask people to think of a time when they were absorbed in school, more often than not, they struggle to come up with an answer. So, if most people cannot think of a time when they were absorbed in school, then it might be possible that absorption in school is impossible. Hence, absorption in school is education's form of a unicorn.

Then, I realized that absorption is not a unicorn, it's a narwhal. Engagement in school at the highest level is possible, but it is unfortunately uncommon and unusual. It does exist, but many people have never seen it, and some don't even believe it's possible because they can't even imagine it. Absorption in school would look like student-driven environments where students initiate the learning and are

i

intrinsically **compelled** to learn. They want to keep at it after the bell rings. After the lesson is over. After the unit is done. Even if they weren't getting graded. It's out there, but it's a narwhal. This book aims to shine light on the mysterious educational narwhal by explaining what engagement is and is not in order to spawn as many narwhals in your school as possible!

Speaking the Same Language

Engagement has become a buzzword in the education profession. We see this term in teacher evaluation tools like the Danielson Framework, where in Domain 3, "Instruction," there is a component called "Engaging Students in Learning." This, for many, is considered a "power component," or a component that is one of the most important of all of the 22 components in the Framework. This prioritization is due to modern thinking about learning, which recognizes that people who learn the most are those who are most invested in their own learning.

The challenge is that it is not easy to design lessons about things that students *have to learn* in ways that students *want to learn*. Indeed, there seems to be a paradox that suggests that if students have to learn X, they won't want to learn it AND what they want to learn about is Y. In other words, the things students want to learn about are not a part of the curriculum and so what is a teacher to do? This is an inverse relationship. As a result, with the ever-growing focus on common and rigorous standards, teachers have reduced the "frills" from their lessons, like projects and choice, in favor of teacher-directed, whole-group instruction. Why bother getting to know your students' interests, learning styles, or preferences if you are handcuffed to curriculum? It's not like you can be responsive or inclusive to this knowledge of your students' differences or needs anyway, right? Ironically, this establishes a mindset that is the exact opposite of what research says are best-practices in terms of having students learn because they want to know more. Thus, we know we're supposed to have engaging lessons, but there is not a shared understanding of what this means.

Filling a Need

Several years ago when I was a Director of Elementary Education, I was responsible for working with the Office of Instruction to design professional development for the principals. We knew we wanted to offer a book study, and at least one of the books should be focused on engagement because, as a district, we identified engagement as a focus for the year. With the theme identified, the challenge became which books? The members of the Office of Instruction did some research, bought some books, and then started reading in a quest to identify which books would be offered to the principals as a choice.

I anticipated that the hard part was going to be narrowing down the books because there would be so many great options to choose from. I was wrong. Though many great books addressed student engagement strategies, they did not define what engagement actually is. This is the problem. How can there be so many books about and expectations around engagement when there does not seem to be a common understanding of what engagement is? A lack of a common understanding leads to conflicts between teachers as practitioners and principals as evaluators. This also leads to conflicts between principals when Principal A says, "The students in this class were engaged," but Principal B says, "I don't think those students were engaged."

This reminds me of the movie *The Princess Bride,* where the character Vizzini kidnaps the princess and the Man in Black pursues them. No matter where they go, the Man in Black isn't far behind. Vizzini repeatedly proclaims that the success of the Man in Black is "inconceivable." After several times of making this proclamation, Vizzini's colleague, Inigo, turns to Vizzini and says, "You keep using that word. I do not think it means what you think it means." I feel like this is what we're doing with the word "engagement" in our profession. We use it, but I do not think it means what you think it means.

This book is designed to create a common understanding of what engagement looks and sounds like so that we can jointly design and gauge instruction against this understanding. For many, this will be a welcomed new starting point. For others, this will be confrontational in the truest definition of the word because it will challenge the way you have always thought about engagement. No matter which one of these descriptions feels more you right now, I challenge you to be open. Take what you think you know and either add to, revise, or unlearn your previous thinking.

The perspective you take on my Engagement Framework is dependent both on what your work is and who you work with. Put differently, if you're a teacher reading this, you might be thinking primarily about students. If you're an instructional leader reading this, you might be thinking simultaneously about teachers and students. Parents might be thinking about their children. The point here is that my goal is to demonstrate that this Framework is not limited to a classroom and extends to all people at all times in all situations.

Theory and Practice

I have been interested in the intersection of knowing and doing for years. In fact, my dissertation, *A Case Study of the Impact of a University-Based Preparation Program on the Reported Thinking and/or Practices of PreK-12 Principals*, explored how theory and practice come together. I wanted to know if the study of educational leadership made a difference in the work of educational administrators. I was especially interested in this because, at the time, I was a teacher-turned-staff-developer, and I felt like getting my administrative certification was an expensive hoop I had to jump through. I also wondered why good teachers could not be promoted to administrative positions without the costly piece of paper.

What I realized through my research was that the best practitioners are those whose actions are informed by research. On one hand, this finding was disappointing because when I started, I wanted to say that training for leadership was unnecessary. On the other hand, learning that the training for leadership improved the practice of leadership was reassuring—it meant that the time and money I spent getting the "piece of paper" was not a hoop, it was a launching pad.

What does this have to do with The Engagement Framework? Everything. Assuming that you have chosen on your own to read this book, you are doing so with a desire to deepen your knowledge of engagement. Even if you have been assigned this book, there is still the possibility that you will walk away with knowledge after reading that you did not consider before you started. While I am honored that you would use my work to do this, *reading this book is just beginning*. It will always remain theoretical if you do not put it into practice.

It reminds me of the difference between planning for a wedding versus planning for a marriage. Thousands of dollars and hundreds of hours are spent planning for a wedding to make sure that it is perfect. Yet, how much money and time do we spend planning for the marriage? In many cases, not much (if any) despite the fact that the wedding is the least important part of a marriage.

This book, I hope, will be just the beginning for you. There will be ideas presented in *Engagement is Not a Unicorn (It's a Narwhal)* that will validate beliefs you already have but may not have been able to articulate. There will also be ideas that will be new to you and will push your thinking. The question is, what will you do with these ideas? Hopefully, reading will be the first of many actions you will take in this journey towards improved understanding of engagement.

Choose Your Own Adventure

This book begins with Section I, which has three chapters. The first chapter explains The Engagement Framework, chapter two explains why The Engagement Framework matters, and chapter three invites the reader to take action. The remaining chapters of the book are categorized into sections that answer three important questions:

1. What
2. So What
3. Now What

Section II begins with the question, "What" and addresses the theory and definition of the four engagement levels. In other words, it creates a common answer to the question, "what does this mean?" It's important to create a common understanding regarding what engagement is because this understanding builds the foundation for Section III ("So What").

Section III, "So What," explains why engagement matters by answering the question, "so why is this important anyway?" In other words, as long as someone is at least compliant, then s/he will be doing what was assigned. Thus, why does it matter if someone is compliant or interested—both are doing what they were told? In "So What," I will explain that it does matter and why.

Section IV, "Now What," provides the reader with ideas, suggestions, strategies, and additional resources to move from one engagement level to the next by answering the question of "how do I take this into my own practice?" Though resources abound regarding how to create engagement, this section provides ideas on how to bridge people from low levels of engagement to higher levels.

Finally, Section V, the last section of *Engagement is Not a Unicorn (It's a Narwhal)*, summarizes the book and invites you, the reader, to reflect on your learning, your actions to date, and your next steps to continue to put into action what you have read.

As you know, *Engagement is Not a Unicorn (It's a Narwhal)* is non-fiction, meaning you do not have to read it from start to finish. Though I have organized it into specific sections, it is possible to read through it according to the points on the Engagement Continuum. In this way, you can choose to read the chapters on non-compliance as a cluster (chapters 4, 8, and 12) and then move on to compliance (chapters 5, 9, and 13), etc. You might choose to skip Sections II (What) and III (So What) and just read Section IV (Now What) because you're curious about applications more than you're curious about the background information regarding engagement. The point is that this book is designed for choice because I know that choice leads to greater engagement.

With this in mind, each chapter in the book begins with a handful of questions to identify your thinking before you read. I encourage you to take a couple of moments before starting the chapter to write down your reflections on your beliefs prior to reading. This provides you with a baseline regarding your thinking. You may want to revisit these questions after you finish each chapter to see what changes, if any, have occurred based on what you read. At the end of each chapter is a brief chapter summary and reflection questions based on the chapter. These questions are easily answered independently, but would also be helpful if you read this with others.

As a former staff developer and a current administrator, I have seen and read a great deal about the challenges of measuring the impact of professional development (PD). If attending PD was enough, then all we would have to do was go to a session, and our work would magically change. Clearly, that doesn't happen. In my experience, even when I go to a great PD session, I struggle to apply what I have learned right away. Then, as time passes, the daily routines overshadow the intention to change. Though the message of the PD was important and powerful, the impact was minor.

Reading a book is also PD, and though your intent right now is to read this to make changes, it will likely be difficult to change your habits. To safeguard against this, I challenge you to do the following:

- **THREE**: Before you read, identify at least three people with whom you will share the ideas you're having as a result of your reading. It doesn't matter with whom or how you will share your ideas, it just matters that you will share.

- **TWO**: As you're reading, find at least two ideas that change you…it may be because you are surprised or unsure or intrigued. It doesn't matter why you change; you're just noting the change.

- **ONE**: When you're done reading, apply at least one idea. Don't limit yourself to a professional application; it could just as easily be a personal one. The point is that you do more than just read and think about engagement—it's that you take what you've read and thought and do something with it.

Each person reads and digests their reading differently. So, if you haven't already done so, grab a pack of Post-Its, a highlighter, and/or a pen and get ready to make this book truly yours! The margins are big so you can write in them. After all, this book is yours. You own it. More importantly, I want you to own the learning and make it personal.

Finally, I chose to include this call to action here, at the introduction, so that you can mindfully read this book with the persistent, even nagging, question, *what am I learning and how will I use it?* While I will celebrate if this book impacts your thinking, for me, this book is the most meaningful if your actions change.

Section I: The Engagement Framework

The next three chapters will address the What, So What, and Now What regarding The Engagement Framework. These chapters set the stage for the rest of the book because this Framework is the foundation on which the rest of the book builds. By the end of Section I, you will understand how The Engagement Continuum and Matrix work together to create The Engagement Framework. The ultimate goal of Section I is to try out in your own school/district what you've read about here.

Chapter 1

The Engagement Framework: *What*

"Don't be mad that I don't care anymore.
Be mad that I once did and you were too blind to see it."
~ Anonymous

Recognizing Your Thinking Before You Read...

- How do you define engagement? Disengagement?

  _____

  _____

  _____

- Is there a difference between being on-task and being engaged?

  _____

  _____

  _____

- What factors influence whether or not someone is engaged?

  _____

  _____

  _____

The Engagement Continuum

Though odd, if I'm being honest, the first time I really started thinking about engagement was in a faculty bathroom at a school I visited. Hanging on to the wall was a poster that outlined Phillip Schlechty's five "Levels of Engagement" (see Figure 1.1). While I certainly wasn't there expecting to learn about engagement—let alone to begin a quest to expand my understanding of engagement that I would ultimately share in this book—that is what happened.

Though Schlechty saw five levels of engagement, there appeared to me to be three major categories: (1) non-compliance, (2) compliance, and finally (3) engagement. Within each of the five levels, Schlechty identifies the parallel threads of attention and commitment with the highest level as "engagement" characterized by high attention and high commitment. Though I cannot disagree with this assessment, the more I thought about his work, the more I felt that something was missing.

Finally, I came to see engagement with four distinct but related markers, which I placed into what I call the Engagement Continuum shown in Figure 1.2. The Engagement Continuum ranges from highly disengaged on the far left to highly engaged on the far right. Since each of these markers is explained in detail in subsequent chapters, I will not dive into each deeply here. The important piece to note for this section is that this continuum is the foundation on which the rest of this book is built.

Figure 1.1 Schlechty's Levels of Engagement[1]

LEVELS OF ENGAGEMENT

According to Phillip Schlechty, there are five ways that students respond or adapt to school-related tasks and activties.

ENGAGEMENT　HIGH ATTENTION – HIGH COMMITMENT

The student associates the task with a result or product that has meaning and value for the student. The student will persist in the face of difficulty and will learn at high and profound levels.

STRATEGIC COMPLIANCE　HIGH ATTENTION – LOW COMMITMENT

The task has little inherent or direct value to the student, but the student associates it with outcomes or results that do have value to the student (such as grades). Student will abandon work if extrinsic goals are not realized and will not retain what is learned.

RITUAL COMPLIANCE　LOW ATTENTION – LOW COMMITMENT

The student is willing to expend whatever effort is needed to avoid negative consequences. The emphasis is on meeting the minimum requirements. The student will learn at low and superficial levels.

RETREATISM　NO ATTENTION – NO COMMITMENT

The student is disengaged from the task and does not attempt to comply with its demands, but does not try to disrupt the work or substitute other activities for it. The student does not participate and learns little or nothing from the task.

REBELLION　DIVERTED ATTENTION – NO COMMITMENT

The student refuses to do the work, acts in ways to disrupt others, or substitutes tasks and activities to which he or she is committed. Student develops poor work sometimes negative attitudes towards formal education and intellectual tasks.

The Highy Enagaged Classroom	The Well Managed Classroom	The Pathological Classroom

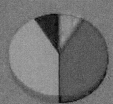

Figure 1.2: The Engagement Continuum

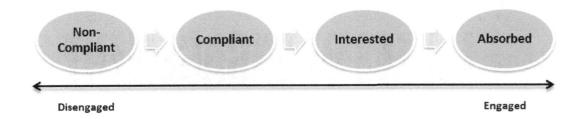

While the terms "non-compliant" and "compliant" are likely self-evident, for the sake of explanation, below are brief definitions for the purposes of The Engagement Continuum.

- **Non-Compliant:** Actively or passively refusing to do what was expected; insubordinate.

- **Compliant**: Doing the minimum of what was expected but only because there is a consequence (positive or negative) if it wasn't completed.

- **Interested**: Going beyond the minimum expectations because the task is stimulating and has temporary value. Generally speaking, the task is enjoyable but not something that would be done unless it was required, and there was a consequence for (not) doing it.

- **Absorbed**: Getting so involved in a challenging task that the person doing it intrinsically wants to continue even s/he doesn't have to.

The Engagement Matrix

I wasn't done thinking about this continuum, which is a linear progression. This additional thinking was likely influenced by several books that I've read, including *Leadership and the One Minute Manager: Increasing Effectiveness Through Situational Leadership II,* where Blanchard, Zigarmi, and Zigarmi create a matrix that contrasts leadership behaviors against the behaviors of the leader's direct reports. This is similar to Max Langsberg's matrix in *The Tao of Coaching* that contrasts skill versus will. Thus, upon continued contemplation, I came to see The Engagement Continuum as bending with both of the poles coming to the middle so that The Engagement

Continuum morphs into the 2x2 Engagement Matrix shown in Figure 1.3. The Engagement Matrix shows that there are two common features between each of the markers on The Engagement Continuum. These features are (1) the relationship you have with the external person and/or consequence[i] and (2) the relationship you have with the task you are doing. The Engagement Continuum shows the linear progression of engagement, and The Engagement Matrix shows the variables that impact the levels of engagement. Ultimately, I encapsulate The Engagement Continuum and The Engagement Matrix under the comprehensive umbrella I refer to as The Engagement Framework.

Figure 1.3: The Engagement Matrix

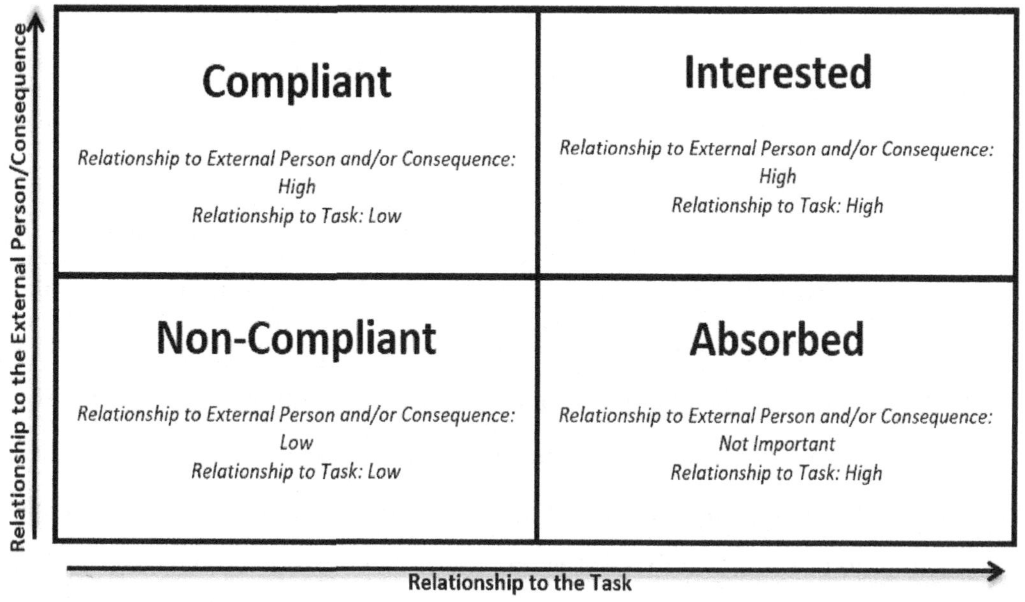

Relationship to the Task

So that you understand how this matrix works, I want to explain the differences between the four quadrants. The left side of The Engagement Matrix shows that the quadrants of Non-Compliant and Compliant share the commonality of having a low

---

[i] With regard to the Engagement Matrix, the term "consequence" is a neutral term that can be seen as either positive (like a reward) or negative (like a penalty).

relationship to the task. The difference between the two quadrants is that even though both types of people *would not* want to do the task they are being asked to do, those who are compliant either care about the person who is assigning the task enough to do the work or they care about the consequence (e.g., grade, money, lack of negative attention, etc.) to do it. Non-compliant people don't care about the person who has assigned the task or are willing to "pay the price," so they opt-out.

The right side of The Matrix shows that the quadrants of Interested and Absorbed share the commonality of having a high relationship to the task. The difference between the two quadrants is that even though both types of people *would* want to do the task they are being asked to do, those who are absorbed are doing so because they are intrinsically motivated to do what was asked; they do not need to be asked to do the work—they would need to be asked to *stop* doing the work. Interested people will do the work when asked, but when it's over, it's over—even though they did enjoy and maybe even found temporary value in what they were doing.

Relationship to the Person Assigning the Task or to the Consequence for Completing the Task

The bottom of The Engagement Matrix shows that the quadrants of Non-Compliant and Absorbed share the commonality of having a low or irrelevant relationship to the person assigning the task or to the consequence for doing the task. The difference between the two quadrants is that even though both types of people *are not* concerned about the external relationship to the person or consequence, those who are absorbed care deeply about the task and are doing it because they are intrinsically motivated to do it. In fact, to them, it is not a task they *have* to do, it's something they *get* to do. Non-compliant people are intrinsically motivated **not** to do what is assigned. What's more, because they do not care about the person who is asking them to do the task, nor do they care about consequences in terms of "payment," they will not do what is assigned.

The top of The Engagement Matrix shows that the quadrants of Compliant and Interested share the commonality of having a high relationship to the person assigning the task or to the consequence of doing the task. The difference between the two quadrants is that even though both types of people *are concerned* about the external relationship to the person or consequence, those who are merely compliant are doing it to get it done since they don't really want to do the assignment. They are *willing* to do it because of their concern for the person assigning the task and/or the consequence associated with (not) completing the task. The mirrored quadrant of Interested is characterized by people who are doing the assignment because it holds their attention in the moment *and* they have a concern for the person assigning the task or the consequence associated with (not) completing the task.

Chapter Summary

This chapter provided the "what" of The Engagement Framework, which serves as the foundation on which the remainder of the Section, and ultimately the book, rests. This Framework was inspired by a poster that outlined the work of Phillip Schlechty.

- There are four markers on the Engagement Continuum. From left to right, these are: (1) Non-Compliance, (2) Compliance, (3) Interested, and (4) Absorbed.

- When the poles are bent towards the middle, The Engagement Continuum becomes The Engagement Matrix.

- The horizontal rows in The Engagement Matrix demonstrate a person's relationship with the task that is assigned; the left side has a low relationship with the assigned task, and the right side has a high relationship.

- The vertical columns in The Engagement Matrix demonstrate a person's relationship with the person assigning the task or the consequence for (not) completing the task. The bottom row has a low or irrelevant relationship with the person or consequence, and the top row has a high relationship.

- The Engagement Framework is the umbrella term for The Engagement Continuum and The Engagement Matrix.

Reflection Questions

1. When in your life have you been non-compliant or compliant? What was your relationship like with the person who assigned the task? If the relationship with the person assigning the task didn't matter, did you care about the consequences (grade, money, etc.) for not doing it?

    _____

    _____

    _____

2. When in your life have you been interested or absorbed? What about the task interested you for that moment but didn't spur you to want to do more after you were done? Why are you so compelled to continue working on those things that you're absorbed with even when they're hard?

    _____

    _____

    _____

3. What questions do you have about each of these markers that you want to learn more about as you continue reading?

    _____

    _____

    _____

4. Are there any areas that you do not agree with in this chapter?

    _____

    _____

    _____

Persistent Questions

1. What have you done so far regarding the three challenges from the Introduction?

   a. **Three:** Find at least three people with whom to share your learning.

   b. **Two:** Find at least two ideas that change you.

   c. **One:** Apply at least one idea from your reading.

   _____

   _____

   _____

2. What have you learned so far, and how will you use it?

   _____

   _____

   _____

Chapter 2

The Engagement Framework: *So What*

"I want, by understanding myself, to understand others."
~Katherine Mansfield

Recognizing Your Thinking Before You Read...

- Do you think it's possible to bypass one level on The Engagement Continuum to get to a higher or lower level of engagement?

_____

_____

_____

- What are the differences between extrinsic and intrinsic motivation?

_____

_____

_____

- When, if ever, is extrinsic motivation an acceptable form of incentive?

_____

_____

_____

Why You Need a 1x4 and a 2x2

The Engagement Matrix intentionally has four distinct quadrants marked by four distinct manifestations of engagement: (1) Non-Compliant, (2) Compliant, (3) Interested, and (4) Absorbed. Let me take a moment to explain why The Engagement Framework has both a continuum and a matrix. With The Engagement Continuum, as people increase their level of engagement, they move to the right. Conversely, if their engagement decreases, they move to the left. While this representation shows movement, it fails to identify what conditions are linked with the progression or regression.

Contrast this with the four-quadrant matrix. Since we know that The Engagement Matrix compares the relationship with the task along the X-Axis (horizontal) and the relationship with the person or consequence along the Y-Axis (vertical), if we change either of the conditions, we will see movement on the matrix. In Figure 2.1, Non-Compliant is identified as Quadrant 1 or "Q1." Each quadrant is labeled in relation to Q1 going clockwise.

Figure 2.1: The Engagement Matrix with Labeled Quadrants

Now imagine that someone is in Q1. How would you move that person to Q2? Since this would be a vertical move, it would require a change in the relationship with the person or the consequence. There are many ways to achieve this. Depending on the time, you could focus on the relationship with the person and get to know him or her better. Certainly, building relationships takes time. So, if you didn't have that kind of time, you could focus on changing the consequence. This could be bribery. *If you do this for me, I will do this for you. If you behave in the store today kids, we can get ice cream on the way home.* That would be what Daniel Pink refers to as a "Carrot" in his book *Drive: The Surprising Truth about what Motivates Us.* The opposite of a carrot is a "Stick." Sticks are threats. If you don't do this, you will have this negative consequence.

What if you wanted to move someone along the horizontal X-Axis of The Engagement Matrix? Since this is the axis that refers to the task, to go from left to right requires a change in feelings towards the task. How would you get people to change their feelings about the task? You have to show them that this is something that they would like or love to do. If you can't accomplish that, then you would have to consider changing the task so that they are still able to accomplish the learning objective in a manner that allows choice and voice. Therefore, while it is important to see the linear progression of The Engagement Continuum, it is critical to understand the relationship between the levels of engagement that The Engagement Matrix provides. Again, the overarching term I use to encompass both the continuum and the matrix is The Engagement Framework.

Side by Side Comparisons

In Figure 2.2, you'll see the different responses that someone at each level in The Engagement Framework would have in relation to the task, person, or consequence. The best way to tap into each of these is to think about situations in which you would qualify under each of these headings. Sometimes this is difficult because if you're wearing your "employee hat," you may think, *I am always at least compliant at work. I would never be non-compliant. I wasn't raised that way.* If that sounds like you, then don't think about work, think about other aspects of your life like house chores or hobbies (although I would argue that there are things that even the most dutiful soldier wouldn't do if it was incompatible with someone's morals, for example).

Figure 2.2: Simplified Responses to the Task, Person, or Consequence at each Level of The Engagement Framework.

	Response to the Task	Response to the Person	Response to the Payment
Non-Compliant	I hate this	Not for you	Not for all the money in the world
Compliant	I tolerate this	For you	Only if you paid me
Interested	I like this	For us	I could do this for pay
Absorbed	I love this	For me	I would pay to do this

I find that the best examples to consider are those that are not related to school.

- If someone went on a show like *Survivor, Naked and Afraid,* or *Fear Factor* and refused to eat a wriggling, plump insect even for a million dollars, that person would be non-compliant.

- If someone didn't want to be on the show but completed the application on a dare, that person would be compliant.

- If someone watched the show if it's on but didn't care if an episode was missed, that person would be interested.

- If someone watched that same show and went to the website to sign-up to be a contestant thinking, "I would TOTALLY do THAT! I wish that were me!" and then started training for it, that would be absorbed.

Consider this example from my life. My daughter can be described as "interested" in playing the piano. She has lessons every Monday that she really looks forward to, but she does not like to practice in between the lessons. She does not get lost in time and space when she plays the piano even though she is the one who wanted to play, and even though I tell her that she can quit if she wants to. She likes playing the piano more than she does not like it, but she definitely does not love to play the piano. In fact, what she really loves is the relationship she has with her piano teacher. If she had a different teacher she didn't like, she might have quit piano a long time ago. Once again, the point here is that we all experience time in each of the quadrants on the Framework, and there are distinct features that characterize one quadrant from another.

You Can't Get There from Here

When I was younger, I used to travel a lot with my parents. When you travel, people often ask you, "Where are you from?" What you need to know is that I grew up in a very, very small town with one stoplight and fewer than 1,000 people. Really. So, when my parents told the kind inquisitors the name of the town where we lived, their response was usually "Where is that?" My parents answered this follow-up question with, "You can't get there from here." Obviously, this is a facetious answer because clearly, you could get there from here, but it wasn't easy. This answer rings true with engagement too. Going from disengagement to engagement is not easy. Depending on where you start, it can be like trying to drive to my hometown without a map in whiteout conditions.

If you are working with people who are disengaged and it is manifesting as non-compliance, you feel like celebrating when they become compliant. Going from non-compliance to compliance can feel so transformational that it is easy to lose sight of the fact that compliance is not engagement. This is not meant to take anything away from the growth—it is simply to say that there is a difference between growth and the final goal, and we should not stop our pursuit of engagement with compliance.

As well, we need to be mindful that one cannot go from zero to sixty without passing through two through fifty-nine. That is just a nice way of saying that there are four distinct points along The Engagement Continuum and we generally pass through each as we travel along the way; it is rare that anyone would switch from non-compliant to even interested, so we should not expect for such a dramatic shift. Instead, we must be vigilant for signs of growth and committed to actively creating opportunities that foster change.

Isn't This Just Intrinsic vs. Extrinsic Motivation?

So at this point, there are going to be some people who are thinking, "It seems like the difference between people who are engaged and those who aren't has to do with whether or not they are intrinsically or extrinsically motivated. Why didn't you just say it like that?"

There is some truth to this observation. When I say "relationship to the task," what I'm really saying is that there is an intrinsic desire to do what you're doing. There is also truth to the observation that when I say "relationship to the person assigning or the consequence for (not) doing the task," what I'm really saying is that there is an intrinsic motivation that does not require a relationship with the person assigning the task or the consequence for (not) doing the task. Put differently, you could say that there is an extrinsic incentive to do the task and to please the person or get the consequence. All of this is true.

However, The Engagement Framework is more than just about intrinsic or extrinsic motivation. Indeed, it is about the source of the motivation. Some people are motivated by a relationship, others are motivated by a reward. Still, others are motivated by a punitive consequence. Depending on the source of the motivation, the location on The Engagement Continuum will be different.

This is critical knowledge for both the person who is assigning the task, as well as the person to whom the task is assigned. After all, if I, as the assigner, notice that there is someone who is being non-compliant with the request, I can probe whether or not we have a strong relationship. If we do, I can assume that this person is **not** opting-out because of a lack of caring about me, so I can move on to asking if there is a problem with the task itself. If the issue is not with the task, then it must be the compensation for the task. In other words, there are distinct reasons that one would be non-compliant, and if I am interacting with someone who is at this point on The Engagement Continuum, there are specific questions I can ask to diagnose what's going on, so I can address it appropriately.

Imagine for a moment that non-compliance simply means that someone is not intrinsically motivated. If that's the case, then the relationship or consequences don't matter since they are not leverage possibilities. This would alleviate the person assigning the task from any accountability in whether or not the person who is assigned the task does the work. After all, if extrinsic motivation is inconsequential, then the person who is doing the assigning is off the hook. "It's not me. I can't help it if the non-compliant person isn't intrinsically motivated." The inaccurate, rhetorical statement that comes when we believe that something is out of our control is, "This person doesn't care, so what am I supposed to do?" The Engagement Framework is the answer to this question. There is much in the way of relationship, consequence, or task that the assigner can do to shift the non-compliant person to a different place on The Engagement Continuum.

> There is much in the way of relationship, consequence, or task that the assigner can do to shift the non-compliant person to a different place on the Engagement Continuum.

There is another problem with saying that engagement is just a function of intrinsic motivation. If engagement is strictly intrinsically motivated, then when someone responds to extrinsic motivation, the person who provided that extrinsic motivation receives no credit for their ability to motivate engagement. If the person assigning the task intentionally designed it so that the person doing it could be interested or absorbed, that means that the person who designed the task had a hand in creating the conditions for engagement to happen. This explains why The Engagement Framework is not just about intrinsic versus extrinsic motivation; it's about the source of that motivation and the impact that has on engagement.

Bringing the Lessons to Life:
A Side-By-Side Comparison

In the field of education, people talk about engagement all of the time. When I go into classrooms and talk with both teachers and administrators, it is common for either and both to say, "The students were really engaged today." The problem is that what they are calling engagement did not match the markers that I have come to look for in relation to The Engagement Framework. This is because engagement is most commonly associated with being on-task (i.e., compliant) and assumes on-task behavior is akin to *interested*.

For example, I worked with a teacher several years ago who struggled. He and I met regularly and talked about his students and his lessons. At the time, I was working in a school that strived to create Project Based Learning (PBL) opportunities for the students, so this was a natural component of our conversations. As a result, this teacher decided to create an environmental conservation project for his students. The goal was to provide students access to the curriculum in an engaging manner.

He eagerly and excitedly invited me to come see the students, and I was just as eager and excited to do so. Unfortunately, what I saw was not engagement. At best, the students were compliant in what they were doing, but most of the students I saw discovered that if they were compliant with the noise level expectations, they could be non-compliant with the learning. This was because there was no real learning expectation; there were activity expectations. The teacher's lesson plan had the following objectives, "Students will work at a voice level of 1 with his/her group members to continue working on how humans positively and negatively affect our environment. Students will continue to use various resources to complete this task. Students will be dispersed to his/her group one group at a time in different areas of the room."

The day I visited, the teacher was in the front of the room, working on the floor with students. He was asking them questions, and what I remember about this was that the questions were about what they were supposed to be doing and required simple recall. At least one of the students who was in the group with the teacher was not following along, but the student was silent, so the teacher wasn't paying attention to him. Another student was off-task but was making noise, so the attention she got was in response to her behaviors and not about the lack of engagement with the learning.

After some time listening in to the teacher's group, I got up to visit the other groups and asked the students what they were learning about. I was told, "We're making posters."

"About what?" I asked.

"Umm. We have to make a playground and put garbage on it," a student told me.

"Really? Why would you do that? Tell me more about it," I probed as I heard another group of students having an off-task conversation that was quiet enough that they would be left alone.

The same student answered me as the others looked at her with hope in their eyes that I wouldn't ask them because they weren't entirely sure. "We're doing it because those are the directions on the board."

"Okay," I said. "What are you learning as a result of making the posters?"

"To make the posters about the playground," the same student offered.

"What do you think?" I asked a different student, trying to get another student to respond.

"I agree with Tasha,"[ii] I was told.

"But why does making a poster about the playground matter?" I questioned.

"Umm. I'm not really sure," the students admitted.

"So is this hard, medium, or easy?" I questioned.

"Easy," all of the students told me, relieved that they could confidently answer one of my questions.

The students in this classroom were performing tasks, but they were not being empowered by their learning. Even more than that, the students did not care about what they were doing or learning for any purpose other than to get a good grade. Though the teacher had the best of intentions, his impact did not match what he hoped to achieve.

Contrast this with Megan Battista, another teacher in the same school who was also struggling. Like the first teacher, Megan and I spoke about the idea of having students learn via PBL. Also like the first teacher, I shared with Megan the idea of student choice and voice in learning. Megan told me about how the upcoming unit was on North America. We talked about some of the important and common pieces of learning that all students must know by the end of the unit. We then talked about how there could be multiple pathways that students could use to demonstrate their learning. Megan left, created a student-centered unit with some common instructions on research, the common learning outcomes, etc., but she also provided students with the opportunity to select how they were going to demonstrate their learning. The students were able to choose which country or region they wanted to study,

---

[ii] This student's name has been changed.

whether or not they would work independently, in pairs, or in a small group, and so forth. As a result, the students' behaviors improved dramatically. More importantly, the students' learning and engagement improved.

Both Megan and the students were excited to come to class. Not only that, but the students also began doing the heavy-lifting of the learning, and the teacher was able to shift from being the proverbial Sage-on-the-Stage to being the Guide-on-the-Side. She conferred with the students to ensure they were addressing the components of the task and to encourage them. At the culmination of the unit, the students proudly shared their work in a learning celebration where they were the experts as other students, teachers, administrators, and families toured and explored their final products. Students ran up and asked me to come visit their area so they could show me what they learned. Even if these students never made it to a place of absorption, they were certainly at least interested in what they did!

The first teacher saw engagement as compliance—if students do what I tell them to do, they are engaged. The second teacher, Megan, recognized that student engagement was more than just doing a task, it was wanting to do a task and feeling empowered through that work.

Chapter Summary

The purpose of this chapter was to help make sense as to how The Engagement Framework works. This is especially true in relation to why there is both The Engagement Continuum (to show the linear progression along a pathway) and The Engagement Matrix (to show the relationships between each quadrant).

- Diagnosing the type of reaction to the (a) task, (b) person, or (c) consequence can diagnose the level of engagement and inform how to respond in order to increase the level of engagement.

- Do not be surprised if most people will likely need to transition through the levels of engagement rather than skipping over one or more to become absorbed.

- While it is important to celebrate growth, there is a difference between growth and the final goal. We should not stop our pursuit of engagement with compliance.

- Intrinsic and extrinsic motivation are associated with engagement. However, there are strategic moves that can be made on the part of the person doing the work and/or the person assigning the work to increase someone's engagement in that work.

Reflection Questions

1. What would you tell someone who hasn't read this chapter to help them understand The Engagement Framework?

   _____

   _____

   _____

2. Do you think there is a meaningful difference between The Engagement Continuum and The Engagement Matrix? If so, what is it? If not, why not?

   _____

   _____

   _____

3. Can you think of an example where someone could jump over a marker on The Engagement Matrix—to go from Q1 to Q3? What, if anything, could cause that leap?

   _____

   _____

   _____

4. In your experiences, is it easier to move people along the horizontal X-Axis or vertically on the Y-Axis? In other words, is it easier to change the extrinsic motivator (person and/or consequence) or to change the task? What are the factors that might influence this?

   _____

   _____

   _____

5. After going into the classroom where the students were learning about environmental conservation, what conversation would you have with the teacher to increase the opportunity to engage students in the learning?

_____

_____

_____

Persistent Questions

1. What have you done so far regarding the three challenges from the Introduction?

   a. **Three:** Find at least three people with whom to share your learning.

   b. **Two:** Find at least two ideas that change you.

   c. **One:** Apply at least one idea from your reading.

_____

_____

_____

2. What have you learned so far, and how will you use it?

_____

_____

_____

Chapter 3

The Engagement Framework: *Now What*

"You don't have to be great to start. But you do have to start to be great."
~Zig Zigler

Recognizing Your Thinking Before You Read...

- How do you define learning?

  _____

  _____

  _____

- What is the difference between theory and practice?

  _____

  _____

  _____

- Is change something that you find easy to do? What helps or gets in the way?

  _____

  _____

  _____

Learning Equals Change

In a presentation I attended in the fall of 2018, I heard Jasmine Kullar, a consultant for Solution Tree, author, and an assistant superintendent for the Cobb County School District in Georgia, ask the audience to define learning. If you're anything like me, you would find this task difficult. After all, learning is a complex series of cognitive functions, I reasoned, and therefore to define what learning is in the moment was tough. However, after that presentation, defining learning will never again be difficult for me.

> Learning equals change. When we learn, we are able to know and/or do something that we did not know or were not able to do prior to the learning.

Here's why. Kullar simplified it in a way that I will always remember. Learning equals change. When we learn, we are able to know and/or do something that we did not know or were not able to do prior to the learning. It's that simple. This simplicity is beautiful. It changed me and the way I see the world.

I think that Jim Knight, speaker and author of many books on instructional coaching, would agree. The first time I heard him speak, he told the audience that he routinely invites them to send him a postcard of what they've done back in their schools after their time with him. He said that he expected, more or less, to be able to wallpaper his office with the postcards he would receive. Yet, he has never received even one postcard.

If you have never been to one of Knight's sessions, you might be thinking that maybe his work is not well done, or maybe he is a jerk, and that explains why no one would send him a postcard. Neither of these assumptions are true. Knight is a prince among men. He is kind and thoughtful, funny and wise. He is a compelling speaker and writer with a wellspring of knowledge. If you are looking for information on instructional coaching, his work will inevitably be included. So, why wouldn't he get even one postcard from one person telling him about one thing they did as a result of their time with him?

Let me pause here and say that when Knight told us this fact, I felt both saddened and called to action. I thought, *I'll do it! I'll go back after this is done and send him a postcard of what I've applied based on my time with him today.* To my surprise, it was actually much harder than I thought. When I went back to work, I realized that as an administrator, I was responsible for the instructional coaching program, but I am not an instructional coach. I did reach out to Knight to ask if he had done any work on the coaching of administrators, but he said he had not. So, even though (a) I helped lead the work of our instructional coaches and the program and (b) much of my leadership was impacted by the time I spent with Knight, I was not able to send him a postcard about how my direct work had changed. For me, instructional coaching is something that I studied (theory), but not something that I personally did (practice).

Now What?

I want *Engagement is Not a Unicorn (It's a Narwhal)* to be more than a theoretical idea generator…I hope it is a practical springboard for next steps. So, I am including some ideas here for how to take what you will read and turn them into actions.

The first action, as you recall, are the three challenges from the introduction:

- **THREE**: Before you read, identify at least three people with whom you will share the ideas you're having as a result of your reading. It doesn't matter with whom or how you will share your ideas, it just matters that you will share.

- **TWO**: As you're reading, find at least two ideas that change you…it may be because you are surprised or unsure or intrigued. It doesn't matter why you change; you're just noting the change.

- **ONE**: When you're done reading, apply at least one idea. Don't limit yourself to a professional application, it could just as easily be a personal one. The point is that you do more than just read and think about engagement—it's that you take what you've read and thought and do something with it.

Have you accomplished any of these yet? If not, that's okay. You may be so engaged in reading that you haven't stopped yet to share. Don't worry. I will continue to remind you of these throughout the book to encourage your actions.

That said, I know that changing behaviors (even when we want to) is very, very hard. Enlisting people who care about us makes the process a little easier. Therefore, even if you're electing to read this book because you want to increase engagement in some aspect of your life or the lives of those around you, it may be difficult to do so. However, have you ever noticed that it is easier to do something difficult if you have an accountability partner (AP)? An AP is someone who you choose to either (a) answer to or (b) do the work with you. For example, an AP can be a friend who you work out with. You do not like to go to the gym, and if you went by yourself, it would be easy to say that you're not going to go today. Nevertheless, you don't want to disappoint your friend by being a no-show, so you go.

An AP could also be someone who you have to share your progress with about your time at the gym. In this case, the AP doesn't meet you at the gym, but is someone who will ask you about how your time at the gym went. In this example, since you know you'll be asked about it, you go to the gym because you want to be able to report out on your progress. APs are part of the reason programs like Weight Watchers or even Alcoholics Anonymous work. In programs like these, the public aspect of sharing progress and having a network helps to create conditions for success.

Another option to help make behavioral changes can be learned from *The Odyssey*. Ulysses knows that when the Sirens call him, he will fatally crash his boat into the sea cliff. In a proactive move, he tells his crew to tie him to the mast of the ship and not to free him until they are past that point in the journey. He takes the measures of having his crew put wax in their ears so they can't hear the Sirens' song and to guard him with swords so that he does not break free. Declaring one's proactive plan is now referred to as a "Ulysses Contract," and there is research that shows that the simple acting of sharing your goals with others improves the likelihood of success. This is similar to but different from accountability partners. With an AP, you enlist a person to help you stay on course, whereas Ulysses Contracts enlist the proclamation of intent to help you stay on course.

I used a Ulysses Contract to help me write this book. I made myself tell people about how I was writing the book so that I kept writing; I can't say that I'm working on a book if I don't work on it. Make a Ulysses Contract and tell people that you're reading this book and that you plan to make changes based on what you're reading. The simple act of talking about the changes will help you go from reading about engagement to changing your actions.

So, take a moment now and find an accountability partner or make a Ulysses Contract. In the age of social media, post something on one of your accounts. Send me a tweet @LyonsLetters or use the hashtag #EngagementIsNotaUnicorn. No matter what you do, I hope that what you learn from this book creates change—for you and your students.

Thus, without further ado, I propose to you the opportunity to say *Yes!* to engagement.

Chapter Summary

The purpose of this chapter was to impart that the goal of this book is to do more than just impact thinking—the goal is to impact action.

- When we learn, we are able to know and/or do something that we did not know or were not able to do prior to the learning.

- Reading this book is just the first step towards change. The change will always remain theoretical if you do not put it into practice.

- Find a way to help you commit to practice by finding an accountability partner, by creating a Ulysses Contract, or by posting on social media.

Reflection Questions

1. What do you think of Jasmine Kullar's definition of learning? How would you have defined it?

_____

_____

_____

2. Think of a time when you have successfully implemented a change in your behavior. What supports led to your success?

_____

_____

_____

Persistent Questions

1. What have you done so far regarding the three challenges from the Introduction?

    a. **Three:** Find at least three people with whom to share your learning.

    b. **Two:** Find at least two ideas that change you.

    c. **One:** Apply at least one idea from your reading.

_____

_____

_____

2. What have you learned so far, and how will you use it?

_____

_____

_____

Section II: What

The next four chapters will provide valuable working definitions and explanations for each of the four levels on The Engagement Continuum and explain how each level works within The Engagement Matrix. By the end of Section II, you will have a common understanding of each level in isolation as well as how each level is related to the other three.

Chapter 4

Non-Compliant: *What*

"If you're going to do something wrong, do it big,
because the punishment is the same either way."
~Jane Mansfield

Recognizing Your Thinking Before You Read...

- What is the first thing you should ask yourself when you see that someone is non-compliant?

  _____

  _____

  _____

- When, if ever, have you been non-compliant?

  _____

  _____

  _____

- What are some reasons why people are non-compliant?

  _____

  _____

  _____

- What are the characteristics you see when people are non-compliant?

  _____

  _____

  _____

Non-Compliance and the Engagement Matrix

The objective of this chapter is to demonstrate that non-compliance can be overt and malicious, subtle and normal, or even intentional and principled. For this reason, and for the purpose of this book, I like the barebones definition from the Oxford Pocket Dictionary of Current English of non-compliance, "failure to act in accordance with a wish or command." This definition does not cast a shadow of malice over non-compliant behaviors; it simply indicates that the behavior and the command do not match.

This Porridge is Just Right

Once upon a time, there was a beautiful little girl with golden curls named Goldilocks. One day, she wandered into the woods and stumbled upon a cabin and walked inside. She saw three bowls of porridge sitting out on the table. Goldilocks was hungry and loved porridge, so she decided to take a bite. The first bowl was too hot. The second bowl was too cold. The third bowl was just right.

I'm sure you know this story. Notice that Goldilocks rejected the first two bowls of porridge. Why? It was not because she didn't like porridge—the story told us she "loved porridge." So why would she not continue to eat either of the first two bowls? When she rejected the porridge that was too hot and too cold, it's not that she was saying, "I don't like porridge," she was saying, "This porridge doesn't work for me." There is a difference.

When we think about why someone would refuse to do something (i.e., be non-compliant), we often think about the person who is being insubordinate, obstinate, and/or defiant. We think, "What's wrong with *you*." What I am suggesting here is that we need to think, "What's wrong with *this*?" In other words, we need to ask if there is something interfering with the person's ability or desire to do the task. Just like Goldilocks, who

> We think, "What is wrong with *you*." What I am suggesting here is that we need to think, "What is wrong with *this*?"

is more than happy to eat porridge that is just right for her but refuses to eat porridge that isn't, when we see someone opting out of doing what was expected, we need to ask the question, *is this task something that is just right for that person?*

In educational terms, this is what Vygotsky refers to as the Zone of Proximal Development (ZPD). The ZPD is the sweet spot where learning is neither too easy nor too difficult. An average ten-year-old, for example, would not want to read *The Cat in the Hat* because it is too easy but would also not want to read *The Taming of the Shrew* because it is too hard. Both of these texts are outside of the average ten-year-old's ZPD. On the other hand, it is within a ten-year-old's ZPD to read *The Lion, The Witch, and the Wardrobe.* When something is too hard or too easy, people tend to opt-out because when things are too easy, we feel disinterested, and when things are too hard, we feel defeated. This is represented visually in Erica Warren's visual of the ZPD (see Figure 4.1).

Figure 4.1 Erica Warren's Visual of the ZPD[2]

On her blog, Warren summarizes the ZPD in this way:

> On the one hand, when learning is too easy, students get bored and their attention drifts away from a lesson. On the other hand, if learning is too hard, then anxiety and confusion can result and when discouraged enough, students can develop a sense of learned helplessness. The "sweet spot" is the ZPD where students are challenged enough to maintain attention and they are able to learn

new concepts with guided assistance and scaffolding. Then, as learning happens, the support structure is slowly pulled away. Eventually, students engage in independent learning and practice until they reach automatization. Learning to automatization means that one has fully learned a concept to mastery and the process of completing a problem is virtually automatic and requires little to no thought.[3]

Asking the question, "Is the person being non-compliant because the task is too easy or too hard?" is the first question one needs to answer when interacting with someone behaving non-compliantly. Remember in Section I, I explained that in addition to disinterest in the task, non-compliance is due to either (a) a problem with the relationship between the person assigning the task and the one doing it and/or (b) that the consequences for doing it are not motivating to the person doing the task. Think, "I don't care about you; I don't care about this." In the event that the non-compliant person is opting out because the task is not within his/her ZPD, working on the relationship and/or the extrinsic consequences is not the right area on which to focus. Change the challenge of the task, and you will change the level of engagement.

> **Change the challenge of the task and you will change the level of engagement.**

The rest of this chapter addresses what is happening if the task is within that non-compliant person's ZPD. Nevertheless, it is important to remember that even the best of us will be non-compliant when we are asked to do things that are too hard or too easy.

Rebel Without a Cause

In his work, Schlechty differentiates non-compliance into two camps: (1) Rebellion and (2) Retreatism. One who falls into the Rebellion side, "summarily refuses to do the task assigned, acts in ways that disrupt others, or attempts to substitute tasks and activities to which he or she is committed in lieu of those assigned or supported."[4] One who demonstrates Retreatism is "disengaged from the tasks, expends no energy in attempting to comply with the demands of the tasks, but does not act in ways that disrupt others and does not try to substitute other activities for the assigned task."[5] This is an important distinction because too often when we think of non-compliance, we think of those who are aggressively opting-out, and we are less inclined to recall that non-compliance can also be passively aggressive.

I don't know about you, but when I think of non-compliant behavior, I think first of those who are rudely and overtly insubordinate and blatantly refuse to do what was expected for no apparent reason. I think of students outright refusing to do what they were told for no other reason than to be obstinate, rude, and disrespectful. The theme here is, "You can't make me!" This is a scene we're all too familiar with. An example from my own career comes from when, as a high school English teacher, my duty was to spend a period in the cafeteria. The rule at the school was that students were not allowed to wear hats inside. There was a boy who had a hat on. I went over to him to ask him to take off his hat, and he blatantly refused. In instances like this, the lack of compliance feels personal. "What did I do to you?" would be a typical and predictable thought for the authority to wonder.

I don't have to be a teacher to experience non-compliant behavior. As a parent of three children, the range of non-compliant behavior from my kids is common and evolves as they grow. Beginning in infancy, my children did not always conform with my expectations or directions. When they were babies, non-compliance would manifest in not wanting to eat the food that I made or not wanting to go to sleep when I put them down. As they have gotten older, I sometimes still have food and bed battles, but I also now have battles over cleaning their rooms or doing their homework. As they get older, I'm going to predict that the battles will be over curfews and maintenance of cars.

As someone who has supervised adults, I have seen examples of non-compliance from this perspective as well. Behaviors such as not coming to work by the expected time, or leaving before the technical end of the day are quite common. Deadlines are often missed—sometimes with a prior request to submit something late and sometimes just not turning it in at all. These are examples that do not have any fanfare because they are not unique.

I refer to people who act in overtly defiant ways to benefit themselves as "rebels." Rebels have an attitude of "You can't make me" because they want to do it on their terms. While there are times when we could chalk up this behavior to a general resistance towards authority, in truth, there are also times when resistance can be personal. This is because a lack of or poor relationships have an impact on behaviors. Rebels are likely not to care about consequences as a result of their actions because rebels often expect a negative outcome since they are very aware of what they are doing. Some rebels may even want a consequence because this justifies their behaviors. After all, if you give me a consequence, you're the bad guy, not me.

> **Some rebels may even want a consequence because this justifies their behaviors.**

Everyone Else is Doing It

There is a fun, interactive game that I have played with people called "Just Like Me." In this game, one person makes a statement like, "My birthday is in June," and if you also have a birthday in June, you stand up and say, "Just like me." The purpose of this game is to show commonalities between people. While it may be difficult for some of us to relate to overt defiance, in truth, we are all non-compliant in many less obvious ways. Have you ever gone to a movie where you were talking or texting even though you were supposed to be silent? Have you ever had an overdue library book or movie rental? The rule was it was due within two days, and you kept it for three. We find it easy to justify our non-compliant behavior when we believe that the rule is arbitrary or unimportant. After all, who does it harm if your library book is late? You're the one who will have to pay the late fee.

If you sit in a fast-food restaurant that has the beverage dispensers available to the customers (rather than the employees) to fill their cups, I would not be surprised if you saw many people taking advantage of the access to the machine by getting free refills even though free refills are not permitted. In so doing, the customer is breaking the rule and being non-compliant. I would suspect that if you interviewed the customers who were doing this, they would admit that this behavior is wrong, but many would likely not classify their actions as stealing. I would also predict that the vast majority of those who refilled their cups would say that shoplifting is wrong. In other words, small acts of apparently harmless defiance are not in conflict with our moral identities—particularly when it seems like everyone else is behaving in the deviant manner. If everyone is doing it, then it cannot be wrong. Think about speeding. How many of us drive *no faster* than the posted speed limit? The point is that even though our first thought in relation to non-compliance is some form of immature and unreasonable defiance to authority, we all are likely to engage in non-compliant behavior on a fairly regular and benign basis.

I call those who behave in ways that are non-compliant but socially acceptable "normalizers." This behavior is justified with the thought that "everyone else is doing it so it can't be that bad." If pressed, normalizers will generally admit that what they are doing is wrong, but since what they are doing is so common, their guilt for non-compliance is non-existent or minor.

Taking a Stand

As a high school English teacher, I used to teach a unit on identity. One of the assignments used the Heinz Dilemma developed by psychologist Lawrence Kohlberg to demonstrate a moral dilemma to determine the stage of growth and development of the subjects. This is because, in more mature stages, people understand that there are differences between arbitrary rules and laws versus those that are "universal ethical principles."[6] The reason that I asked my students to debate what Heinz should do was that I wanted them to understand that what is "wrong" isn't always wrong and what is "right" isn't always right. I used this to help set the stage for when we read books like Harper Lee's *To Kill a Mockingbird* and Nathaniel Hawthorne's *The Scarlet Letter*.

It's important to remember, though our first response to the term "non-compliant" is likely to be an image of someone who is maliciously and carelessly behaving insubordinately, not all non-compliant people are rebels. There are also those who are non-compliant for very purposeful and intentional reasons that are not meant to challenge authority, per se, but meant to challenge arbitrary or immoral rules.

Kohlberg's Heinz Dilemma[7]

A woman was near death. There was one drug that the doctors thought might save her. It was a form of radium that a druggist in the same town had recently discovered. The drug was expensive to make, but the druggist was charging ten times what the drug cost him to produce. He paid $200 for the radium and charged $2000 for a small dose of the drug. The sick woman's husband, Heinz, went to everyone he knew to borrow the money, but he could only get together about $1000, which is half of what it cost. He told the druggist that his wife was dying and asked him to sell it cheaper or let him pay later. But the druggist said: "No, I discovered the drug, and I'm going to make money from it." So Heinz got desperate and broke into the man's laboratory to steal the drug for his wife. Should Heinz have broken into the laboratory to steal the drug for his wife? Why or why not?

If you've ever read "Letter from a Birmingham Jail," Martin Luther King, Jr.'s response to his 1963 imprisonment after his non-violent actions taken in response to systematic racism, you've seen King, Jr.'s thinking on non-compliance in the form of activism. While the actual letter is too long to include here (an excerpt from the "Letter" is included at the end of this chapter), King's point is that breaking laws is wrong, but it is not wrong to break "man-made" laws that violate "moral law." In fact, he argues that it is important to engage in civil disobedience when the laws are unjust and that doing so demonstrates the "highest respect for the law."

King Jr.'s letter and Kohlberg's Heinz Dilemma illustrate that non-compliance is not always an act of stubborn or insubordinate behavior that lacks purpose or motivation. Many times people who are being non-compliant do so with great care,

> Many times people who are being non-compliant do so with great care, intention, and principle.

intention, and principle. In fact, taking a stand, marching to the beat of your own drummer, and speaking up are all values that America was founded on and ones that we still revere. People who are non-compliant for moral reasons I refer to as "activists." Their desire is really about doing what they believe is right, rather than to not do what was asked. Further, depending on your beliefs, one person's non-compliance is another person's absorption—*I'm not disregarding your tasks, I'm holding true to my values.*

Non-Compliance and The Engagement Framework

If we go back to Section I of the book and review non-compliance in relation to The Engagement Framework, then we can see that there are two features to non-compliance, one having to do with the task and the other having to do with the external person or consequence associated with (not) doing the task (see Figure 4.2). Clearly, those who are non-compliant have a low relationship to the external person and/or consequence and a low relationship to the task. This does not mean that s/he does not care about the task or the person; we should not mistake a low relationship to the external person, consequence, or task to be a lack of caring. In fact, in many instances of non-compliance, it is quite the opposite. Activists intrinsically care greatly about *not* doing what is asked. Their choice is commonly personal and deliberate. It is not that they do not care about what they are asked to do, it's that they strongly care about not doing what they are asked to do. Those who take a stand may want to be noticed because they are trying to draw attention to a cause.

Schlechty's "retreaters" are more passive in their refusal. They are not trying to draw attention to themselves. Retreaters are likely not to care about what they are assigned, what they would get from doing the assignment, nor do they care about who assigned it. They are not taking a moral or personal stand; they are just disinterested in doing what is assigned, and they do not care enough about the external drivers to do it in spite of their internal apathy.

Figure 4.2 The Engagement Framework Highlighting Non-Compliant Behaviors

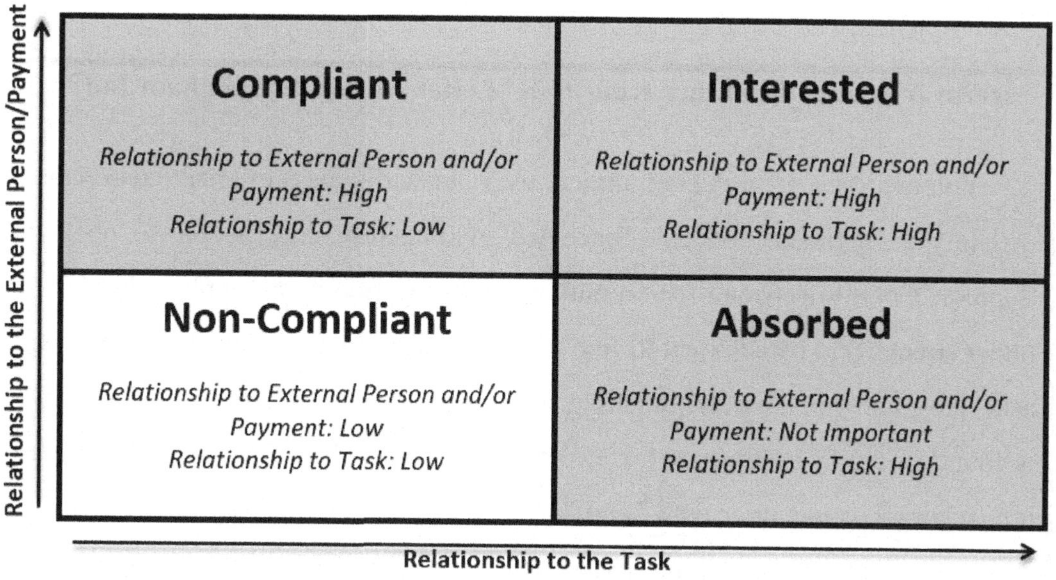

A Fine Line

It is worth noting that reasoning behind behavior can change over time. In other words, the reasoning behind rebellion is frequently due to an inability to do what is expected. What manifests as a lack of skill is hidden behind the mask of a lack of will. Put differently, if I cannot do what you ask me to do, I may prefer to pretend to be unwilling rather than expose that I am actually unable. In this way, in its simplest form, rebellious behaviors may actually be a manifestation of a rebel's fears of being unable to do what is asked. If I can't do it, I won't do it.

It does not take long for rebellious behaviors to become the status quo behaviors for a rebel. This means that the initial and intentional refusals can turn into habits and patterns of behaviors. This is how a rebel can transition into a normalizer.

On the opposite end, there are activists. Unlike rebels, activists have the skill to do what was asked. What they lack is the will. Those who disagree with an activist will interpret the behaviors as resistance. True activists are those who blaze the trail. Those who follow the path that is already there normalize the path for others to follow. Ultimately, depending on how well-traveled the path becomes, those who do not go down the path can become non-compliant.

Excerpt from Martin Luther King Jr.'s "Letter from a Birmingham Jail"[8]

You express a great deal of anxiety over our willingness to break laws. This is certainly a legitimate concern. Since we so diligently urge people to obey the Supreme Court's decision of 1954 outlawing segregation in the public schools, it is rather strange and paradoxical to find us consciously breaking laws. One may well ask: "How can you advocate breaking some laws and obeying others?" The answer is found in the fact that there are two types of laws: There are just and there are unjust laws. I would agree with Saint Augustine that "An unjust law is no law at all."

Now, what is the difference between the two? How does one determine when a law is just or unjust? A just law is a man-made code that squares with the moral law or the law of God. An unjust law is a code that is out of harmony with the moral law. To put it in the terms of Saint Thomas Aquinas, an unjust law is a human law that is not rooted in eternal and natural law. Any law that uplifts human personality is just. Any law that degrades human personality is unjust. All segregation statutes are unjust because segregation distorts the soul and damages the personality. It gives the segregator a false sense of superiority, and the segregated a false sense of inferiority. To use the words of Martin Buber, the Jewish philosopher, segregation substitutes an "I-it" relationship for an "I-thou" relationship, and ends up relegating persons to the status of things. So segregation is not only politically, economically, and sociologically unsound, but it is morally wrong and sinful. Paul Tillich has said that sin is separation. Isn't segregation an existential expression of man's tragic separation, an expression of his awful estrangement, his terrible sinfulness? So I can urge men to disobey segregation ordinances because they are morally wrong.

Let us turn to a more concrete example of just and unjust laws. An unjust law is a code that a majority inflicts on a minority that is not binding on itself. This is difference made legal. On the other hand, a just law is a code that a majority compels a minority to follow that it is willing to follow itself. This is sameness made legal.

Let me give another explanation. An unjust law is a code inflicted upon a minority in which that minority had no part in enacting or creating because they did not have the unhampered right to vote. Who can say that the legislature of Alabama which set up the segregation laws was democratically elected? Throughout the state of Alabama, all types of conniving methods are used to prevent Negroes from becoming registered voters and there are some counties without a single Negro registered to vote despite the fact that the Negro constitutes a majority of the population. Can any law set up in such a state be considered democratically structured?

These are just a few examples of unjust and just laws. There are some instances when a law is just on its face and unjust in its application. For instance, I was arrested Friday on a charge of parading without a permit. Now there is nothing wrong with an ordinance which requires a permit for a parade, but when the ordinance is used to preserve segregation and to deny citizens the First-Amendment privilege of peaceful assembly and peaceful protest, then it becomes unjust.

I hope you can see the distinction I am trying to point out. In no sense do I advocate evading or defying the law as the rabid segregationist would do. This would lead to anarchy. One who breaks an unjust law must do it openly, lovingly, (not hatefully as the white mothers did in New Orleans when they were seen on television screaming "nigger, nigger, nigger") and with a willingness to accept the penalty. I submit that an individual who breaks a law that conscience tells him is unjust, and willingly accepts the penalty by staying in jail to arouse the conscience of the community over its injustice, is in reality expressing the very highest respect for law.

Of course, there is nothing new about this kind of civil disobedience. It was seen sublimely in the refusal of Shadrach, Meshach, and Abednego to obey the laws of Nebuchadnezzar because a higher moral law was involved. It was practiced superbly by the early Christians who were willing to face hungry lions and the excruciating pain of chopping blocks, before submitting to certain unjust laws of the Roman empire. To a degree academic freedom is a reality today because Socrates practiced civil disobedience.

We can never forget that everything Hitler did in Germany was "legal" and everything the Hungarian freedom fighters did in Hungary was "illegal." It was "illegal" to aid and comfort a Jew in Hitler's Germany. But I am sure that if I had lived in Germany during that time I would have aided and comforted my Jewish brothers even though it was illegal. If I lived in a Communist country today where certain principles dear to the Christian faith are suppressed, I believe I would openly advocate disobeying these anti-religious laws.

Chapter Summary

Understanding non-compliant behavior provides a background that personalizes these behaviors and minimizes judgment. Those who are non-compliant are often intrinsically motivated to opt-out of compliance and/or they do not have a vested interest in the person assigning the task nor the reward for doing the task itself. We would all like to believe that, at first blush, we are rule-followers, or at least, law-abiding citizens. However, this is not always the case.

- The first question we need to ask when someone is being non-compliant is whether or not the task being asked is within that person's Zone of Proximal Development (ZPD). If the task is too easy, the person will refuse due to disinterest. If the task is too hard, the person will refuse the task due to discouragement.

- We are all non-compliant at times.

- The first thought when hearing the phrase, "non-compliant" is generally one of insubordination.

- There are at least three different types of non-compliance. Those who are actively disengaging to be obstinate (rebels), those who are breaking the rules that no one seems to follow anyway (normalizers), and those who are practicing civil disobedience to create change (activists).

Reflection Questions

1. In your own words, how would you define non-compliance? How does your definition align with what you read in this chapter?

_____

_____

_____

2. With regard to the Heinz Dilemma, what form of non-compliance is Heinz taking if he steals the medicine? What form would it be if he didn't?

_____

_____

_____

3. How is the perspective of non-compliance different based on if you are the person in violation or if you are the person whose rule is being violated?

_____

_____

_____

4. Do you feel that there are times when non-compliance is appropriate? Why or why not? How do you draw the line?

_____

_____

_____

5. Where would you plot a rebel, a normalizer, and an activist in the Non-Compliant Quadrant? Would the plot points for each overlap or be in distinct areas of the quadrant?

_____

_____

_____

Persistent Questions

1. What have you done so far regarding the three challenge questions from the Introduction?

    a. **Three:** Find at least three people with whom to share your learning.

    b. **Two:** Find at least two ideas that change you.

    c. **One:** Apply at least one idea from your reading.

_____

_____

_____

2. What have you learned so far and how will you use it?

_____

_____

_____

Chapter 5

Compliant: *What*

"Working hard on something you don't care about or have a say in
is not perseverance or 'grit,' it's compliance."
~Sylvia Libow Martinez

Recognizing Your Thinking Before You Read...

*   How do you define compliance?

    _____

    _____

    _____

*   When, if ever, is compliant behavior desirable?

    _____

    _____

    _____

*   Is it possible for one person to be compliant and another to be absorbed while doing the same thing? Why or why not?

    _____

    _____

    _____

*   What are examples from your life when you are currently compliant?

    _____

    _____

    _____

Compliance and the Engagement Matrix

Remember that compliance falls in the upper left quadrant of the Engagement Matrix. This means that the relationship to the external person and/or consequence is high and the relationship to the task is low (see Figure 5.1). Compliant people will do the task, but we cannot confuse doing a task because you have to with doing the task because you want to. For this reason, compliance can be in service to the relationship, as a path of least resistance, as a means to an end, or because the task is too unfamiliar to know any other way to do it.

Figure 5.1: The Engagement Matrix Highlighting Compliant Behaviors

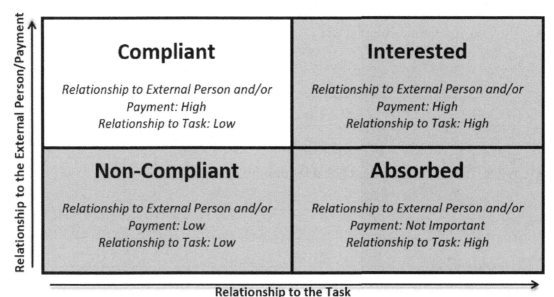

When I Say "Jump" You Say "How High"

For me, the easiest way to think about compliance is to think about a time when I am doing what I was told to do simply because I was told to do it. This is because, at the heart of it, compliance is about getting the job done in response to one or more of the following potential outcomes:

1. I don't want to disappoint or disrespect the person who told me to do it (my boss, my parent, my spouse, my friend, etc.)

2. I want the reward I will receive when I'm done (my paycheck, my grade, to be right, my lights remain on, etc.)

3. I am avoiding the punishment I would receive if I didn't do it (being grounded, being wrong, getting an Improvement Plan, being fired, etc.)

Compliance is a path of least resistance and is a "give to get." This means that there is an expectation from the person doing the task that goes something like this: *If I **give** you what you want, in return, I will **get** what I want.* This is a transaction. Compliant people, at best, aim to make the other person happy. At worst, compliant people just want to end the task as soon as possible. Nowhere in this dynamic do compliant people find intrinsic value in what they are doing.

If you are anything like me, when you were a child, your parents said something like, "When I say 'jump,' you say, 'how high?'" or "Because I said so." These replies highlight the nature of compliance well. There are countless situations where this would apply from parent to child. Take out the garbage. Clean your room. Do your homework. Go to bed. While in our heads (or under our breaths), we thought all kinds of retorts for these demands, we did it anyway.

Though our emotions have likely mellowed with age and experience, the truth is that even adults comply. When you go to an airport, you would likely prefer not to take off your shoes when you go through security. It's not that you don't understand why doing it is necessary, but if left to your own devices, the long lines and inconvenience of going through that process are something you would choose to avoid. Yet, you do it anyway. When your boss tells you that you have a new task to do, you may ask why it needs to be done and/or even propose a different task to do instead. At the end of the day, however, you'll likely do the task anyway because your boss told you to. This is compliance.

Path of Least Resistance

Sometimes less obvious, but equally compliant, is the response to a child who asks why something is done a certain way, and the adult responds, "I'm not sure" or "That's the way it's always been." If we are doing something for no other reason than conventional practice, what we're doing falls under the heading of compliance. This type of compliant behavior is the personification of traits I associate with a "rule-follower." Rule-followers generally don't ask questions, they just do what they need to so they can get the job done. Give them a list, they'll follow it. The boxes will be checked off. The goal here is task completion. This robotic obedience doesn't mean that they enjoy what they're doing, just that they've done it.

In a previous job, I was responsible for approving the elementary principals' time-off requests. Every two weeks, I had to sign-off on their timecards. The thing was, the principals were salaried employees who never used timecards. I could not understand why there was a timecard sign-off for them but, every other week, I logged onto the computer to complete this task. I wished I did not have to do it at all, but I did it anyway. Just about anything you do blindly is probably done out of rule-follower compliance because, if you were given the opportunity to no longer do it, you would choose not to.

Traditional math instruction is a good example of a rule-follower scenario. When I was in school, I was taught to compute numbers to solve an equation, but I was not taught the reason why the computation worked. I thoughtlessly plugged in numbers and came up with answers. If I asked my parents or teachers, "Why do I do it this way," there was a good chance that they could not tell me mathematically why the computation worked—just that it worked. We were all just following the rules.

Anything for You

When talking to people about compliance, invariably, someone will say to me something like, "I know what you're talking about when you said that compliance might be done because of your relationship with the other person. That's why I did _____ with my spouse (dad, child, sibling, friend, etc.)." At the end of a presentation, a woman came up to me and said she learned how to knit because her mom wanted to. Even though she wasn't really interested in knitting, she wanted to spend time with her mom. When you are compliant because you want to make the other person happy, you are what I call a "people-pleaser." People-pleasers are a little tricky because there could be such a strong relationship with the other person that the people-pleaser is interested or even absorbed in the *person*. However, the specific *task* that the people-pleaser is doing is neither interesting nor absorbing. For this combination of reasons (i.e., I care about you and our relationship but not about this task),

> For this combination of reasons (i.e., I care about you and our relationship but not about this task), people-pleases will avoid non-compliance.

people-pleasers will avoid non-compliance. At the same time, the engagement in the task is only as high as compliance.

This happens all the time in schools and starts when children are very young. Primary-aged children are generally much more driven to make their teacher happy than they are to voice an objection to the task. While primary-aged children are those whose curiosity is arguably the most overt and strongest, they will dutifully do what they need to if it means their teacher will be happy.

Leave Me Alone

Another form of people-pleasing is doing the task because you do not want to upset the other person. Whereas the initial example was doing something because you wanted to spend time with another person, you may want to please someone else to avoid spending (more) time with them. In this case, the goal is to do whatever needs to be done so you can make that person happy and reduce or eliminate the interactions you have with that person. Examples of this manifestation of people-pleasing tend to have negative consequences if the task isn't done. Here the relationship with the person assigning the task is low, but the motivation to do the task is to avoid the negative consequence. At the same time, pleasing the person who assigned the task can be seen as a positive consequence despite the poor relationship.

We've probably all heard the bad advice, "Don't let the students see you smile until Christmas." The intention of this recommendation is if you want the students to take you seriously, you need to be serious (and maybe a little cruel). Did you ever have the "mean" teacher when you were a student? This was the teacher who probably yelled at students, belittled them, and/or was overly strict? I'll bet you didn't want to upset that teacher because you didn't want to draw attention to yourself. Out of fear, you were probably the most compliant in that teacher's classroom than anywhere else. If compliance is all you're hoping for, then this might work for you. However, since compliance is disengagement, then generating people-pleasing out of fear should never be a tactic we use.

I'm Drowning

I once had the pleasure of being coached by Paula Bevan, a Senior Consultant for the Danielson Group. From Dr. Bevan, I learned a great deal about coaching, including that there are people who do not benefit from coaching. At first blush, you might expect that she felt the very best people don't need coaching—and you'd be wrong. After all, she would say, *Even Michael Phelps, the most decorated Olympian of all time, has a coach. Why? It's not because his coach can swim better than Phelps—obviously, that's not true. It's because his coach can do something Michael cannot do. Watch him as he swims.*

So, if it's not the best people who wouldn't benefit, then who else could it be? There are four types of swimmers (see Figure 5.2). Those who are the best, like Phelps. Those who are pretty good, like lifeguards. Those who are adequate, like recreational swimmers. And, those who are drowning because they can't yet swim. *Since coaching is a collaborative act that invites input (from the swimmer in this case), you would never seek input from someone who is drowning* Bevan taught me. In the midst of flailing about and gasping for air, you wouldn't invite collaboration by asking, "So what stroke do you think you might want to try right now?" This critical situation requires the person on the pool deck to be directive (not collaborative), "Grab this," as the lifesaver is tossed out or "I've got you. Put your arms around my neck."

Figure 5.2: How to Help People Who Can and Cannot Swim

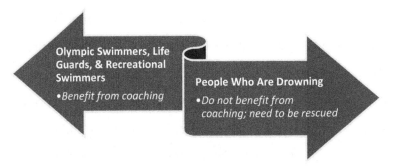

You don't have to be drowning to want direction. Those who are doing something for the first time like it too. For first-timers, what they need to do is new(er). In this way, direction is not micro-managing, but clarifying and helpful. When I went through AED (defibrillator) training, I learned that when using an AED, the machine will talk me through each step of the process as I'm doing it. I can't tell you what a relief it was to hear that in a real-life emergency. I would not have to remember how to use the

AED—a device that I was briefly trained on and never really needed to use. It goes without saying that complying with the steps for using the AED is not just appropriate, but a matter of life and death. This, after all, is not a time to be either non-compliant or look for ways to infuse choice and voice into the task.

Most of us are never in the position that requires this level of strict compliance or someone might get hurt. However, most of us are occasionally in the position of being a first-timer and find that following the provided directions helps to create a bridge from our current level of inexperience to a deeper level of knowledge. The column labeled "Calibrating" in Laura Lipton and Bruce Wellman's Learning-Focused Conversations chart (see Figure 5.3) highlights how to best interact with first-timers (and beyond). Notice how "Calibrating" has no input from the learner. The point here is that there are times when direction that elicits compliance is important for success and not something to be avoided.

I've Never Done This Before

There is a difference between how first-timers and those who are drowning feel. First-timers are eager to do the work but are new to the work being done. For this reason, their compliance stems from a lack of awareness of other ways to do the work. Put differently, first-timers are compliant because they need the direction to successfully do what they need to do. As their skill develops, their compliance may diminish because they will know more about the task to know when or where they could cut-corners than the normalized non-compliant people do. On the other hand, they may morph from compliant to interested over time when they can shift from focusing on "am I doing this right" to "I enjoy doing this."

Figure 5.3: Learning-Focused Conversations: The Continuum of Interaction[9]

Learning-focused Conversations: The Continuum of Interaction

Supervisor/Specialist	Calibrating	Consulting	Collaborating	Coaching
	Information, analysis, goals		*Information, analysis, goals*	
Guiding question	What are the gaps/growth areas indicated for this teacher based on present performance levels and the standards?	What information, ideas and technical resources will be most useful to this teacher at this time?	What are some ways to balance my contributions with this teacher's experiences and expertise?	What mental and emotional resources might be most useful for this teacher at this time?
Function	• Articulating standards • Using data to identify gaps between expected standards and present results • Defining problems • Prescribing results	• Clarifying standards • Using data to analyze gaps between expected standards and present results • Offering information and ideas • Providing problem analysis and perspectives • Naming principles of practice	• Jointly clarifying standards • Using data to co-analyze gaps between expected standards and present results • Co-generating information and ideas • Co-analyzing problems • Expanding perspectives	• Referencing standards as a focal point • Using data to explore gaps between expected standards and present results • Facilitating teacher idea production • Mediating teacher problem-framing and analysis • Enhancing teacher capacities for planning, reflecting, problem-solving and decision making
Role in planning for action	• Determining teacher actions/goals • Naming success criteria • Establishing timelines	• Proposing teacher actions/goals • Defining success criteria • Confirming timelines	• Co-constructing teacher actions/goals • Co-developing success criteria • Agreeing on timelines	• Exploring teacher actions/goals • Eliciting success criteria • Clarifying timelines
Cues	• Credible voice • Using neutral language, as in *"These data ... "* *"This example ... "*	• Credible voice • Using neutral language or personal pronouns, as in, *"I think that ... "* *"It is important to ... "* *"Here is one way to think about that"*	• Approachable voice • Collective pronouns, as in *"Let's think about ... "* *"How might we ... "*	• Approachable voice • Second person pronouns, as in *"What are some of your ...?"* *"How might you ...?"*
Cautions	• Take care not to let personal preferences become prescriptions. Judgments must be supported by clear, external criteria. • Use literal observation notes, classroom artifacts and assessment data to avoid subjectivity or bias.	• Monitor and manage the impulse to help or rescue. Stay learning-focused and don't let personal passion overcome patience with the developmental process. • Be aware that overuse of the consulting stance may build dependency on the supervisor for problem solving.	• Resist the impulse to dominate the conversation and provide the bulk of the analysis and thinking. • Monitor for balance in idea production. Don't allow personal enthusiasm or preferences to override the intention to co-create ideas and options.	• Reduce potential frustration by posing developmentally appropriate questions. Questions should stretch not strain thinking. • Be sure that questions allow for multiple responses and do not signal that there is a preferred answer.

This excerpt from *Leadership and the One Minute Manager: Increasing Effectiveness Through Situational Leadership II* shows how first-timers are both appreciative and compliant with direction.[10]

"I'm interested in finding out how the One Minute Manager works with you," said the entrepreneur. "Would you call him a collaborative manager? I've been reading a lot about collaborative leadership."

"He's far from being collaborative with me," said Larry. "In fact, he is very directive with me. People development is his baby. So my job is essentially to follow his direction."

"But why doesn't he just assign you the projects he needs you to do and then just let you figure them out?" wondered the entrepreneur. "He must trust you if he put you in this job."

"I think he trusts that I'll develop in the role but he's the expert," said Larry. "So he assigns me projects and then works very closely with me on almost every aspect of them. This role is a big stretch for me. I'm just learning about several of the responsibilities that come with this job."

"Don't you resent that?" asked the entrepreneur. "It sounds pretty controlling to me."

"Not at all," said Larry."

In schools, student teachers, subs, and new hires tend to fall into this level of first-timer compliance. Student teachers, for example, have spent countless hours and money learning about how to be a teacher but they have never been in front of students for any meaningful period of time or the students they have worked with are not the ones they're working with now. They are chomping at the bit to do the work, but they are eager to get input about how to do it well in this situation. In fact, another way to think about first-timers is that they have a high level of will and a low level of skill. Compliance, then, for the first-timers, is a scaffold. This temporary structure is a support to assist in success that will hopefully transform their compliance into *interested* or *absorbed*. If they don't like it, their first-timer compliance may transform into rebellious non-compliance.

Even so, people who are drowning benefit from directions which require compliance too. Like first-timers, drowning people have low skill, but their discouragement from drowning likely causes them to also have low will. They would rather not do the task since they have not been successful, so if we don't catch it in time, they will also become non-compliant.

Progress Over Perfection

To an authority, regardless of why someone is being compliant, compliance can be a success if the subordinate was previously non-compliant. You told me to finish my peas. I did not want to. I tried to get out of it (non-compliant). Ultimately, however, I did it (compliant). The authority feels better that I finished my peas and did as I was told. I may feel better because we can move on. Then again, I may feel worse because I did something that I did not really want to do, and that has a negative impact on how I feel about myself and erodes how I feel about the authority.

As well, if I'm a first-timer, compliance feels good because I needed guidance, not choice, to do the task. Thus, there are times when both the authority and the subordinate agree that compliance can also feel successful. You told me I had to go to practice. I didn't want to, but you told me that if I did, you would buy me an ice cream after. I went to practice. You felt good that I went, and I got my ice cream afterward, so I felt good too. In this sense, compliance is a victory because progression away from non-compliance has occurred. Of course, there is also the version where I did not want to practice, but you told me to, and I did it compliantly. I feel better though at the end because I improved as a result of the practice. In this example, I am probably interested in the thing I'm practicing even if the practice, itself, is done compliantly.

No matter how good compliance may feel in comparison to non-compliance, compliance is a deceptive state. While compliance means the task is getting done, it is deceptive because one can easily forget that compliant behavior is doing the minimum to get positive consequences or to avoid negative consequences, including punishments and/or

> No matter how good compliance may feel in comparison to non-compliance compliance is a deceptive state.

harm to a relationship. No matter how willing someone looks on the outside, anyone who is operating compliantly is behaving this way out of a feeling of obligation.

Duty, Honor, Country

Some reading this may have a background in sports or the military where honor and respect are paramount characteristics. Though I have never served, it is my understanding that there is an expectation in the military of compliance to authority. West Point, one of America's finest military preparation schools, has as its motto, "Duty, Honor, Country." The term "duty" can easily be viewed through the lens of compliance. For civilians like me, duty may very well be doing a task compliantly. This is not true for those who are true believers in this motto or others like it. Their beliefs about duty run so deep that they are actually absorbed or at least interested in doing what is required.

When searching for quotes to place at the start of this chapter, I Googled "obedience quotes." The overwhelming majority of quotes about obedience are religious in nature. The authority, in this case, is the ultimate authority—God. Those who have deep religious beliefs would not see obeying the word of God or their spiritual guide (i.e., pastor, priest, rabbi, etc.) as being compliant; they would agree with Joseph B. Wirthlin, a leader in the Mormon faith, who said, "When we love the Lord, obedience ceases to be a burden. Obedience becomes a delight."

In this way, one person's compliance is another person's absorption because the feelings about the task and/or the external consequence are perceived differently. This will be discussed in more depth in the chapters on Interested and Absorbed. Suffice it to say, the motivation behind the behavior varies from person to person, and this is what distinguishes whether someone is non-compliant, compliant, interested, or absorbed.

Chapter Summary

This chapter introduced the nature of compliance. In comparison to non-compliance, compliant people do what they are told to do even though they would rather not. Their motivation for compliance is linked to their external consequence (or lack thereof) and/or their relationship with the person assigning the task.

- Doing something because you were told to do it is compliance. This was true when you were a child, and a parent told you to clean your room. This is still true when you are an adult, and you are assigned a task at work that you would rather not do, but you do it anyway.

- There are also many examples in life of blind compliance where you do something, but you don't know why you're doing it. For example, you probably do not know the science behind why you don't put metal in a microwave, but you comply with that rule anyway.

- There are at least three different types of compliance. Those who are doing what they need to get a disinteresting task done (rule-followers and those who see it as a means to an end), those who care about the person assigning the task but not about the task itself (people-pleasers), and those who are unfamiliar or unsuccessful with the task and need clear direction (first-timers and drowning people).

- If you are interacting with someone who was previously non-compliant, compliance feels like a victory. Even so, compliance is still doing the bare minimum to get by.

- Depending on your beliefs, what one person does compliantly, another does willingly and with desire.

Reflection Questions

1. In your own words, how would you define compliance now? How does your definition align with what you read in this chapter?

_____

_____

_____

2. How is the perspective of compliance different based on if you are the authority assigning the task or if you are the subordinate who is completing the task?

_____

_____

_____

3. Do you feel that there are times when compliance is appropriate? Why or why not? How do you draw the line?

_____

_____

_____

4. Think of a time when you shifted from non-compliance to compliance. Was it the incentive, punishment, and/or relationship that caused the shift?

_____

_____

_____

5. Give an example of something that you are blindly compliant with now, but you are not sure of the reason you need to do it at all.

_____

_____

_____

6. Where would you plot a rule-follower, people-pleaser, first-timer, and a drowning person in the Compliant Quadrant? Would the plot points for each overlap or be in distinct areas of the quadrant?

_____

_____

_____

Persistent Questions

1. What have you done so far regarding the three challenge questions from the Introduction?

    a. **Three:** Find at least three people with whom to share your learning.

    b. **Two:** Find at least two ideas that change you.

    c. **One:** Apply at least one idea from your reading.

_____

_____

_____

2. What have you learned so far, and how will you use it?

_____

_____

_____

Chapter 6

Interested: *What*

"To waken interest and kindle enthusiasm is the sure way to teach easily and successfully."
~Tryon Edwards

Recognizing Your Thinking Before You Read...

- How do you define *interested*?

  _____

  _____

  _____

- What are reasons why people are interested?

  _____

  _____

  _____

- What are the characteristics you see when people are interested?

  _____

  _____

  _____

- How can you increase the likelihood of someone being interested?

  _____

  _____

  _____

Interested and the Engagement Matrix

This chapter aims to show interest as the entry point to engagement. Interest can take the shape of those who really like the task they need to do, those who really like the consequence for doing a task they enjoy, and those who understand that the task is a small price to pay for the chance at the consequence. At this point, we have made the steep climb from the furthest depths of disengagement in the quadrant of non-compliance to the more shallow waters of disengagement in the quadrant of compliance. Though this felt like a victory, compliance should not be the stopping point. We know that the way to move vertically in the Engagement Matrix is by improving the relationship to the external person and/or to find a more compelling consequence. The goal now is to make the shift towards true engagement by focusing on the task (see Figure 6.1).

Figure 6.1: The Engagement Matrix Highlighting Interested Behaviors

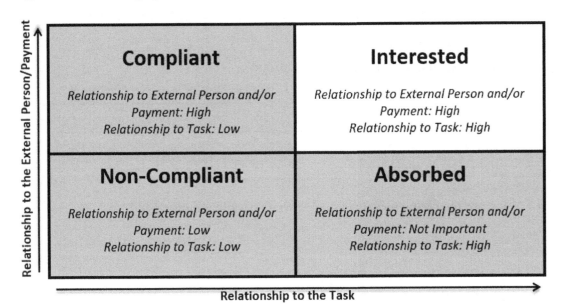

The entry point into engagement is interest in the task. In this quadrant, students are interested in the activity that they are doing in the class, and teachers can celebrate this as engagement. Interest gets students to a point whereby they are more than just willing to do the work—they want to do the work. At least for that moment. However, when the bell rings or the unit is over, the student is no longer willing to continue.

Like compliance, interest is deceptive since interested people are temporarily engaged. People often observe that when working with others who are interested, enjoyment in the task is noticeable. Often overlooked, though, is that when people are at the interested level, the enjoyment is both temporary and also extrinsically motivated—the student enjoys the task but would give up if the extrinsic consequence(s) was taken away. This is why interest is in the upper right corner of the Engagement Matrix. In other words, the enjoyment is short-lived and motivated by the consequence for (not) doing the task.

We have all experienced this. We were given a task that we actually enjoyed doing. Nevertheless, when given the opportunity to stop, we were not compelled or motivated to continue on our own time. This is what I call a "willing participant." There should be equal billing here of both words—willing and participant. Compliant people do the work, but interested people do more than the minimum because they willingly participate in the task. In classes, willing participants raise their hands before being called on. When working in groups, students' "heads are down and butts are up" (in the air) because they're leaning in to see what's going on. When it is time to share their learning, willing participants volunteer to go first because they want others to hear what they did. While having discussions, willing participants offer their ideas. In fact, willing participants may even be on the cusp of absorption because they may be absorbed in the *process* of learning even if the topic, content, or other variables are only interesting (or vice versa).

> **Compliant people do the work, but interested people do more than the minimum because they willingly participate in the task.**

Locus of Control

In order to shift from compliance to interest, the task must be changed. The question is, who is able to change the task? Chances are, it's the authority. For students, that means it is the teacher, for teachers, that means it is administration. No matter who the authority is, if the tasks are designed without input from those doing the tasks, then the highest level of engagement the authority is likely to see is interest (more information about why this is will be explained in the "Absorbed: What" chapter of this book).

In fact, you can think of the horizontal axis of the Engagement Matrix, which emphasizes the task, in the same way you think of the gradual release method of I Do, We Do, You Do (see Figure 6.2). I am not speaking about the modeling portion of completing a task. That is something else altogether. In this case, I use the phrasing of the gradual release method to give insight into how releasing control impacts the feelings of engagement. The more the authority controls the creation of the task for those who are doing the task, the more likely the feelings towards that task will be compliant (at best). The more voice and choice those doing the task have in the creation, selection, and/or execution of the task, the more likely the feelings towards that task will be interested (at worst). After all, which would you rather do, the one thing you were told to do or the one (or more) thing(s) you chose to do?

> **The more voice and choice those doing the task have in the creation, selection, and/or execution of the task, the more likely the feelings towards that task will be interested (at worst).**

Figure 6.2: Engagement Increases as Control by the Assigner is Released

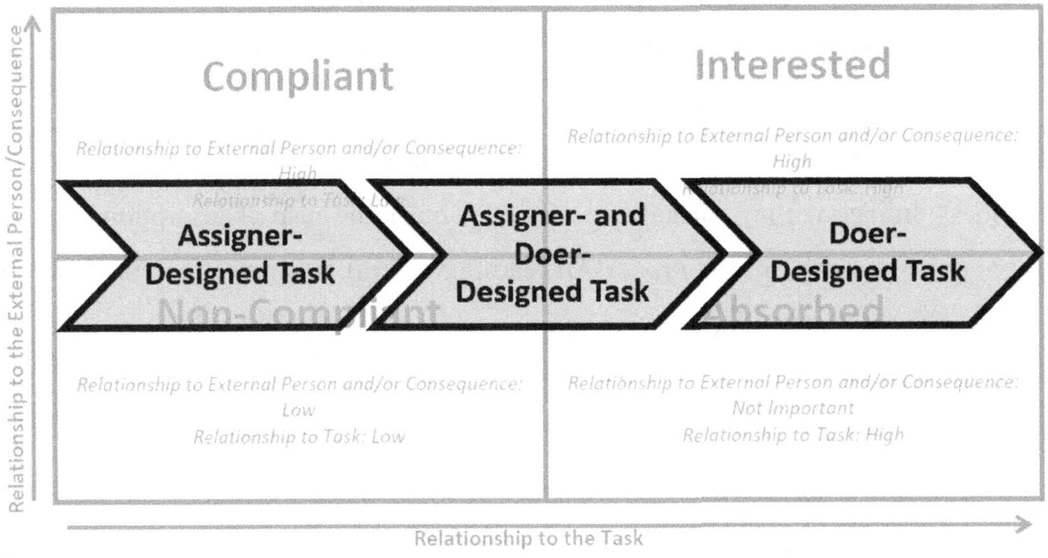

Again, the difference between those who are compliant or interested is their relationship with the task. The stronger the relationship with the task, the more engaged they are. If we want to increase engagement, we must strengthen the relationship with the task for the person doing the task. Doing so happens through focusing on the person(s) doing the task as much as we focus on what needs to be done.

Show Me the Money

Another key feature of being interested is that those who are at this level of engagement are motivated extrinsically. If you recall, Figure 2.1, "Simplified Responses to the Task, Person, or Consequence at each Level of The Engagement Framework," identified that those who are interested like the task and like/respect the person who assigned the task. Additionally, their feelings towards the payment for doing the task are "I could do this for pay," meaning that they still want compensation for their efforts. This is a key distinction for the interest level of the Engagement Matrix. *Interested people need an extrinsic reward for doing the task.* This explains why students will stop doing something if their grade goes away. Students who do interesting work want a grade. If the grade is off the table, they will move on to other things that are going to be graded despite the fact that they are interested in the work.

Yes. Interested students will stop doing interesting and even enjoyable work if they are not rewarded via a grade for doing the work. How many people (kids or not) would do the "extra credit" for fun? "Don't worry about adding this on to my grade (or paycheck). The joy of doing it was all I needed." If people are expected to do the work, they expect to be paid in return. As such, in most cases, if you remove the grade for students, the students will shift their attention to something that is graded. Once that work is finished, the students will ultimately move on to things they find absorbing, and that will most likely not be something studied in school. This is not to say that people cannot find absorption in schoolwork; it simply means that this is less likely or nearly impossible to happen when what is being officially studied is dictated externally to the person who is doing the work.

I am surprised at how difficult it is for adults to understand this concept regarding students and yet how easy it becomes when I switch the example to adults. Think about things you do as an adult that are the enjoyable parts of your work. I'm not talking about the things that fuel your soul; I am talking about run-of-the-mill things that are a part of the work you do. For example, think about professional development (PD). Most people I know are not fans of useless PD, but can get excited about attending a session that they find valuable for their work. Yet, what if I told you that this PD was (a) on a Saturday or (b) after work or (c) to attend you had to pay with your own money or (d) to attend you would need to use a personal day? Would you still go? If you answered yes, then you are likely beyond interested in this topic—you are absorbed. If you said no, then this topic was only at the interest level; you want extrinsic compensation for your attendance, and your compensation is your pay and/or time. Students are the same way. Though they may be interested in the various projects, assignments, and/or topics you are studying in class, if they do not continue to learn or do more after the point that the unit, lesson, or period is over, then it doesn't matter how engaged they were during the task, they were only interested.

Look at the tweet from @pernilleripp after she finished two days of PD. I'm sure you can relate to this feeling. I'm sure she was interested in her learning during the PD, but she wants to be able to go home and process, not produce. How can we use this to think about our students?

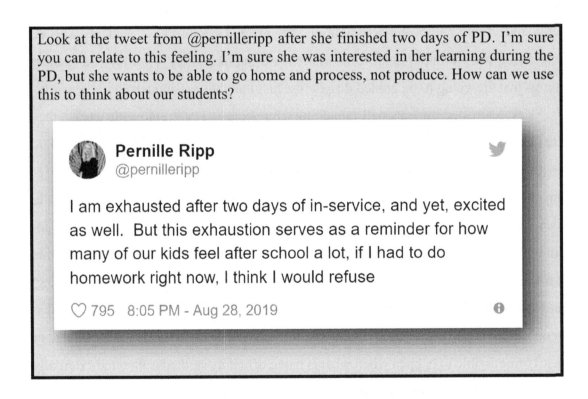

Let me make this even clearer. Think about your job as a whole. Whatever that job is, you call it your job because you get paid to do it. I sincerely hope that you are at least at the interested level in relation to your job, but here's a way to tell if you are not beyond the interest level. How do you feel on Friday afternoon when you leave work for the weekend? Are you looking forward to having time away from work, or do you work *for fun* on Saturday and Sunday? On Sunday evening, as the workweek approaches, do you wish you could extend your weekend so that you can have more time not working, or are you itching to get back to work? If you're like most people, you probably like (and hopefully even love) your job, but on the weekend, you'd rather not do your work. If that sounds like you, then you are interested in your work (not absorbed). If you are at a level of compliance, the question you would want to ask is, "If all jobs paid the same amount, what would I want to get paid to do?" This is a fundamentally different question than the one you would ask to determine absorption, "Even if I needed to make money, what would I still pay to do?" Think about it this way...

- When we are at the **non-compliant level**, we dislike the work so much that the compensation (consequence/relationship) for doing the work is less than what it would take to get us to do the work.

- When we are at the **compliant level**, we are only doing the work for the compensation (consequence/relationship) since there is no enjoyment in the work.

- When we are at the **interested level**, we want compensation (consequence/relationship) to do the work even though we like the work.

- When we are at the **absorbed level**, we do not need compensation to do the work because doing the work is the compensation.

These statements hold true regardless of what type of "work" the person is "compensated" for. As such, the work could be a multi-million dollar contract for a construction company or a coloring sheet for a child in Sunday School. A kindergarten child will be non-compliant for the same reasons that Bill Gates would be non-compliant—they don't care about the task, and they don't care about the consequences. This is why once you understand the underlying factors of engagement through The Engagement Matrix, you can begin to take actions to universally identify and change levels of engagement in yourself and others.

Just Doing My Job, Ma'am

This level of interest exemplifies the second manifestation of interest, which I call a "professional." The term professional actually has two meanings. The first refers to how people behave. You might say, "Wow, you were such a professional in how you approached that angry person. You acted like it didn't bother you even though it must have been difficult when she raised her voice at you." The second refers to people who are paid for their work. Here you're talking about the difference between an amateur (someone who does the task recreationally) and a professional (someone who is paid for doing the work). Both of these meanings of professional apply to this type of interest since a hallmark of being interested is that you like the work (therefore, you behave professionally), and you like the compensation (meaning you are a professional who is paid).

The area(s) in which we became a professional was probably influenced by areas in which we were once absorbed. This is because many of us tried to find a way to get paid to do the thing(s) we loved to do. In a sad twist of fate, when we make money doing the thing we love, we often decrease our engagement in the task. Why? Simply put, when we did the thing we loved for the joy of doing it, we never had to worry about extrinsic compensation. When we do it professionally, we have pressures that we didn't have before—can I make my car payment doing this? Can I pay my rent this month if I do this? How will I eat? These pressures can have a depleting impact on our level of engagement, meaning our desire to do the task is replaced by our need to make money by doing the task. Consequently, the thing we were once absorbed in becomes the thing we're now only interested in.

> These pressures can have a depleting impact on our level of engagement meaning our desire to do the task is replaced by our need to make money by doing the task.

Eye on the Prize

Interested people can also be "strategists." Strategists are those who do the task because they are very attracted to the consequences. In comparison to professionals who liked what they were doing and found a way to get paid to do it, strategists liked the payment and found a way to do the task.

Strategists are students who take an AP course in a subject that they minimally like (at best). They're smart enough to do the work but, more than that, they recognize that there is a certain prestige in taking APs. Strategists start doing the work not because they really like the work, but because they think others will like them more because they did the work. If they find they actually like the work, they shift from being *compliant* (I'll take this because it looks good) to *interested* (it looks good and I like it). Another example is when students commit to volunteering so that they can have something to include on their National Honor Society applications. Though they started for the outcome, if they are interested (and not compliant), they end up enjoying the experience. With both of these examples, though, because the students are only interested in the AP course and volunteering, they would not continue doing it unless they got the reward for their time and effort.

We do not outgrow this. As adults, we are just as likely to say "yes" to additional work or even a promotion because we want others to view us as capable, we want a raise, and/or we want the status that comes with the title that we acquire. This doesn't mean we're selling out; it means we're getting ahead. Again, what we're interested in is our job, and if we're going to do it, why not get the highest pay we can? If I like this and you're willing to pay me to do it, that's a win-win.

Is "Good" Enough?

One of the major reasons I wrote this book is because we use the term "engagement" all the time in the field of education, yet we never take the time to create interrater reliability about what we mean when we say "engaged." You and I can both sit in a classroom and observe the students, and without a common understanding of what we are looking for, I can say, "The students **were not** engaged," and you can say, "The students **were** engaged." Even though we observed the same classroom and came to different conclusions, we would both be right if we do not take the time to create common understandings.

People at the interest level **are** engaged. I want to emphasize this point because some see a scale with four markers and struggle to accept anything less than the fourth marker to be a sign of success. In the same way that the highest level of the Danielson Framework for Teaching is "a place you visit, not a place you live," the same is true for The Engagement Framework. This is because it is not easy for someone to create tasks that are interesting for others. Further, depending on your own beliefs and practices, releasing control of assignments, adding choice and voice to tasks, and learning about those with whom you are working so that you understand the consequences that motivate them could be challenging. This is why it is not a bad thing to aim for getting to the interest level.

Think about it. What level of defeat exists when people who have to do something

> **What level of defeat exists when people who have to do something enjoy what they are doing?**

enjoy what they are doing? Most of education is compulsory, even at a collegiate level when there are prerequisite courses. Rarely, if ever, do students in elementary or middle schools select what courses they enroll in. The teachers, administrators, the board of education, and the government determine what is required. So, we take students and put them in classes they are required to take and the teachers are required to teach. While all of this sounds painful and demotivating, there are teachers and students every day who find real interest in what they are doing. Students who are excited to work on the project, read about the topic, or learn the skill. Teachers who are eager to take the requirements and personalize them so that even if it is something that must be taught, that students will want to learn about it. This is where engagement starts. This is not to say that authorities should not seek ways to move beyond the interest level; it is simply to say that the interest level is worthy of both celebration and the label of real engagement.

Interest Is Easy

On a final note regarding interest, it's important to note that to be interested doesn't mean that the task you are doing is relevant, challenging, or appropriate. There are students in classrooms every day who like what they're doing, but what they're doing is unintentionally not aligned to the expected learning outcomes.

Take, for example, the students in Chapter 2 who were supposed to be learning about humans' impact on the environment. Even if the students had been interested in making the posters, they could have been incorrect in what they put on the posters. Or, the learning outcome may have been meant for a different grade level. You get the point. When we focus on learning activities at the expense of the learning outcomes, we can increase engagement in the process of doing the task but have a negative or neutral impact on the learning of the task. Interesting things like group work, poster creation, games, etc., can be fun and, when done well, can also be educational. In schools, we need to ensure that we find ways to do both at the same time—not one at the expense

> When we focus on learning activities at the expense of learning outcomes we can increase engagement in the process of doing the task but have a negative or neutral impact of the learning of the task.

of the other. After all, learning without fun is too common, but so is fun without learning.

Bringing the Lessons to Life
History Came Alive…And Then Departed

When my oldest son, Nolan, was in fifth grade, he was assigned a History Comes Alive project. This is where students research someone who is dead in order to learn as much as they could about the person. Ultimately, students "bring the person to life" in a presentation where they dress up and "become" that person. Speaking in the first person, a student will talk about *my* childhood and *my* work, as though that student *is* the researched person.

In my son's class, he was able to choose the person who he researched, Steve Jobs. Nolan spent hours reading about Jobs and creating the speech he would ultimately share during his presentation. He spent even more time rehearsing his speech so that he had it memorized. None of this includes the time he spent in class on his tri-fold board and helping others with their boards. This was all Nolan talked about for months when he talked about what he was doing in school. He could not have been prouder of himself and I could not have been more surprised by his level of engagement.

Prior to the fifth grade, Nolan's teachers most commonly described his work style as "rushed." Historically comments on his report cards always included sentiments like, "Nolan is bright but needs to slow down and take his time" and

"Nolan often has errors because he is rushing." This was not the case with his History Comes Alive project. I wouldn't say that he went slower, but I would say that because he cared so much about the details, his accuracy improved. I would commonly find Nolan in his room rehearsing his speech or drawing an Apple logo even when he could have been doing other things like playing video games. He was unquestionably engaged in this work.

As I worked on this book, a year after he finished, I asked him, "Did you like doing the History Comes Alive project?"

His answer was quick and to the point, "Yeah."

"What did you like about it?"

In the way a sixth-grade boy's response would be, Nolan said, "I don't know." When probed a little further, he said, "I liked History Comes Alive because it was fun to do and dress up and know more than anybody else about the person I was."

"Nolan, would you have liked it as much if you were assigned a person?"

"No."

"Why not?"

"Because what if I got someone who wasn't interesting and I didn't have as much to learn or say about that person. I wouldn't have liked that."

"If your teacher changed her mind and told you at some point after you started that you no longer had to do the project, what would you have done?"

"Stopped."

"I thought you liked doing the project."

"I did," Nolan said, "But, I still would have stopped if I could have."

I wish that I could say that I was surprised. I wasn't. I knew that Nolan would say that because he didn't continue doing anything in relation to the project once it was over. Though Nolan has always been interested in reading short biographies about historically famous people (one of his perennially favorite books when he was younger was *Superstars of History,* a book for kids of 40 biographies by R. J. Grant), he did not want to know more about Jobs. He did not want to research another person. He did not become more interested in history. In short, despite his willingness and commitment to this project, his engagement level extended only as high as interested.

Yet, as a parent, I was *thrilled* to see Nolan so engaged. I did not need to coax him to do his homework; he did it without prompting. I'm sure his teacher was happy too. The other students in his class were equally interested; Nolan's interest in the project was the norm. Accordingly, when given time to work on their projects in class, the students were eager to do their work. It was a win-win.

Chapter Summary

This chapter crossed the threshold from *disengaged* to *engaged* because *interested* is the most basic level of engagement. Whereas the direction previously explored is vertical and related to extrinsic motivators (consequences and relationships), shifting from compliant to interested is a horizontal shift with the relationship to the task.

- Interest gets students to a point whereby they are more than just willing to do the work—they want to do the work. At least for that moment. However, when the bell rings or the unit is over, the student is no longer willing to continue.

- When people are only at the interested level, the enjoyment is both temporary and also extrinsically motivated—the student enjoys the task but would quit if the extrinsic consequence(s) was taken away. For students, the consequence is in the form of grades, for adults, it's in the form of their paycheck.

- To increase engagement, we must strengthen the relationship with the task. Doing so happens through focusing on who is doing the task as much as what needs to be done.

- The more the authority controls the creation of the task for those who are doing the task, the more likely the feelings towards that task will be compliant (at most). The more voice and choice those doing the task have in the creation and/or selection of the task, the more likely the feelings towards that task will be interested (at least).

- It is not a bad thing to aim for getting to the interested level. This is where engagement starts.

- There are at least three main types of interested people: (1) willing participants, (2) professionals, and (3) strategists.

- Since people can find interest in unnecessary tasks, being interested doesn't mean that the task you are doing is relevant, challenging, or appropriate. We need to guard against making tasks that sacrifice the learning for enjoyment.

Reflection Questions

1. Most people are surprised that interest isn't the highest level of engagement. Were you?

   _____

   _____

   _____

2. In your current role, think of a task that you are interested in doing? What about that task is interesting? Why do you not continue to pursue doing that task beyond the point you have to?

   _____

   _____

   _____

3. Think of a task that you are doing at a level of compliance. What about that task could be changed to move it towards the interested level for you?

   _____

   _____

   _____

4. If all jobs paid the same amount of money, what job would you want?

   _____

   _____

   _____

5. Most teachers feel like if they took grades away from their students, the students would not do the work. How do students learn to focus on grades (extrinsic) and not on learning (intrinsic)?

    _____

    _____

    _____

6. Where would you plot a willing participant, a professional, and a strategist in the Interested Quadrant? Would the plot points for each overlap or be in distinct areas of the quadrant?

    _____

    _____

    _____

Persistent Questions

1. What have you done so far regarding the three challenge questions from the Introduction?

    a. **Three:** Find at least three people with whom to share your learning.

    b. **Two:** Find at least two ideas that change you.

    c. **One:** Apply at least one idea from your reading.

    _____

    _____

    _____

2. What have you learned so far, and how will you use it?

    _____

    _____

    _____

Chapter 7

*"Excellence isn't about working extra hard to do what you're told.
It's about taking the initiative to do work you decide is worth doing."*

~ Seth Godin

Recognizing Your Thinking Before You Read...

• How is motivation linked to absorption?

_____

_____

_____

• Is absorption more common within the workplace for adults or the classroom for students? Why?

_____

_____

_____

• What is the relationship between absorption and challenge?

_____

_____

_____

• Is it possible to be too absorbed?

_____

_____

_____

Absorption and the Engagement Matrix

In the bottom right side of The Engagement Matrix, you will find *absorption*. Though it's on the bottom, this is the highest form of engagement. This is because to be absorbed, you are highly interested in the task, and you have no regard for the external consequence or relationship related to the task; you are intrinsically motivated. This means that the task you are doing is so enjoyable for you that you would choose to do it even if you didn't have to. As such, it is probably the state of engagement that you are least likely to find in most classrooms or workplaces. This chapter will explain why absorption in the workplace and in schools is so challenging but also why it is so important. As with the other levels of engagement, absorption manifests in a variety of ways from those who are exploring a new pursuit to those who have found a passion for a task to those who take their absorption in the task too far.

Figure 7.1: Absorbed and the Engagement Matrix

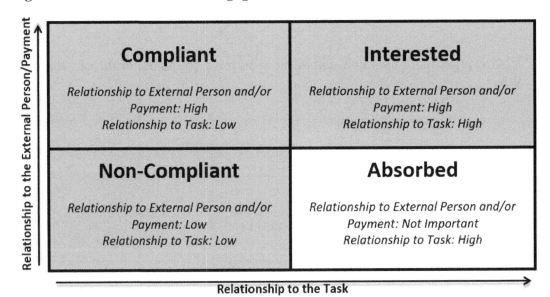

Let There Be Light

Thomas Edison famously remarked, "Genius is 99 percent perspiration and 1 percent inspiration." Of course, his advice is meant to spotlight the fact that no matter how great an idea is, it will take a tremendous amount of effort to go from the thought to the tangible creation. He should know. "In the period from 1878 to 1880 Edison and his associates worked on at least three thousand different theories to develop an efficient incandescent lamp."[11] His commitment to his idea and his ability to continuously work despite failure is the definition of absorption. This is because when a person is absorbed, the work, though challenging, does not feel like work in the traditional sense.

When doing work at the absorption level, time passes differently. We know when we're not there. A ten-minute activity feels like it lasts an hour because we are disengaged and want it to be over. On the other hand, we have all been doing something for an hour where it feels like only ten minutes have passed and we want more time. In his book, *Flow*, Mihaly Csikszentmihalyi posits that people strive to find experiences in their life that they find optimal, which he terms "flow." Flow is "the state in which people are so involved in an activity that nothing else seems to matter; the experience itself is so enjoyable that people will do it even at great cost, for the sheer sake of doing it."[12] Though I am sure that Edison had days of despair and drudgery, his persistence in the creation of the lightbulb demonstrates both the aspect of great costs but also great involvement. Indeed, Csikszentmihalyi lists numerous examples in his book of people working with great effort who find themselves in a "zone" where time and effort are lost in a blur of total engagement in the actions they are doing despite the fact that the actions require challenge.

In the introduction of the book *Flow*, Csikszentmihalyi explains that flow is not a state of ease, but a state of purposeful challenge that leads to accomplishment.[13]

"Contrary to what we usually believe…the best moments in our lives, are not the passive, receptive, relaxing times—although such experiences can also be enjoyable, if we have worked hard to attain them. The best moments usually occur when a person's body or mind is stretched to its limits in a voluntary effort to accomplish something difficult and worthwhile. Optimal experience is thus something that we make happen. For a child, it could be placing with trembling fingers the last block on a tower she has built, higher than any she has built so far; for a swimmer, it could be trying to beat his own record; for a violinist, mastering an intricate musical

---

passage. For each person there are thousands of opportunities, challenges to expand ourselves.

"Such experiences are not necessarily pleasant at the time they occur. The swimmer's muscles might have ached during this most memorable race, his lungs might have felt like exploding, and he might have been dizzy with fatigue—yet these could have been the best moments of his life. Getting control of life is never easy, and sometimes it can be definitely painful. But in the long run optimal experiences add up to a sense of mastery—or perhaps better, a sense of *participation* in determining the content of life—that comes as close to what we meant by happiness as anything else we con conceivable imagine."

Challenge and Engagement

Csikszentmihalyi is clear about how challenge is a critical aspect of flow. Ironically, when people are disengaged, those who assign the task are often quick to decrease the challenge and make it easier. Several years ago, I was at a New York State Education Department Common Core roll-out session. Kate Gerson, a Senior Fellow for the University of the State of New York Regents Research Fund at the time, matter-of-factly remarked, "The consequence of most of our lessons is that students leave the lesson informed about what has happened in the text…[because we teach in a way that] rescues, that dives in, that scoops students up and does the analysis for them."[14]   For numerous reasons, teachers can shelter students from struggle as though struggling is a state to be minimized—or worse yet—avoided.

> For numerous reasons teachers can shelter students from struggle as though struggling is a state to be minimized—or worse yet—avoided.

The impact of challenge on engagement is echoed by Angela Duckworth's work on "grit." Duckworth defines grit in this way:

Grit is passion and perseverance for long-term goals. One way to think about grit is to consider what grit isn't. Grit isn't talent. Grit isn't luck. Grit isn't how intensely, for the moment, you want something. Instead, grit is about having what some researchers call an "ultimate concern"—a goal you care about so much that it organizes and gives meaning to almost everything you do. And grit is holding steadfast to that goal. Even when you fall down. Even when you screw up. Even when progress toward that goal is halting or slow.[15]

In other words, rather than rescuing students from challenging tasks, we need to teach them how to have grit.

Remember, to be absorbed means that you are willing to do the task beyond the point that you are able to stop; it is not limited to a timeframe. As well, tasks that are absorbing are those that require persistence because we cannot achieve the highest levels of success in that task the first time we embark. If we did, it would be too easy, and we would lose interest. Tasks that are absorbing are those that require us to be gritty for the very fact that we will need to (a) devote a great deal of time and effort to it before we achieve the end goal and (b) because we will need to be resilient since we will experience failure along the way.

Grittiness pairs beautifully with Carol Dweck's work on a growth mindset, or the belief that success is a result of effort, not predestined ability. Those with a growth mindset recognize that even though there are people who may have more initial skill in one area or another, that long-term success is dependent upon the time and effort a person is willing to contribute towards growing their skills. Contrast this with a fixed mindset where someone believes that success is a function of innate and finite abilities. Therefore, fixed mindset people believe that if they are not good at something when they try it for the first time, they should quit trying because their lack of initial success is an indicator that this is a skill they do not have. Growth mindset people would approach the same experience very differently and say, *I will probably not be good at something when I try it for the first time, but with practice, I will improve.* Lack of initial success is not a deterrent; it's a reminder that practice and dedication lead to success. Grit and growth mindset are clearly connected. Both highlight traits of commitment and resilience, and these are traits that are critical to engagement, particularly when it is at the absorption level.

Therefore it is imperative for teachers who truly want engaged learners to create the conditions in which engagement can happen. Every educator is familiar with the idea of intrinsic motivation. We learn about it in our undergraduate courses, and we compare it to the demonized extrinsic motivation, its opposite. Where extrinsic motivation is all about a carrot or a stick, intrinsic motivation is all about the inner compass. *The joy of doing this comes from what I give to myself for doing this, not from what you can give me for doing it.* As Kendra Cherry's article, "Intrinsic Motivation: Why You Do Things," reminds us, if you think about what intrinsic motivation is, it is the desire to do something

> for the pure enjoyment of it...Your motivations for engaging in the behavior arises entirely from within rather than out of a desire to gain some type of external rewards such as prizes, money, or acclaim. Of course, that isn't to say that intrinsically motivated behaviors do not come with their own rewards. These rewards involve creating positive emotions within the individual.[16]

The reality is, however, we need to explicitly teach students about intrinsic motivation so that they can recognize what it feels like and so that they seek out that feeling.

What Is Your Hobby

This brings the conversation about engagement full circle. When explaining the WHAT of non-compliance, there was the discussion about Goldilocks. This was the idea that people will disengage when things are either too hard or too easy, that is, outside of their Zone of Proximal Development. *It doesn't matter how hard I try, this is just too hard.* On the other hand, there's the feeling of *I was doing this years ago...this is so boring.* Either one of these scenarios creates a dynamic that is ripe for disengagement. This is why you cannot consider whether or not people are non-compliant for one of the three other reasons (rebellion, normalization, or activism) unless and until you determine if what is being asked is something that they could legitimately do in the first place. When someone is in a state of absorption, there is no need to ask if the task is too hard or too easy; the very fact that the person is deeply engaged is a sure-sign that the task being done is within the Zone of Proximal Development.

> **When someone is in a state of absorption, there is no need to ask if the task is too hard or too easy; the very fact that the person is deeply engaged is a sure-sign that the task being done is within the Zone of Proximal Development.**

Interestingly, it is not uncommon for someone who is struggling greatly to become deeply engaged if the conditions are changed. People who may struggle to read will resist reading. However, if given a book on a topic of interest, those same struggling readers will become engaged and not want to put the book down. In this way, one's ability is directly related to one's interest.

In speaking with many people about engagement, before I share my thinking with them, I ask them three questions.

1. Tell me about at least one of your hobbies?
2. How do you know if someone is engaged?
3. What can you do to increase engagement for yourself or others?

I ask the second question because I know that I will change their thinking, but I want to create a baseline for them. This is also an important question because when I ask people question two, they often point to compliance-based behaviors. Further, even when people identify characteristics of engagement, they are often not able to identify the common leverage points to increase engagement.

More important to this chapter, however, is the first question about someone's hobby. What I want to elicit is not really what the hobby is, but help people identify the complexity of what the task entails. Interestingly, because of their experiences and/or psychological proximity to the task, many people are unable to see the challenge in what they willingly do. Therefore, I want them to consider how often they do their hobbies, how they feel when they're doing them, how much their hobbies cost (both in terms of time and money), and how their proficiency within their hobbies has evolved over time. Unless the hobby is new, there is surely growth in one's abilities, but these changes are gradual and can be easily missed. Therefore, tasks that are absorbing have these common traits:

a. I really want to do even when I don't have to
b. I give my own resources to do
c. It is appropriately difficult for me

It's important to state explicitly that I use the term "hobby" when introducing people to the concept of absorption for two reasons. The first is literal. Everyone has at least one hobby making it easy for people to understand what is meant by the term. Though people quickly grasp that hobbies are pastimes we do of our own free will, it can sometimes take a little more convincing to demonstrate the inherent level of challenge. Nevertheless, people tend to get there. The second reason I use the term hobby is figurative. This is where I make the transition from home to work/school. If you can understand how a personal hobby functions, then how can we take these traits and transfer them into the school setting for both students and educators?

For example, it is common for those who are absorbed to have a goal regarding their hobby. *I want to finish this race in this time. I want to beat this level before the end of the week. I want to complete this painting by the time winter comes.* Not only that, most of the time, absorbed people also have their next task in mind before they achieve their current task. *When I finish with this, I'm going to move on to that.* Csikszentmihalyi tells us this is because "One cannot enjoy doing the same thing at the same level for long. We grow either bored or frustrated, and then the desire to enjoy ourselves again pushes us to stretch our skills, or to discover new opportunities for using them."[17] It is this type of thinking that we could and should be using in schools but, for whatever reason, is uncommon in traditional classroom settings where everyone is expected to learn and do the same things even though we know that every student in the room is different.

I Think I Like You

In a manner that is similar to non-compliance, with its different archetypes of non-compliance (rebel, normalizer, activist), absorption also has a range of manifestations. This is important because even though the goal would be to create tasks that are at the absorbed level, not all absorption is the same, and we need to be alert to when absorption crosses over into an unhealthy place. More of that in a moment. For now, let's enter into the lowest form of absorption, being a "novice." When you're a novice, you are smitten with the idea of the task. You may or may not have yet really tried to do it yet, but the idea of it is really appealing.

In Disney's *Beauty and the Beast*, there is a song called, "Tale As Old As Time" that says, "Barely even friends, then somebody bends unexpectedly." This is an example of those first moments of desire that may ultimately lead to love. The thing is, in the beginning, a novice is not quite sure if a long-term relationship with the other person is appropriate, but a novice is curious about whether or not there may be something there. This is the feeling of being intrigued. It's the feeling of thinking about that person all of the time and thinking about your future and if that person is in it. You know that feeling. It's not yet love, but there is potential.

That same feeling is present with absorbing tasks. Maybe you saw someone doing something that looked exciting—*hmmm, that rock climbing looks like something I might like.* Maybe you read something that mentioned another book, and you considered buying it—*that book sounds like it's right up my alley.* There are a million entry points of introduction to a new task, but no matter the method, the person's interest is piqued, and this new activity becomes a welcomed part of that person's free time. Novices sample tasks they think they might like in order to see if they like the reality of doing it as much as they liked the idea of doing it. The truth is that since the novice is trying the task on for size, there is a good chance that the task may not be nearly as engaging as the novice hoped. It may be too hard, too easy, too expensive, too time-consuming, too isolating from others, etc., and the task then becomes a tried-and-failed relationship rather than something long-term. This task was a "phase."

The rejection of possible absorption tasks is actually a perfectly healthy and important behavior. After all, we can't do everything, and it would be very unhealthy if people continued to do things they did not like doing in their free time. As well, learning what you do not enjoy

> The rejection of possible absorption tasks is actually a perfectly healthy and important behavior.

is just as important as it is to learn what you do enjoy. In other words, just like in your dating life where it is important to kiss a lot of "frogs" before you find your "prince(ss)," it is critical to try on a lot of different tasks before you find your true loves.

We have all be novices as students when there was a topic, course, book, club, or extra-curricular, that we found ourselves being attracted to. The most ready examples of this tend to be things that occurred beyond the school day rather than during it; it is the sport you tried out for and played for only one season or the play you participated in and enjoyed but wasn't nearly as fun as you thought it would be.

In college, I had the opportunity to take a course called, "The Beauty and Art of Chess." I was very excited because I didn't really know how to play chess but had always wanted to learn how. I was eager to get my own chess set and to come to class. At the end of the course, I thought I would be a decent chess player and would play chess as often as I could. My novice optimism about what I was doing and how I would feel about it were high. In reality, I found that even though I understood how to play chess, playing it was much more difficult than I anticipated. What's more, the difficulty was not one that motivated me to persist even though I enjoy difficulty in other areas of my life. Thus, for whatever reason, I never became more than a novice chess player and, in fact, realized that I was really only interested in playing chess since it would provide me quality time with someone who I wanted to spend time with (extrinsic relationship consequence).

True Love

You become an "enthusiast" at the point in which you find a task that you truly enjoy. Enthusiasts become engrossed in a task, and the rest of the world falls away. They're so focused on the task that nothing else matters. This is "flow." It does not mean that you cannot stop, but that if given a choice, you would keep going. This is not just a flash-in-the-pan, it's a commitment of time and resources.

We all have these areas in our lives. Tasks that we spend our free time doing and, in our downtime of our work, we daydream about. It's the feeling of getting lost in playing your instruments, and even when you're not playing, you find yourself thinking about the next piece of music you are going to attempt or that tough spot in the piece you are currently working on. It's playing multiple games of chess and then when you're lying in bed, reminiscing about the opening moves you used and how they impacted the games' trajectories. These behaviors of investment and reflection are familiar to all of us even if we may not play an instrument or chess because we can all relate to being engrossed in a task that we don't want to end.

In thinking about this, I realized that hobbies come and go. What was engrossing for us at one point in our lives may not be something that lasts forever. For example, when I was two, I started dancing. If you asked me what I wanted to be when I grew up, even through the ages of eight or nine, I would have told you, "I want to be a ballerina." That changed when I was ten. I moved to a new town and started attending a new dance class. At the same time, I entered a self-aware-preteen stage of my life. This combination of circumstances led me to shy away from wanting to be in a leotard, and I backed away from dancing. Though I gave up dancing and the desire to be a ballerina that does not diminish the feelings for dance I had as a child or the role that hobby had in my life. Just like you have to kiss a lot of frogs, you will go through stages in your life where the things that you enjoy doing will change. This, too, is healthy and to be expected.

Whereas being a novice is a phase, being an enthusiast means that ***the thing we do becomes the thing we are***; it is our identity. We are not just someone who goes running (the verb), we are a runner (the noun). When Nolan was absorbed in Thomas trains (see "Bringing the Lesson to Life" at the end of the chapter),

> Whereas being a novice is a phase, being and enthusiast means that *the thing we do becomes the thing we are*; it is our identity.

his identity could have been called a Thomas Enthusiast. You can be an athlete, a knitter, a cat-lover, a YouTuber, or a disciple. People who are truly absorbed embrace the identity of the thing they are passionate about.

This reminds me of when I was a student-teacher. In my second placement, I taught eleventh-grade students. At some point, I asked them, "Who in here is a writer?" Not one student raised a hand. I was shocked (though I wouldn't be now). I said, "Wait. Why is no one raising their hands? You can all write, correct? So why wouldn't you call yourself a writer?" It's a silly question now, I realize. Being able to do something—like write or chemistry or run—does not mean that someone sees that as their identity—I ***am*** a writer, a chemist, or a runner. Claiming an identity suggests a deeper level of both skill and absorption for the task that is being done.

Further, in our culture, we place a great deal on formal education and preparation before we allow people to claim a moniker. In this way, one could not have a title unless one has the pedigree or endorsed preparation. This is something that schools need to be on guard for so that we can help students understand that they have the opportunity to adopt a writer's, scientist's, or athlete's mindset. In other words, anyone can get absorbed in the tasks that these people do.

We Have a Problem

In *The Odyssey*, sailors who were once on a desperate journey to get home became so distracted by their consumption of the lotus (a food) that they completely forgot what their true mission was. These men were beyond smitten or engrossed in the lotus, they were obsessed, and this obsession was not just a temporary distraction, but a life-altering addiction that impaired their ability to do the other things that they once valued. While it is appropriate and essential in living a good life to have things in which we will be absorbed, it is also inappropriate and dangerous to cross the line and become a lotus-eater.

The Odyssey **is an epic poem about Odysseus' trials and tribulations in his journey home after war. In book IX, Odysseus' ship lands on the island of Lotus-Eaters.**

I was driven thence by foul winds for a space of nine days upon the sea, but on the tenth day we reached the land of the Lotus-eaters, who live on a food that comes from a kind of flower. Here we landed to take in fresh water, and our crews got their mid-day meal on the shore near the ships. When they had eaten and drunk I sent two of my company to see what manner of men the people of the place might be, and they had a third man under them. They started at once, and went about among the Lotus-eaters, who did them no hurt, but gave them to eat of the lotus, which was so delicious *that those who ate of it left off caring about home, and did not even want to go back and say what had happened to them, but were for staying and munching lotus with the Lotus-eaters without thinking further of their return*; nevertheless, though they wept bitterly I forced them back to the ships and made them fast under the benches. Then I told the rest to go on board at once, lest any of them should taste of the lotus and leave off wanting to get home, so they took their places and smote the grey sea with their oars.[18] (emphasis added)

A modern metaphor might be that we cannot survive if we only eat ice cream. Though the idea of that sounds great at first, the reality is that ice cream cannot sustain us in the long term, and we would quickly feel sick. When we cross the line from a healthy, balanced lifestyle and abuse those things that are meant to be consumed in moderation, we become unbalanced and unhealthy. This is true if we're talking about drugs, alcohol, food, and—as it relates to engagement—personal or professional (school) diversions.

There is nothing inherently wrong or bad in relation to, say, gambling. Many of us enjoy an occasional night of poker or cards with friends. However, if people spend their full day playing these games and neglect themselves or their responsibilities, that is a problem. It's a problem if this impacts others like your spouse, children, and/or parents. It's a problem if you cannot stop even when you recognize the negative impact of your choices on others. Therefore, we would be wise to follow the advice of Epicurious, who said, "Be moderate in order to taste the joys of life in abundance." This is why people who become consumed by an absorbing task are addicted to it. Addicts, then, are the third type of absorbed person.

Both unfortunately and surprisingly, for many students, parents, and educators, the thing we are most addicted to in schools is not a task, but the consequence we give students for doing the tasks—grades. It's hard to determine what you are absorbed in when the things that are most absorbing are things that are challenging. Since challenging tasks are ones that require perseverance through repeated failure before achieving success, if graded on attainment of success, absorbing tasks would routinely be scored low. If the grade matters—and we have *taught* students that grades matter—then in courses where tasks are graded (particularly in a traditional manner), students will not become absorbed.

Adults expose even PreK students to grades not as a form of feedback regarding progress, but as an extrinsic motivator to acquire. Even before students are taught about percentages and averages, we place "100%" on their papers with stickers or smiley faces. We tell them implicitly and explicitly that doing well means getting good grades. Though we may give lip service to effort and persistence, we instill a fixed mindset whereby doing well means doing well the first time, and your grade will reflect that. We then also tell students that they need to figure out what they love to do and find a way to get paid to do it. This is not a mixed message as much as it is an afterthought or conciliatory axiom meant to make us feel like we are not just concerned about grades. Fueled by an obsession for class rank, honor roll, academic awards, etc., our addiction to grades is most prevalent with students who get good grades (or parents who want their child to get them). Though we would never equate grades to obsessive over-eating, spending, gambling, or drugs, in schools, grades are as ubiquitous and harmful as over-consumption of toxic substances like nicotine, alcohol, drugs.

Bringing the Lessons to Life:
Absorption Through Life

My son Nolan was a Thomas the Tank Engine enthusiast as a toddler. He spent a lot of time at his train table, watching Thomas cartoons, reading Thomas books, and we would take him for train rides. Now that he's older, it does not surprise me that he is no longer interested in trains—in fact, it would be more surprising if he was. Many of the things he likes now are probably not going to be the things he will like a decade from now. There are many reasons for this. Of course there are things related to physiological changes that will influence his preferences, but there are also environmental impacts. The people he will encounter throughout his life change and impact the things that he may be exposed to and, ultimately, what he will enjoy.

At the same time, there will be tasks that Nolan is enthusiastic about now that he will always be engrossed in. Nolan is passionate about soccer. I'd be willing to bet money that Nolan will always play soccer. He may or may not go on to play collegiate or professional soccer, but I think in some way, he will play and, if he has children, so will they.

Chapter Summary

This chapter provided the background to explain absorption—the highest level of engagement. When you are absorbed, you are drawn into the task and have no regard for the external reward or relationship related to the task; you are intrinsically motivated. This means that the task you are doing is so enjoyable for you that you would choose to do it even if you didn't have to.

- Mihaly Csikszentmihalyi calls absorption "flow" and emphasizes the importance of challenge regarding activities that cause us to lose track of time and derive focus. Ironically, in schools, we often shelter students from challenge because we think that they will resist. Angela Duckworth's and Carol Dweck's research supports the belief that those who embrace challenge are more likely to find success and satisfaction.

- Everyone has something in which they are absorbed...they call this their hobby. When they are engaged in their hobbies, they are willing to spend time and money on it and, as a result, improve as they work within their Zone of Proximal Development.

- There are at least three types of absorbed people—novice, enthusiast, and addict. Novices are just "trying on" activities, enthusiasts who are willing to make a long-term commitment of time and resources, and addicts who neglect their responsibilities and others.

- In schools, grades are the most common form of addiction.

Reflection Questions

1. What is something that makes you feel absorbed in your current work? What is something that could be done to increase your absorption in your current work?

    _____

    _____

    _____

2. Consider the conditions you have created for others. How could you alter the conditions to increase absorption?

    _____

    _____

    _____

3. Do you think we need to explicitly teach students about intrinsic motivation so that they can recognize what it feels like and that they need to seek out that feeling? What is an example of how you could do that?

    _____

    _____

    _____

4. I hear adults say all the time that students will give up when they get to something that is challenging. Do you see this in your experiences, and how do you encourage students to approach challenge rather than giving up?

    _____

    _____

    _____

5. What is a hobby of yours? How much time do you spend doing it? What do you need to buy or pay for to do it? Why is it so absorbing to you?

_____

_____

_____

6. Think of a hobby that didn't make it past the "novice" phase. What was it that attracted you to this hobby, and why do you think you didn't become an enthusiast?

_____

_____

_____

7. What is the role of grades in your classroom? Do grades interfere with engagement?

_____

_____

_____

Persistent Questions

1. What have you done so far regarding the three challenge questions from the Introduction?

    a. **Three:** Find at least three people with whom to share your learning.

    b. **Two:** Find at least two ideas that change you.

    c. **One:** Apply at least one idea from your reading.

_____

_____

_____

2. What have you learned so far, and how will you use it?

_____

_____

_____

Section III: So What

The next four chapters will provide valuable insight as to why each of the four levels in The Engagement Framework matter. By the end of Section III, you will be able to recognize how you can have a direct impact on your own and others' levels of engagement and use that to increase engagement.

Chapter 8

Non-Compliant: *So What*

"You are always responsible for how you act, no matter how you feel."
~Robert Tew

Recognizing Your Thinking Before You Read...

- What influence do the following have on non-compliance?

  Perspective • Relationship • Motivation

  _____

  _____

  _____

- How could you assist rebels, normalizers, and activists to shift towards compliance?

  _____

  _____

  _____

- When motivating someone, are there times when carrots work better than sticks and vice versa? How can you tell?

  _____

  _____

  _____

Reflecting on Non-Compliance

As you recall, when non-compliance manifests, we must ask if the task is within the Zone of Proximal Development (ZPD) of the person doing the work. If the task is too hard or too easy, people will be non-compliant because they are defeated (too hard) or disinterested (too easy). If this is the case, there is a simple solution for disengagement—change the challenge of the task, and you'll increase engagement. Given this, it's obvious why it's important to understand the underlying motivation behind the non-compliance. Once you understand, you can respond accordingly. This chapter explains the importance of understanding non-compliance, in all its forms and the impact that can have on engagement.[iii]

The Wind and the Sun

When my youngest son, Oliver, was in the first grade, he brought home a book to read on the fable of "The Wind and The Sun." This has always been one of my favorites, and I was excited for him to read it. If you are not familiar with it, this fable personifies the sun and the wind. Each thinks himself stronger than the other. They see a man walking up the road and decide that the one who can get the man to remove his coat is the strongest.

The Wind goes first. He blows and blows, but rather than the man taking off his coat, the man clutches his coat closed and shivers. The images of The Wind blowing make The Wind look like he is exerting great effort—his cheeks are puffed out, and his eyebrows are knitted together. It is clear that The Wind is exhausting himself to get the man to remove his coat.

When it is The Sun's turn, his tactic is different. The Sun, rather than try to bully the man into removing his coat, simply begins to smile. The Sun's warmth is bright and friendly. The once hunched-over, distressed man begins to relax. When you turn the page, The Sun's smile has grown even larger, and the man is removing his coat. By the end of the story, the man's coat and hat are off, and he has unbuttoned his shirt and rolled up his sleeves. The moral of this story is that through kindness and warmth, you can accomplish more than you can if you are cold and aggressive.

[iii] This chapter assumes that the task is within the doer's ZPD and, therefore the non-compliance is a manifestation of disinterest in the relationship or consequence for doing the task.

In "The Wind and the Sun," to be compliant means to remove a coat. This means that when the man clutched tighter to his coat to protect himself from the blustery blowing of The Wind, the man was being non-compliant; he did not do what The Wind wanted. In response, The Wind did not ease up or change course—he doubled down and became more aggressive. The more the man attempted to protect himself from The Wind's actions, the more non-compliant he became. It was only when The Sun shined warmly on the man did the man choose to comply. Eventually, not only did the man take off his coat, he willingly rolled up his sleeves and did more than what The Wind or The Sun even expected him to do.

> **Eventually, not only did the man take off his coat, he willingly rolled up his sleeves and did more than what The Wind or The Sun even expected him to do.**

So much can be gleaned from this fable if read through the lens of engagement. It speaks to the importance of relationships and motivation. Trying to force people to do things they do not want to do is hard enough. Getting aggressive towards people will not only demotivate them from doing the task, but it will also negatively affect the relationship. The interesting thing is, when most people read the story, they put themselves in the shoes of the man. With regard to your work and engagement, I suspect that you are just as often the weather.

Why People Resist

Based on the last chapter, there are three types of people wearing coats.

1. **Rebels**: You can't make me take my coat off.
2. **Normalizers**: If so many people are wearing coats and no one gets hurt, is it really wrong?
3. **Activists**: Wearing coats is the best and only the thing to do, and trying to get me to take it off would go against my beliefs and values regarding coats.

It is important to understand the motivation behind the person wearing the coat because it will impact the approach needed to get the person to remove the coat, though warmth would likely help no matter what the motivation is.

Unfortunately, it can be very difficult to be warm and sunny when someone refuses to do what was asked—especially if you are in a position of authority and the person is a subordinate. By definition, a subordinate is someone who is lower in position and, according to the standard hierarchy, this person should, as my mother would sometimes say to me, "only ask 'How high?' when told to 'Jump!'" If you are someone who takes this perspective, then the idea that as a superior you would have to be warm might cause you to feel *heated* instead. Nevertheless, if you are the superior and your goal is to have the subordinate do what you have directed, understanding the other person aids you in achieving your goal. The good news is, this may not be as hard as you may first suspect.

Seek First to Understand

In his book, *The Seven Habits of Highly Effective People*, Stephen Covey explains that after years of research, he discovered that there are seven universal and timeless principles that effective people recognize, embrace, and embody; Covey labels these principles "habits." The fifth habit is "Seek First to Understand, Then to Be Understood." The thinking behind the fifth habit is the notion that we need to listen without an agenda or judgment to truly hear what the other person is saying.

If you're like most people, you probably seek first to be understood; you want to get your point across. And in doing so, you may ignore the other person completely, pretend that you're listening, selectively hear only certain parts of the conversation or attentively focus on only the words being said, but miss the meaning entirely. So why does this happen? Because most people listen with the intent to reply, not to understand. You listen to yourself as you prepare in your mind what you are going to say, the questions you are going to ask, etc. You filter everything you hear through your life experiences, your frame of reference. You check what you hear against your autobiography and see how it measures up. And consequently, you decide prematurely what the other person means before he/she finishes communicating.[19]

> "And consequently, you decide prematurely what the other person means before he/she finishes communicating."

We do this not because we're bad people, it's because we have bad habits. We think that others either (a) think like we think or (b) should think like we think. Accordingly, we treat them how we want to be treated. The problem is the way they want to be treated is not what we want—it's what *they* want.

Keeping in mind the notion of seeking first to understand and then to be understood, there are two reasons why someone would shift from non-compliant behavior to compliant behavior, and they can be seen if you look at the left side of The Engagement Matrix (see Figure 8.1). The difference between Non-Compliance and Compliance is not in how people feel about what they are being asked to do because in both quadrants people don't want to do the task; the difference is the relationship they have with the person asking them to do the task and/or how people feel about the extrinsic consequences they are receiving. Thus, the two features you can work on if you want to shift someone from non-compliance to compliance are (1) the relationship the person has with the person asking or (2) the consequence for doing it.

Figure 8.1 The Engagement Framework Highlighting the Differences Between Non-Compliant and Compliant Behaviors

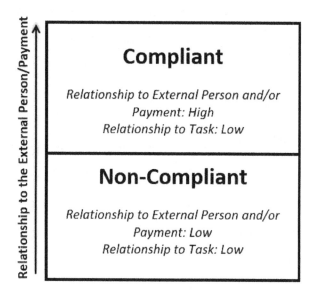

Only for You

The first reason why people would transition from being non-compliant to compliant is that they care about the person who is asking them to do it. Thus, one would need to work on the relationship between him/herself and the other person. This is why there are times when someone will do what Person A says but would not do it for Person B. If someone would do the behavior for one person and not the other, this may be a sign that the reason for the non-compliance is rebellion.

If someone is exhibiting signs of rebellion, then an antidote could be to improve your relationship with that person. The thing about growing relationships is that it is not quick nor easy. This is true if you just met someone, but it is even harder to build a strong, trusting relationship if the relationship before this point has been challenged, strained, or antagonistic. The other person is likely to be suspicious and feel as though your reasons for trying to build a better relationship are self-serving. Furthermore, that person would be right if your goal is to get the task done. Indeed, the goal of building a better relationship with someone should be the goal. Period. It must be the only reason to improve the relationship. The more I invest in our relationship, the more we will care about each other.

> A common side-effect of caring more about someone is that you are more likely to do something for people you care about—including things you may not otherwise do.

A common side-effect of caring more about someone is that you are more likely to do something for people you care about—including things you may not otherwise do. If my own children wanted to go to see a cartoon movie, I would probably take them even if I really did not want to watch the movie. I would not do the same thing for other children because my relationship with the other children is not the same as the relationship I have with my own children. Ultimately, the stronger the relationship is, the more likely I will do for you things I would not even do for myself. Through seeking first to understand, we can build and nurture our relationships with others.

What's in it for Me

Relationships are not the only benefit to understanding others. We are all familiar with the question, "What makes you tick." The meaning of this phrase highlights the things that someone is interested in, passionate about, and motivated by. These are the things that get someone out of bed in the morning—their raison d'etre. This leads me to the second reason why someone shifts from non-compliance to compliance, and that is because the extrinsic motivation (consequence) has changed.

We see this in schools. A student is having a tough day and refuses to do the work. Another adult comes over and talks to the student, and the next thing you know, the student is complying. The task didn't change. The person who is working with the student did. Another example can be seen when teachers work on teams, like they often do in middle schools. The science teacher could bring up a student who is struggling behaviorally, asking, "What is Emma like in your class?" Perhaps every teacher except the math teacher says something like, "Yeah, Emma shouts out," or "Emma isn't doing her homework for me either." The math teacher, on the other hand, says, "Emma is great in my class now. At the beginning of the year, she acted that way, but I reached out to her and asked her what was going on. She wasn't ready to open up to me, but I persisted. Now, I know that she likes basketball a lot, so I find ways to talk to her about it and to use basketball examples when we work on math. I'm not saying that she loves math, but I feel like she's working hard for me because she knows I'm trying to get to know her."

Relationships are not the only way to change behaviors from non-compliant to compliant. Extrinsic motivation can help too. Take, for example, normalizers who have let their health slide. People like this see their non-compliance with their health as a personal choice. If my non-compliance impacts just me (I am out of shape or unhealthy), then I am the person who is asking to do something different. Rather than go to the gym today, I will stay home. I will buy another pack of cigarettes. I will have dessert. Certainly, some people become motivated if someone they love frames the argument that they need to improve their health. This is also sometimes true when a medical professional tells them that they need to lose weight or quit their bad habits.

More often than not, however, the challenge to become compliant with good lifestyle choices is an intrinsic battle that can be assisted through extrinsic means. This is why things like "Biggest Loser" competitions at work are so effective. The initial motivation is the desire to lose weight, but that desire isn't compelling enough in isolation. Something external is needed, be it the prize at the end, the competition, and/or the publicity of the effort. As well, since many people tend to participate in these types of competitions, it becomes the new normal. This makes it easier for a normalizer to change behaviors and harder to continue with the old behaviors.

Finally, it is very common for behaviors that were once motivated extrinsically to shift to being intrinsically motivating as a result of seeing the positive effects of those changes. That is, I started dieting because of my office's Biggest Loser challenge, but I continued to watch what I ate and exercise after the competition was over because I saw the health benefits I gained through the process. In this way, the extrinsic motivation was a temporary scaffold on the journey from Point A (a place I initially preferred) to Point B (a place that I now find preferable to Point A).

Even if you didn't work in a school or have children who attended school now, since you were once a student, you would know that extrinsic motivation is as common in schools as reciting the Pledge of Allegiance. In the absence of intrinsic motivation, extrinsic consequences can go a long way. Primary age students love stickers and stars on their papers (many older students do too). Older students aspire to be on the Honor Roll. Schools use grades as motivators for students. Do this and get a 100 percent, don't do it and get a 0 or I'll call home, or you can't participate in recess or the dance or the game. The problem is that the thing that was meant to be a scaffold (i.e., the carrot or the stick) never goes away. The goal of the scaffold was to momentarily help encourage compliance on the way towards interest—you don't know that you'll like to do this yet, so to help you get there. In other words, I'm going to create a consequence that will move you from non-compliance to compliance. Unfortunately, the focus on the task is overshadowed by the focus on the consequence. In this way, the task becomes getting or avoiding the consequence rather than the learning.

Rewards and Punishments

Extrinsic motivation comes in many shapes and sizes, and the better I understand you, the better I am able to select a motivator that will shift you towards compliance. Positive motivators include offering a better grade or more money if you do what was asked. For adults, other positive extrinsic motivators might include a bonus like more time off or a promotion. For children, it could be lunch with the teacher, staying up later, or even dessert. There are also negative extrinsic

> Extrinsic motivation comes in many shapes and sizes and the better I understand you, the better I am able to select a motivator that will shift you towards compliance.

motivators. We can all relate to some version of the line, "If you don't take out the garbage, you'll go to your room for the rest of the night."

There are, of course, horrific and extreme examples of how knowing someone's likes and dislikes can assist in designing extrinsic motivators. Bribes, for example, are a way of manipulating someone's likes so that one could entice someone else to do something that the other person would not otherwise do. This is the classic, "You scratch my back, I'll scratch yours." Extreme examples of this could include lobbyists and politicians or criminals and lawyers. The opposite is also true. "If you don't tell me what I want to hear, something bad will happen to people you love." The first set of examples are positive extrinsic consequences, and the last example is a negative extrinsic consequence.

In Orwell's classic, *1984*, Big Brother knows everything about everyone. So, when the Thought Police imprison criminals, they administer the worst punishments in Room 101. Once they arrest the protagonist, Winston, he easily confesses to crimes he committed as well as those he did not to minimize the torture he receives. Throughout his confessions, however, he does not betray his love Julia. That is, not until he is taken to Room 101. His torture before Room 101 was generic in nature in that it was physical assault, sleep and food deprivation, etc. that all the prisoners experienced. In Room 101, rats were introduced to his punishment simply because Winston feared rats more than anything else. It was only under these conditions that Winston betrayed Julia and shouted out, "Do it to Julia."[20]

More often, however, benign and everyday examples of extrinsic motivators abound. While shopping, extrinsic incentives to get you spend more money include offering you free shipping when you spend a certain amount or giving you a higher discount as your total bill increases. When I was in school, I participated in Book It. I would be able to get a coupon for a free pizza at my local Pizza Hut every time I read a specified number of books. The now-ubiquitous Elf on a Shelf operates in this way. The elf is there to watch the children's behavior on Santa's behalf. The better the children behave, the more presents they will receive for Christmas from Santa. In a school district I once worked, teachers were paid to accrue professional development hours. At the same time, the state department of education required teachers to accrue a certain number of professional development hours every five years, or their certification will be revoked. This example about professional development highlights two sides of the same coin. Some people need the reward of an incentive to motivate their accrual of professional development; some people need the threat of revocation of their certification.

I cannot talk about rewards and punishments without mentioning Daniel Pink's work in his thought-provoking book, *Drive: The Surprising Truth About What Motivates Us*. Briefly, Pink's research found that carrots (incentives) and sticks

Learn more about the ideas in *Drive* by watching this animated video: https://cutt.ly/RSADrive

(negative consequences) have an adverse effect on motivation, actually serving to demotivate rather than to encourage engagement when the task requires more than just rote completion. That is to say, when you try to offer carrots or sticks to motivate doing tasks that are what Pink calls, "heuristic," i.e., innovative, creative, and/or something other than "plug and play," you shift the focus away from doing the task towards receiving the consequence, and that leads to an inferior outcome.

Anyone who has read *Drive* knows that the summary I have provided has grossly simplified Pink's work. Nevertheless, understanding motivation is directly related to non-compliant behavior. I would hope that much of the time that there is non-compliance, the task is what Pink would call an "algorithmic" task, or one that requires the doer to do the same thing every time; people generally do not refuse to do things that are creative or innovative. What's more, the goal is to shift the non-compliant person to compliance—*please just do what I'm asking even if you don't want to.*

If the non-compliant person refuses to do something heuristic, that's a different matter. In fact, understanding the motivation behind the behavior is just as important as understanding what to do about it since if you don't understand the why, you will risk responding incorrectly to the problem. This is the crux of "Section III: So What." Whereas "Section IV: Now What" will provide some ideas about how to respond to a non-compliant person, you may also want to read *Drive,* which does a terrific job with this, particularly when there are heuristic tasks.

Same Behavior, Different Understanding

While you can work on the relationship and the extrinsic motivators to shift someone from non-compliance to compliance, compliance is the best you could hope for if you only worked on the left side of the matrix. You would have to work on the right side of the matrix in order to shift someone to absorbed (see Figure 8.2). This would be needed if you were working with an activist who was being non-compliant.

Figure 8.2: The Engagement Framework Highlighting the Differences Between Non-Compliant and Absorbed Behaviors

Non-Compliant	**Absorbed**
Relationship to External Person and/or Payment: Low *Relationship to Task: Low*	*Relationship to External Person and/or Payment: Not Important* *Relationship to Task: High*

Relationship to the Task →

Therefore, in the event that someone is non-compliant because of activism, no relationship is likely to change the behavior because even though that person may have a respectful relationship with you already or may grow into one, that person's ideology is fundamentally opposed to what you want. As such, changes to external factors, be them carrots, sticks, or relationships, will not alter the justification for the person to do what is being asked or expected. True activists are willing to sacrifice almost anything, including their freedom or life, for their cause. As a result, it is very unlikely you could shift them towards compliance because they see themselves as absorbed in the task of resistance. There are exceptions. It can happen that as the relationship changes, your ability to have open dialogue exposes the other person to different ways of thinking, which leads to alterations in the other person's beliefs. This is the work of missionaries, for example. However, the best one could hope for is that the two parties may simply resolve at a respectful position of agreeing to disagree because the worst outcome can be deadly.

This is why the likelihood of a transition from non-compliant towards another quadrant is very low for an activist. When people feel strongly that their position is not only right, but righteous, they are most likely to see themselves as absorbed in their stance rather than non-compliant with yours. In other words, there are two different interpretations of the same behavior. In 2013, the Black Lives Matter (BLM) movement started in response to what the BLM activists saw as the systematic racism experienced by Black Americans, specifically from law enforcement. Those who supported the movement saw themselves *not* as non-compliant with the law but as absorbed with combatting race inequality in the United States. Those who opposed the movement saw those same actions differently. Rather than seeing the BLM supporters as activists, they saw them as normalizers (at best) or rebels (at worst).

> **When people feel strongly that their position is not only right, but righteous, they are most likely to see themselves as absorbed in their stance rather than non-compliant with yours.**

The problem is that if the other person's behaviors are motivated through a means that is different from the one you identify, the likelihood that the behaviors will change is small since you will be working on X when the true leverage point is Y. Sticking with the BLM activists example, there is no amount of extrinsic motivation in the form of rewards or punishments that would create compliance for a true activist. Sending BLM activists to jail will not change the way they feel about the cause (it may actually serve to reinforce the belief). So if working on rewards and punishments won't work, then the other option to achieve compliance is the relationship. This is a better bet, but it still will not create compliance for a true activist. Though an improved relationship could lead to important conversations, the relationship between some people and some other people does not have a large enough impact on the cultural inequities that the activist identifies.

Parents, more often than students, tend to be activists in school settings. How many students protested the Common Core, required immunizations, specific curriculum, or books? It can happen, but parents are those who are more likely to fall under this heading in schools. Parent activists may run for the school board, transfer their child(ren) into a different school, or decide to homeschool their child(ren). These reactions to the school demonstrate how deep activist parents' beliefs are.

More than being non-compliant with school rules, students tend to become activists for causes that are likely larger than their specific school. The most well-known example of this happened after the school shootings at Marjory Stoneman Douglas High School (MSDHS) in Parkland, Florida in 2018. Following this horrific tragedy, a handful of outraged MSDHS students formed "Never Again MSD," a group dedicated to advocating for gun control to prevent gun violence. Not only did they organize, they got others to do the same. Students from across the country participated in school walkouts in honor of those who died and as a way to evoke action, not just awareness, to ending mass shootings. Students did this even when it was not condoned by their parents or schools, and even if it meant disciplinary actions because they were committed to the cause.

This can happen on smaller scales too. When a student goes against the group and sits with a new kid at lunch, that child is being an activist. When a student voluntarily writes a letter to the administration or the board to seek a change in a policy or a procedure, the child is practicing activism. When a child sticks up for another child who is being mistreated by others (students or adults), this is an example of social non-compliance that manifests as activism.

Bringing the Lessons to Life:
The Dollars to Doughnuts Example

The following is a personal example of non-compliance and how all three leverage points (relationship, positive, and negative consequences) were utilized over time to eventually lead my children to compliantly get ready on time for school.

My husband's work schedule is such that he leaves the house a little after 5:00 A.M. As such, I have always been the sole parent responsible for ensuring that my children and I get out of the house on time. Getting three kids ready in the morning is not easy but it is something that needs to be done. Complicating matters is the fact that I am not a morning person. So, I prepare as much as possible the night before so we do not have time to dilly-dally. In order to get everyone in the car on time, I proactively created a plan before there was a concern about non-compliance.

I told the kids that if they all made it into the car before I did, that was worth one point. If we got to daycare before it opened at seven, that was also worth one point. As a team, they were able to earn two points per day. When, as a team, they earned eight points, I would buy them each a doughnut on the way to daycare. I figured that eight points meant that four out of five days a week they would be ready and waiting for me. This seemed like a reasonable goal for them—no one is perfect.

I also decided that I would allow them to continue their point tally from one week to the next. Specifically, if one week was a short week or they missed more than two points, they still had the opportunity to accumulate the points the next day. Doing so meant that the full week was not going to be a washout from their perspective if they missed those points early on. If that were the case, then in a week where they had a bad Monday (no points) and they only got one point on Tuesday, they could have decided the rest of the days that week didn't matter since mathematically they could not achieve eight points that week. That would mean they had no incentive to get in the car before me and that would have been a lose-lose scenario for all of us.

With this plan, they acted as a team. If only one of them made it to the car before I did, that was as good as none of them being in the car. I needed all of them there. I also figured that the team design of this incentive would create positive peer pressure and foster relationship building. For example, rather than one or two of them hopping in the car and feeling good that they beat me, they would know that unless they were all there, they all lost. This could encourage them to help each other if one was lagging behind. "I'll get your coat out for you," for example, or "Mom's on her way. Hurry up!" Let's call this Plan 1.0.

Though the positive peer pressure did not go as well as I would have liked (it was more like two children to one child, "It's your fault we didn't get the point today!"), Plan 1.0 worked well for years. Eventually, though, I started to notice non-compliance. It became more and more common for me to get to the car before one or more of my kids. I realized that the doughnuts were losing their novelty and allure. Around this same time, my older children began to get more interested in actual money. Since the cost of a doughnut was a dollar, the incentive morphed into Plan 2.0 "You can choose a dollar or a doughnut and you do not have to select the reward as a team. It's completely up to you which one you get." That reignited the incentive and my children hustled again to get their points.

In the winter of 2015, I accepted a new position that was closer to home. As a result, I did not need to get the kids to daycare by seven. That meant I had to come up with a new strategy for earning that second point. Enter Plan 3.0. I altered the plan so that they received one point each for getting in the car before me and another point for the group if they were all in the car before I was. This meant rather than keeping a team tally, I now had to switch to individual children tallies. It still accomplished the three musketeers' goal of "All for one and one for all."

My daughter, Lilia, who is also not a morning bird, struggles to get out of bed in the morning. Despite waking up Lilia first and having her get her clothes out the night before, the boys and I would find ourselves waiting in the car for her. As a result, she didn't earn as many points as they did. I thought her non-compliant behavior would be ameliorated by having to be in the car as we went through the drive-through and she watched her brothers eat their doughnuts. In other words, I thought that the natural consequence of watching her brothers eat doughnuts would be the motivation she needed to get compliant. It wasn't. Rather than feeling motivated, she felt alienated. Her non-compliance had nothing to do with her relationship with her brothers or me, but watching her brothers eat their doughnuts and watching me buy her brothers the doughnuts negatively impacted our relationships with her. My solution caused a bigger problem and her normalized non-compliant behavior became rebellious. When I treated her like I was The Wind, she was even less inclined to get in the car before I did because she didn't want to contribute to her brothers earning points because she was hurt. Over time our relationships in the morning improved again, but I still struggled to find a solution to her non-compliant behavior, i.e., getting to the car before I did.

In the fall of 2017, my oldest, Nolan, started middle school. In my children's school district, the middle and high school students start earlier than elementary school students. This meant, for the first time, Nolan was going to get the bus from home and just two of my kids were going to need to go to daycare. My youngest, Oliver, is not difficult to wake or get ready and I falsely believed that getting ready in the morning would be easier. I was wrong. Since Nolan was almost always in the car before I was, his not being involved in the team had no impact on assisting or preventing Oliver and Lilia's arrival to the car before me. In fact, in 2017, the months of September-December were rough. Oliver was accruing one sad point most days because Lilia was not getting to the car before I was. Once again, her non-compliance was her normalized behavior.

I was frustrated. I really did not care about the points; I cared about getting to work on time. I tried to penalize her by saying, "I am going to start the timer on my phone when I get in the car. For every minute you are late, that will be the amount of time you have to wait to use your electronics." This was a short-lived Plan 4.0. The problem was that I would forget to time her or I would forget to tell my husband her time since he was the one who got them off the bus. My carrots were no longer working for her and neither were my sticks. She was non-compliant with my expectations and I was growing ever more irritated with her lack of concern for the fact that she was letting down her brother and me.

Finally, just before the holiday break in 2017, I had an idea…I knew that Lilia was not as motivated by getting a dollar anymore (in part because she was nine and even when she had money, we still were likely to buy her things rather than her needing the money for what she wanted). But I also knew that the idea of paying me would be unbearable to her. In Late December, as I was driving Lilia and Oliver to daycare (after I got to the car before both of them), I announced Plan 5.0.

"Here's the deal. When the new year starts, if you get to the car before I do in the morning, you will still earn a point. If both of you get to the car before I do, you will earn your second point. When you get to eight points, I will still give you a dollar or a doughnut. Here's the new twist…if I get to the car before you, I get your point. When I get to eight points, YOU owe ME a dollar."

"WHAT?!"

"You heard me. I am tired of waiting for you when I have to get to work. I don't like getting up early any more than you do. It's a part of our responsibilities. We do everything we can to sleep as late as we can. I am not getting you up early because I want to get up early. We get up when we do because I have to be at work. When you are late, it could make me late to work and that's not okay. There is nothing more I can do except wake you up earlier. Would you prefer that?"

"No."

"Okay. Then this is the new plan. I will keep track daily of the points and you will only owe me a dollar when YOU have been late eight times. You do not owe me if it wasn't you."

Literally overnight my daughter changed from being non-compliant to compliant because I found the right combination of positive and negative consequences. In fact, in the first month alone she got in the car before I did 100 percent of the time. This was a 180-degree change compared to her behavior prior to the new plan when every day she was late. This proved that she was always capable of getting in the car before me, she just wasn't doing it.

For a summary, you can see the evolution of the plan over time in Figure 8.3. Notice that the changes from one version to the next are noted in bold, italic font. What worked when my kids were ages four, two, and zero worked for years. However, as they grew, their motivations changed. The difference between Plan 1.0 and Plan 2.0 was not the plan, it was the reward; just a doughnut (1.0) to an option between a dollar and a doughnut (2.0). Eventually I had to change the plan because my job changed (Plan 3.0). When I realized that the incentives I was willing to offer were not enticing enough, I added a negative consequence (Plan 4.0). Finally, I realized that I did not have the right combination of positive and negative consequences (Plan 5.0).

Regardless of the complexity of this or the motivations being offered, notice, **the task itself never changed**—my kids always had to get in the car before I did. The variable was the extrinsic consequence. I knew they were only compliant because if the consequences went away, they would revert back to getting in the car whenever they wanted since they lacked intrinsic interest in the task. In other words, if left to their own devices, they would have been non-compliant. This plan exemplifies how important it is to understand motivation in order to move from one level of engagement to the next.

Figure 8.3: The Evolution of the "Get to the Car Before Mom" Plan

Version 1.0: Get a Doughnut	
Plan: Earn 2 Points	
1. One point as a team for everyone getting to the car before mom	
2. One point for arriving to day-care before the door is unlocked	
Positive Consequence	**Negative Consequence**
A doughnut	No points

Version 2.0: Get a Doughnut or a Dollar	
Plan: Earn 2 Points	
1. One point as a team for everyone getting to the car before mom	
2. One point for arriving to day-care before the door is unlocked	
Positive Consequence	**Negative Consequence**
A doughnut OR *a dollar*	No points

Version 3.0: One for Me, One for Us	
Plan: Earn 2 Points	
1. One point as a team for everyone getting to the car before mom	
2. Each child could earn one point for getting to the car before mom	
Positive Consequence	**Negative Consequence**
A doughnut OR a dollar	No points *and your siblings may get points and rewards when you don't*

Version 4.0: Your Time is My Time	
Plan: Earn 2 Points	
1. One point as a team for everyone getting to the car before mom	
2. Each child could earn one point for getting to the car before mom	
Positive Consequence	**Negative Consequence**
A doughnut OR a dollar	No points, your sibling may get points and rewards when you don't, *and take away time from things you want*

Version 5.0: You Get a Point or I Get Your Point	
Plan: Earn 2 Points	
1. One point as a team for everyone getting to the car before mom	
2. Each child could earn one point for getting to the car before mom	
Positive Consequence	**Negative Consequence**
A doughnut OR a dollar	No points, your sibling may get points and rewards when you don't, *mom earns your points, and you'll owe mom money*

Chapter Summary

The fable of "The Wind and the Sun" reminds us that the story of non-compliance depends a great deal on which character is telling the story. If you are the man, you are just responding to the weather; if you are the weather, your goal is to get the man to do what you want. This means that we need to be aware of our position. When we are acting as an authority, seeking first to understand and then to be understood assists us in improving our intended outcomes. As we seek first to understand, there are two main results. The first is improved relationships with others, and the second is an improved understanding of what the other person likes and dislikes.

This chapter also identified three different motivations related to non-compliance, why it is important to recognize the cause for the behavior, and how it differs for rebels, normalizers, and activists.

- Doing so allows you to begin moving from a position of non-compliance towards compliance (if you are working on extrinsic features) or towards absorption (if you are working on intrinsic features).

- If they are going to transition, rebels and normalizers will move towards compliance because the reason they are non-compliant is due to their relationship or their consequence for compliance. In other words, there is no moral justification for their non-compliance.

- Activists are likely not going to become compliant because they do not see themselves as non-compliant; they believe they are absorbed in their behaviors.

Reflection Questions

1. How does your "weather" affect the compliance (or not) of rebels? Normalizers? Activists?

   _____

   _____

   _____

2. What are some examples of things that you find motivating?
   a. Give an example of a reward.
   b. Give an example of a punishment.
   c. Give an example of a relationship.

   _____

   _____

   _____

3. Think of an area in your life where you could be seen by someone else as an activist. What is that area, and is there anything that someone could do to have you become compliant with a request from someone who disagrees with you?

   _____

   _____

   _____

4. What advice would you give your friend who asked for your help to this problem: _My ten-year-old son's room is always a mess. I have told him repeatedly to clean his room but he never does, or he does it but then it is a mess again the next day._

   _____

   _____

   _____

5. Think of a plan that would work to help motivate you or someone you know to achieve a task. For that plan to be successful, do you need just incentives or just negative consequences? Would a combination of both "carrots" and "sticks" be more successful? Why or why not?

_____

_____

_____

Persistent Questions

1. What have you done so far regarding the three challenge questions from the Introduction?

    a. **Three:** Find at least three people with whom to share your learning.

    b. **Two:** Find at least two ideas that change you.

    c. **One:** Apply at least one idea from your reading.

_____

_____

_____

2. What have you learned so far, and how will you use it?

_____

_____

_____

Chapter 9

Compliant: *So What*

"If you must have motivation, think of your paycheck on Friday."
~Noel Coward

Recognizing Your Thinking Before You Read...

- If compliance is in the upper left quadrant of the Engagement Matrix, what does this tell you about the connection to the external motivators and the assigned task?

  _____

  _____

  _____

- What are common characteristics of tasks that lead to compliance?

  _____

  _____

  _____

- Is it possible to make a task easier even if you are still only compliant?

  _____

  _____

  _____

- Why is compliance a deceptive quadrant to be in?

  _____

  _____

  _____

Reflecting on Compliance

As you recall, compliance is about doing what you're told even though you would prefer not to. Compliant people are no more interested in doing the task than non-compliant people, but compliant people have the right combination of extrinsic motivators. This chapter explains the importance of understanding compliance and the impact that can have on engagement.

Making Moves

In the "So What" chapter related to non-compliance, there was a great deal written about how to move away from non-compliance. Located in the bottom left quadrant of the matrix, there were two directions to go—left towards absorbed or up towards compliance. Now that one has achieved compliance, that is certainly worthy of celebration; compliance is far better than non-compliance! However, what are the options now that someone is in the upper left corner of the matrix?

Obviously, someone can downshift away from compliance towards non-compliance. At this point, you are aware that the reason for this move would be because something negative happened to the relationship between the two people (the person doing the task and the person assigning the task). If this is not the case, then there must have been a change in the way the person doing the task related to the extrinsic motivator…the person's feeling about the consequence has changed and/or the consequence itself has changed. I used to be offered $100 to do this, but now I'm being offered $50 and I won't do it for less than $100, for example.

Going back to The Engagement Matrix, remember what it says about someone who is compliant. Compliant people have a "high" relationship to the external person and/or consequence and a "low" relationship to the task. That means that in order to shift from compliance to higher levels of engagement, there needs to be an improvement towards the feelings connected to the assigned task.

The Grunt Work

Most of the time, we are compliant because we just don't enjoy doing whatever that particular task is. This boring task is the price you pay to do the work you enjoy doing, which is most of the work you get to do. There are going to be some things in life that we *have* to do. That's just the way it is. In those instances, we simply need to be at peace with the fact that being compliant beats the alternative to being non-compliant.

> There are going to be some things in life that we *have* to do. That's just the way it is. In those instances, we simply need to be at peace with the fact that being compliant beats the alternative to being non-compliant.

Let's get real. The truth is, it is not always possible to alter the assigned task. Most people do not like standardized tests, for example. You may not enjoy completing the required paperwork for your job. I'm not the biggest fan of doing laundry. I know, however, that I have to do the laundry, so I have developed ways to make it more tolerable. I almost never do laundry during the week, but I will sometimes sort the accumulated laundry during the week, so it makes it easier to get the first load in on Friday night after work. It used to bother me when my children would leave their clothes inside-out for me to turn the right way. I tried to get them to do it correctly before putting their clothes down the laundry chute. When that didn't work, I would have them come and right their clothes as I was sorting it. That only led to irritation on their end and irritation on my end because I was irritated that they were irritated. I have now come to peace with the fact that it does not matter if the clothes are inside-out or not in order for them to get clean. Now, I wash and fold them in whatever state I get them. I figure eventually my kids will get tired of getting the clean clothes inside-out, but even if they don't, that's okay because it doesn't impact me. My change in how I approach the laundry does not make me enjoy doing laundry more, but it makes doing this task easier.

Compliant rule-followers are focused on getting the task done, not because they care about the task, but because getting the task done is a means to an end. Once the task is done, they can move on to other things. What's more, when the task is done, there is some consequence that is awarded (for a positive) or avoided (for a negative) that is achieved. For example, how many times as a student did you complete the end of chapter questions (task) so that you didn't get a zero (consequence)? I highly doubt you cared about answering the end of chapter questions even if you did them anyway. The motivation was the consequence, not the task. In fact, I'm going to guess that there were times when you were non-compliant with the behavior of learning (because you copied the answers from someone else), but you were compliant with the task completion. In this case, you followed the rules of getting the work done and disregarded the rules of academic honesty because breaking the academic honesty rules was an example of normalized non-compliance.

Since this type of compliance is rampant in schools, we must be on the lookout for it. I'm not talking about cheating. I'm talking about students who superficially meet our expectations regarding behavior, and we accept this as meeting our expectations for learning. Wouldn't you rather have students who are so excited and eager to share their learning or ask questions of each other even if that means they're blurting out versus having a classroom full of students who are quietly disengaged and going through the motions? Wouldn't you rather be a teacher who is working in a school where you are encouraged to try new things even if it's messy versus working in a school where you are just expected to do what you're told? If that's what we want for ourselves, we should also want (and create) it for our students.

Classroom Visits

I worked with an administrator, Michelle Jaros, who spends half of her job as an independent evaluator conducting formal classroom observations. In her role, she has the opportunity to observe teachers across the district in kindergarten classrooms through twelfth grade—including honors, Advanced Placement, and International Baccalaureate. She told me what stood out the most to her from the observations is the change in instructional techniques as students progress through school. In elementary schools, she observed students working collaboratively more often than at upper levels. At upper levels, students are more often lectured to but have accountability to produce something either at the end of the lesson or for the next day. That doesn't ensure that the quality of what they produce is high necessarily, just that the expectation is there.

Michelle's take-away was that students at the younger levels needed to be asked to produce more to demonstrate what they have learned, and students at the upper levels needed to be allowed to interact more with each other rather than sit-and-get. This will be addressed later in this book, but the premise is important to understanding compliance. If you have a classroom where students have the chance to work collaboratively, how do you know that the students are actually working on and learning what you expect? If you have a classroom where students are independent observers to the learning due to structures like lectures or modeling by the teacher, how do you know that the students are actually paying attention and learning what you expect?

I have visited countless classrooms for a variety of reasons. In many of the classrooms I go into, I see very common patterns of behavior when students are working in a small-group or one-on-one with a teacher while other students are working independently or in small groups. The first thing I see is that the teachers are positioned with their backs towards a wall so that they can face the students in the teacher-group while maintaining eye contact with the students who are working independently. This positioning gives the appearance that the teacher is able to monitor the students who are not working directly with the teacher. In reality, however, the teacher is tethered to the small-group because the teacher is providing some form of teacher-led instruction. Even students in kindergarten eventually catch on to the fact that the teacher is not going to leave the small-group often (if ever) to come over to the students who are working independently *unless* the students who are working without supervision are drawing attention to themselves.

The second thing I see is that there is little to no accountability for the work that the independent students are doing. By accountability, I mean a product that each student has to produce and submit at the conclusion of the independent time. So, if the teacher is engaged in a guided reading lesson with Jose, Bella, and Booker, while the rest of the class reads silently, how does the teacher know that the rest of the class actually read? I am sure your mind is racing with at least half a dozen ideas for how to hold the students accountable for reading in this scenario. The problem is, this doesn't always happen.

As a result, and this is HUGE, the third thing that I commonly see when I visit classrooms is that students are *compliant with behavioral expectations and non-compliant with the learning*. Students learn that if they can be rule-followers and/or people-pleasers and remain quiet, which is a behavioral expectation, they can stare into space or talk to their neighbor in a whisper. Quiet

As a result, and this is HUGE, the third thing that I commonly see when I visit classrooms is that students are *compliant with behavioral expectations and non-compliant with the learning.*

students can leave to go to the bathroom—particularly in classrooms when students do not need to ask permission to leave. There are many examples of behaviors that allow students to avoid learning as long as they are quiet. Even in a classroom when students are not working independently but are answering questions out loud, if the teacher calls on students who raise their hands, the students who never raise their hands are able to be non-compliant with the learning and can fade into the background.

Some of you reading this may not have structures like this in your class, and so you may be thinking that this does not apply to you. You're only half right. If you don't use structures like this in your classroom, the actual example doesn't apply to you. However, I would encourage you to reflect on what ways students can be rule-followers who are behaviorally compliant and still be non-compliant with the learning. For example, if you do a lot of lecturing, like you may do in a secondary social studies class, I am sure that there are many times when you have said something to a room full of respectful but passive students. Then, when you tested the students on what you told them, they were not able to pass the test. In a math classroom, you may have modeled the work for the class, and some students raised hands and volunteered answers while those who didn't sat there without disruption. Yet, when the students were asked to do the work themselves, they couldn't do it. We cannot mistake quiet, respectful (people-pleasing and/or rule-following) students with students who are learning. I am not saying that quiet, respectful students are not learning; I am saying that there is a difference between meeting behavioral expectations and meeting learning expectations. If you are thinking that it is the students' responsibility to learn and the teachers to teach, even if this is true (which is debatable), there are still ample, proactive, and strategic methods to increase the likelihood of learning.

> **I am not saying that quiet, respectful students are not learning; I am saying that there is a difference between meeting behavioral expectations and meeting learning expectations.**

What's Wrong with Compliance

The differences between compliant and engaged learners is beautifully highlighted in Allison Zmuda and Robyn R. Jackson's book *Real Engagement: How Do I Help My Students Become Motivated, Confident, and Self-Directed Learners?* Zmuda and

Jackson share a powerful side-by-side comparison of what a compliant learner looks and sounds like in comparison to engaged learner (see Figure 9.1). In workshops I've given on engagement, I take each of the characteristics in Figure 9.1 and put them on separate slips of paper. Then I have the participants see if they can determine which statements relate to compliance and which relate to engagement. It's not as easy as you think it would be. The best comment I received when doing this came from a kindergarten teacher who said, "All of the descriptors of engaged learners are the behaviors of my students when they start school!"

Think about students who have time to independently read—be it during a Reader's Workshop or during sustained silent reading like Drop Everything and Read (D.E.A.R.). What happens when the reading time ends?

- Non-compliant students weren't reading even if they were pretending to read because they were compliant with the noise-level/behavioral expectations.

- Students who were compliant with the learning expectations will stop reading since they were only reading during that time because you told them to do it.

- Truly engaged students, on the other hand, may have to be repeatedly told to put their books away because reading time is over.

Engaged students, unlike compliant students, were reading something they at least enjoyed and want to continue reading. They are not interested in your timeline or agenda. Compliant students play by your rules; engaged students play by their own. Compliant students do what they are told, don't make waves, and meet your expectations; they are on-task. This compliance lulls you into believing that they are more than willing passengers on your train—you think they want to go along on this ride. Compliant students may do school well, but what you actually want are students who do learning well.

> **Compliant students may do school well but what you actually want are students who do learning well.**

Figure 9.1: Zmuda and Jackson's "A Compliant Learner and an Engaged One"[21]

Compliant, Dutiful Learner	Engaged Learner
1. Follows oral and written directions with minimal prompting	1. Follows oral and written directions with minimal prompting but may pursue an alternative approach to personalize the experience
2. Completes explicit procedures and requirements in a timely manner	2. Pursues own train of thought regardless of task at hand or feedback from staff, which may make it difficult to finish in a timely manner
3. Intently focuses on task completion to finish the assignment	3. Focuses on the learning and wants to talk about it regardless of prompting and without consideration of others
4. Participates in group activities and discussion when prompted	4. Actively participates in group activities and discussion when interested in the material but can be reticent while still mulling over ideas and information or when still actively immersed in the previous task
5. Responds to straightforward questions but needs scaffolding to pursue a more complex question	5. May be bored or unmotivated to respond to straightforward questions but is fascinated by questions that require teasing out ambiguity and complexity or questions that are personally interesting and relevant
6. Seeks approval, credit, or high marks because of effort, quantity, or adherence to directions	6. Seeks recognition for the thoughtfulness of the work or originality of the work, even if it isn't complete or doesn't adhere to the directions
7. Plays it safe by electing to follow known procedures, explore familiar topics, and use tools that have been mastered; dismisses or avoids alternative points of view or approaches	7. Chooses to take risks by exploring something new, attempts to solve a problem in a novel way, and considers alternative points of view
8. Completes work with no expectation for finding personal relevance, connection or interest	8. Seeks work that is interesting – or seeks to make work interesting
9. Takes information at face value and does not question the credibility or validity of "experts" (e.g., a teacher, an online source, the textbook's interpretation)	9. Questions both text and people to better understand an issue, topic or problem
10. Waits patiently for assistance to get help or decides not to ask a question because the conversation would require more work	10. Demands immediate assistance or attention and feels justified for doing so in light of curiosity, interest, or investment in the task or topic

The best example I have seen that highlights how schools tend to reward compliance is in Erica Goldson's 2010 graduation speech. Goldson was the valedictorian of her class. Yet, despite her obvious intelligence, in her description of herself on her blog, she says of her graduation that, "A new chapter unfolded after I stepped down from the podium on the 25th of June, 2010. I was free. No more school legally mandated by the State for me. I now could choose how, when, and where to educate myself."[22] How and why is it that this could have happened to Erica? Who is in your class now who is compliantly doing the assigned reading but not ever reading for pure enjoyment? Who is seeing learning as answering your questions rather than creating their own? Moreover, what are you compliantly teaching, and how can you become engaged in what you're doing?

Read the full transcript of Erica Goldson's speech or watch the video of her delivering it by visiting her blog: https://cutt.ly/Goldson

An excerpt from Erica Goldson's valedictory speech.[23]

Some of you may be thinking, "Well, if you pass a test, or become valedictorian, didn't you learn something? Well, yes, you learned something, but not all that you could have. Perhaps, you only learned how to memorize names, places, and dates to later on forget in order to clear your mind for the next test. School is not all that it can be. Right now, it is a place for most people to determine that their goal is to get out as soon as possible.

I am now accomplishing that goal. I am graduating. I should look at this as a positive experience, especially being at the top of my class. However, in retrospect, I cannot say that I am any more intelligent than my peers. I can attest that I am only the best at doing what I am told and working the system. Yet, here I stand, and I am supposed to be proud that I have completed this period of indoctrination. I will leave in the fall to go on to the next phase expected of me, in order to receive a paper document that certifies that I am capable of work. But I contest that I am a human being, a thinker, an adventurer – not a worker. A worker is someone who is trapped within repetition – a slave of the system set up before him. But now, I have successfully shown that I was the best slave. I did what I was told to the extreme. While others sat in class and doodled to later become great artists, I sat in class to take notes and become a great test-taker. While others would come to class without their homework done because they were reading about an interest of theirs, I never missed an assignment. While others were creating music and writing lyrics, I decided to do extra credit, even though I never needed it. So, I wonder, why did I even want this position? Sure, I earned it, but what will come of it? When I leave educational institutionalism, will I be successful or forever lost? I have no clue about what I want to do with my life; I have no interests because I saw every subject of study as work, and I excelled at every subject just for the purpose of excelling, not learning. And quite frankly, now I'm scared.

I Learned It by Watching You

As a child in the 1980s, I clearly remember the Say No to Drugs campaign that Nancy Regan lauded. As a result of this focus, there were

Never seen this commercial? Watch it here: https://cutt.ly/ByWatchingYou.

numerous public service announcements and commercials created to warn children and parents against the dangers of drugs. Anyone who was alive then remembers the one with a teenage boy who is in his room when he's confronted by his father, who has a cigar box in his hand. The boy is on his bed, listening to music on his headphones. The father walks in with cigar box in hand and turns down the music. The boy sees the cigar box, looks worried, and removes headphones.

Father: Is this yours?

Boy: Yeah….[stammering]

Father: [interrupts] Your mother said she found this in your closet.

Boy: I don't know. One of the guys must've…

Father: [interrupts] "Must've" what?!

Boy: [defensively] Look, dad, it's not mine!

Father: Where did you get it?

Boy: Dad I...

Father: [interrupts] Answer me! Who taught you how to do this stuff?

Boy: You! Alright?! I learned it by watching you.

Dad looks embarrassed and sheepish. The voiced-over narrator says, "Parents who use drugs have children who use drugs."

Educators know the value and impact of modeling. In fact, our profession is one that values modeling so much that student teaching and administrative internships are par for our course. We are all familiar with the gradual release method that prioritizes modeling during the "I Do" phase of the learning. We do all of this because we hope that the children will imitate what we have shown them. Though there are times when we may intentionally give non-examples—we hold the scissors like this not like this—in most instances, however, when we explicitly intend to model behavior, we provide exemplary demonstration of what we are hoping to see the other person do for first-timers. For example, if I went to a dance class, the instructors are going to show me how to dance well by dancing well; they will not show me how they dance poorly and then expect that I would be able to infer from their mistakes how to dance well.

Notice here that I have said, "explicitly intend to model behavior." That is because there are many times when we model behavior without awareness. This happens when we have grown so accustomed to our own mindless habits or beliefs that we do not know what we are doing or saying. You can see this when children are playing house, for example, and the child who is acting as the parent innocently says something in the right tone and using the exact words so that the child sounds like the mini-me of the parent. This occurred with my children. A bad habit that I was previously unaware of happened to me when my youngest son, Oliver, was learning how to talk. His brother, Nolan, is four years older and must have been around five when Oliver was learning how to speak. Nolan was a mischievous boy who I would refer to (sometimes affectionately, sometimes with exasperation) as "Naughty Nolan." I knew that there were times when my husband or I would raise our voices. It became apparent, however, when Oliver started talking that we must have been raising our voices with Nolan more than we knew because rather than calling his brother, "Nolan," Oliver said in an angry voice, "NOLAN!" every time he said his brother's name as if that was the correct way to pronounce it. Oliver wasn't saying it like this because Nolan had done something to him or because he was upset with Nolan; Oliver was saying it because that's how he heard us say it.

What does this have to do with compliance, you may be asking yourself? Everything. People are usually not very good at hiding their inner feelings. Their body language and/or tone in their words exposes their real feelings about what they are doing. Therefore, if someone is behaving in a compliant manner, others are more than likely going to notice. If you are a teacher, that means that your students are going to feed off of your energy. Are you teaching a unit or lesson that you do not like? Are you giving a test that you do not want to give? Do not be surprised when your students start to ask why they have to do it too. It is not that they had an opinion about it to begin with—it's that they are reflecting back to you what they have implicitly observed.

Energy is contagious. This is the premise of bestselling books like *The Energy Bus* and *The No Complaining Rule* both by Jon Gordon. You do not have to be a believer in warm and fuzzy movements to know that this is true. If you smile at a baby, the baby will smile back. The opposite is also true. If you make an angry face at a baby, the baby will respond with fear. If I want my children to try a food, I will be more successful if I talk about how much I enjoy the food, and I eat it in front of them. This does not guarantee that they will like the food, but it does increase the odds that my kids will try it. My husband is notorious for his enthusiastic behavior about the movies he enjoys. He will talk up how great the movie is to the kids, and they will get themselves worked into a frenzy about seeing the most amazing movie based on my husband's salesmanship. This does not mean they will always agree with him after the movie is over. However, his enthusiasm increases their interest.

Don't believe me? The modeling effect has been studied for years, particularly in the impact that modeling has on aggression. In these experiments, children were shown cartoon videos and/or real-life models of someone being physically aggressive with a doll (hitting, kicking, etc.). When given a doll to play with, children who were shown these models were more likely to be aggressive than children who were not shown these models.[24] This doesn't mean that all modeling is bad. First-timers need models to learn how to do most things. This is how babies learn to talk, feed themselves, get dressed, use the toilet, etc. What it means is that, in addition to all of the wonderful uses of modeling, we need to be mindful that we also model our feelings, consciously and unintentionally.

What does this mean in schools? We need to question what we are doing compliantly with and for students in the name of learning. Granted, there are things that are unavoidable, like mandated state assessments. For tasks like that, I refer you back to what I wrote earlier about finding ways to make doing compliant tasks easier (like I do with laundry). Perhaps shift the focus from *having to take the tests* to *getting to show what you know*. Go from *we need to do this because it will be on the test* and replace that with *we're going to do this briefly, and we're also going to have time to spend on many other opportunities*. In other words, keep the mandated tasks in perspective.

Let's not forget about those things that we're doing compliantly that we may not need to do at all. My best example of this is assigning homework. In reality, a major reason why students do not do their homework is because the homework is disengaging. You wouldn't want to do it either and, when you were a student, you probably rarely had homework that was even interesting. Why do we do to our students what we didn't enjoy for ourselves?

What if you stopped assigning homework and started offering students the choice to do it? Or, what if the assignments students had to do were not low-level, rote regurgitations? As an adult, I'm guessing that you do not enjoy grading this type of assignment since you are forced to read the same answers over and over. Yet, YOU have control over what the students are assigned to do. After all, if the focus is on completing the homework for a grade versus something (anything) that emphasized the *purpose* of the work and its relationship with learning, then we've missed the mark. Focusing on learning means we have to model a shift from compliance to a focus on learning. We know what focusing on compliance sounds like, "You didn't do your

> **If we want our students to be learners, we need to model what that looks and sounds like.**

homework, so you get a zero," or "This homework is late, you get a lower grade." Focusing on learning would sound like, "I need to get a sense of where you are with what I've been teaching you. This task will let me know if I should move on to the next part of this learning or if we still need more time here, so it's important you do the task as well as you can." Focusing on learning could also sound like, "Here are some problems I think you should be able to do. Give them a try so we can see how you're doing so far." If we want our students to be learners, we need to model what that looks and sounds like.

Deal Breakers

There needs to be a word of caution. Even though compliance is often better than non-compliance, that doesn't mean that there are not what I call "deal breakers." I would never encourage anyone to be compliant with things that they are morally opposed to doing. If you are in a position where you are being asked to do something that you fundamentally do not agree with, then you should give careful consideration to whether or not that is the right position for you to be in. Yes, I am saying you may need to quit a job or no longer be friends with someone or any other number of choices. This is because you have choice. No one is forcing you to do something you don't want to do. You are forcing yourself due to the relationship or extrinsic motivators. You. Have. Choice. You may not be able to leave your job that day or end the friendship at that moment, but you may want to consider an exit strategy.

Chapter Summary

The purpose of this chapter was to explain why compliance is important. Compliance is located in the top left quadrant on the Engagement Matrix, meaning compliant people have a high relationship to the external person and/or consequence and a low relationship to the task. That means that in order to shift from compliance to higher levels of engagement, there needs to be an improvement towards the feelings connected to the assigned task.

- Compliant tasks are generally boring or repetitive. Though the task may never be interesting, there are probably things you can do to make the task easier.

- In classrooms, be on the lookout for students who are compliant with the behavioral expectations but non-compliant with the learning.

- Compliant people do what they are told, don't make waves, and meet your expectations. This compliance lulls authority figures into believing that they are more than willing passengers on your train—you think they want to go along on this ride. Compliant people may do what they're told, but what you actually want are people who want to do the work/learning.

- Energy is contagious. When authority figures behave compliantly rather than being interested or absorbed, they model that compliance is acceptable and their subordinates notice.

- You always have a choice. Do not be compliant with things that you fundamentally disagree with. If you cannot end that relationship or responsibility immediately, you may want to consider an exit strategy.

Reflection Questions

1. Think of a task you're currently doing compliantly. What are some ways that you could make doing the task easier, even if you cannot avoid doing it at all?

_____

_____

_____

2. Are there ways right now in your classroom where you have students who might be compliantly slipping through the cracks? What about your classroom design allows this to happen?

_____

_____

_____

3. Name a time when you saw an authority who was obviously being compliant. How did you know, and what impact did that behavior have on those who were being led by this person?

_____

_____

_____

4. As you looked at Zmuda and Jackson's "A Compliant Learner and an Engaged One" T-Chart, what surprised you and why?

_____

_____

_____

5. Watch the full graduation speech by Erica Goldson. Would you consider her to be a successful student based on her admission about being a compliant student? Why or why not?

_____

_____

_____

Persistent Questions

1. What have you done so far regarding the three challenge questions from the Introduction?

   a. **Three:** Find at least three people with whom to share your learning.

   b. **Two:** Find at least two ideas that change you.

   c. **One:** Apply at least one idea from your reading.

_____

_____

_____

2. What have you learned so far, and how will you use it?

_____

_____

_____

Chapter 10

Interested: *So What*

"It's easy to get people's attention, what counts is getting their interest."
~A. Philip Randolph

Recognizing Your Thinking Before You Read...

- If *interested* is in the upper right quadrant of The Engagement Matrix, what does this tell you about the connection to the external motivators and the assigned task?

_____

_____

_____

- What are common characteristics of tasks that lead to interest?

_____

_____

_____

- Is it acceptable to be satisfied with engagement at the interested level?

_____

_____

_____

- How do you create interest for employees?

_____

_____

_____

Reflecting on Interested

As you recall, *interested* is the entry point into true engagement. Like compliance, interest can feel really good to the person assigning the task when those who are doing the work like the work they are doing. This is especially true when the interested people were once in a place of disengagement—either non-compliance or compliance. The more people like the task they are doing, the less it feels like work for the people doing it or those who are monitoring the work being done. This is accomplished by changing the task. This chapter explains the importance of understanding interest and the impact that can have on engagement.

Freedom Within Form

Imagine for a moment that students, even at the youngest of ages, are both (a) taught to communicate in ways that express their interests and abilities to design tasks that matter to them and (b) that they are in an environment that is responsive to their needs. Picture classrooms where students can say, "I have some natural strengths when it comes to X, but I'm working to grow in Y. That means that right now tasks that challenge me in Z way are ones that I am attempting to do." Does this sound like an engagement unicorn or narwhal to you?

Empowering students to be able to communicate around what engages them does not need to be as mythical as it sounds. Obviously, it would require teaching students about the features of the Engagement Framework, or at least teaching them to communicate their likes and dislikes in terms of consequences and tasks. It would also necessitate clarity from the teacher about the necessary outcomes and flexibility about the pathways towards those points.

What is challenging about this idea is that there is often rigidity around curriculum because people mistake curriculum for the standards. These two things are not the same, but are so commonly confused that it is no wonder people can often feel handcuffed when given a curriculum. The bottom line is that while the standards themselves are not negotiable, we should seek curriculum and instruction that is. This is what Dr. Zoila Morell

> The bottom line is that while the standards themselves are not negotiable, we should seek curriculum and instruction that is.

meant when she wrote in the "Introduction to the New York State Next Generation Early Learning Standards":

> **Rather than prescribe a lockstep progression of lessons or curricula for all children in all settings, the Standards serve to articulate the expectations of what children can learn and do as a result of instruction that is not standardized, but personalized, differentiated, adapted, culturally and linguistically relevant, and context-based. While we may have the same learning objectives for all children, our means for meeting these objectives are highly responsive to the individual child.**[25] (emphasis in the original)

Morell's point is that there is a difference between standards and standardization of curriculum and instruction. She's right.

It can be confusing to understand the differences between standards, curriculum, instruction, and assessment. Each of these is described below using a metaphor of travel. That is, if the standards are the destination (let's say Chicago), the curriculum is the vehicle (car, boat, bus, plane, etc. used to arrive at the destination). The instruction is the approach or route used to get to Chicago—I chose the scenic route, you chose a shortcut. Finally, in this metaphor, the assessment is the GPS that tells us if we actually arrived in Chicago, if we broke down along the way, or we made even better time, got past our destination, and are in Kansas City.

- *Standards:* Standards are the *expectations* for what students should know and be able to do at each grade level. The standards answer the question, "What is the destination for the intended learning?"

- *Curriculum*: Curriculum is the *content* that gives students access to the standards. According to Robert Marzano,[26] it should be both:
  - *Guaranteed* (i.e., all students, regardless of their teacher or school, will have access to the same content, knowledge, and skills across the district).

o *Viable*[iv] (i.e., the curriculum is realistic in scope and has made careful decisions to narrow the universe of knowledge into developmentally appropriate and challenging learning targets for the students in the district).

Ultimately, the curriculum is the common and reasonable plan used to teach students the learning goals embodied in the standards and prepares students for success for the next grade level. The curriculum answers the question, "What is/are the best vehicle(s) for all students to arrive at the destination?"

- **Instruction**: Instruction is the *approach* (route) a teacher uses to ensure that all students learn the content. Instruction is fluid and changes depending on the teacher's abilities and the students' needs. Instruction is a variable in the learning "equation" since how a teacher chooses to teach the content is highly dependent on the students, the resources, and the teacher's own knowledge of the content and pedagogy. This explains why two teachers can tackle the same curriculum differently. The instruction answers the question, "What are the best approaches I can use to ensure all students arrive at the destination?"

- **Assessment**: Assessment is the *measure* of what students have learned. This is fundamentally different from what teachers have taught because students may not demonstrate learning of taught material, and this explains why not all students answer all questions correctly all of the time. Assessment is able to identify what students know as well as identifying if the curriculum and/or instruction are meeting the needs of our students or require revision. The assessment answers the question, "Where are the students in relation to where they are supposed to be?"

[iv] I strongly agree with Marzano's research on a guaranteed and viable curriculum I would also add that curriculum needs to be contextual. In other words, though a curriculum could be both guaranteed and viable, if the contextual constraints (time, human or other resources) cannot support the curriculum, it doesn't matter if it's the best curriculum ever because its implementation in that context is not the best ever.

Teach the Students Not the Curriculum

Morell's statement explains why teachers in the same state have the exact same standards but do not use the exact same curriculum. Though, even if they did (as I know there are some states that do), the instruction from one teacher's classroom to another teacher's classroom is unique. This variance is linked to the differences between the teachers, of course. Teacher A has been teaching for thirty years, and Teacher B just graduated, and therefore, their knowledge and experiences are different.

What is also important to note in the variance is the difference between *the students*. Even in thinking about my own three children, for the holidays, I will buy them some of the same things, but I will also buy them things that are distinct and different even though they are all my children with the same genetics and parents. Now imagine the range of students teachers encounter.

- Teacher C teaches in a rural part of the state and Teacher D in an urban part.

- Teacher E has bilingual students whose parents work at the local university and speak English fluently, and Teacher F has second language learners whose parents do not speak English and are refugees.

The background, experiences, and so forth that the students bring are different, and the experiences the students have in school should be responsive to these differences. The students should be seen as more than just passive receptacles of the content; they should be valued as active agents in learning. As the hierarchical authority in the relationship, the teacher is the person who controls if the students have equal billing in the learning dynamic.

Educational Bankruptcy

John Locke is credited with the notion of "tabula rasa" or blank slate. This is the belief that knowledge is only derived through experience or perception. In the simplest of explanations, Locke believed that people learn through doing, also known as empiricism. In fact, many educators subscribe to this approach to learning. In their research on engagement, Appleton, Christenson, and Furlong found that involving students in the learning process in active, rather than passive ways, increased engagement. "Given that education typically requires students to learn content and accept social values imposed by others," they write, "there is potential value to increased understanding of the process involved in transitioning students from externally regulated compliance to self-regulated collaboration in the pedagogical process."[27]   In other words, students need to be participants, not just recipients, of learning.

While there is much to be said about being an active agent in learning, when the idea that students are genuinely "blank" is taken to an extreme, teachers rob the learners of their instincts, interests, or existing experiences. Paulo Freire, author of *Pedagogy of the Oppressed*, cautions educators against seeing students as blank. Using a banking metaphor, Freire explains that when teachers look at students as empty vessels waiting to be filled, they dehumanize students as though the students come to the teacher without their own experiences, knowledge, and contributions. This dichotomy creates an imbalance whereby the student has nothing to contribute and is waiting to be filled by the teacher. "The teacher presents himself to his students as their necessary opposite; by considering their ignorance absolute, he justifies his own existence."[28] Freire further asserts that this premise is a stance of oppression. Liberation from this paradigm occurs when learning is seen as a mutual exchange between the teacher and students once the teacher acknowledges that the students are complete beings. It is easy to imagine that students who are seen as co-creators of their learning are likely to have a greater sense of engagement in what they are learning and doing.

Below are two brief excerpts from Chapter 2 of *Pedagogy of the Oppressed* to demonstrate Freire's ideas.

Narration (with the teacher as narrator) leads the students to memorize mechanically the narrated content. Worse yet, it turns them into "containers," into "receptacles" to be "filled" by the teacher. The more completely she fills the receptacles, the better a teacher she is. The more meekly the receptacles permit themselves to be filled, the better students they are. Education thus becomes an act of depositing, in which the students are the depositories and the teacher is the depositor. Instead of communicating, the teacher issues communiques and makes deposits which the students patiently receive, memorize, and repeat. This is the "banking" concept of education, in which the scope of action allowed to the students extends only as far as receiving, filing, and storing the deposits. They do, it is true, have the opportunity to become collectors or cataloguers of the things they store. But in the last analysis, it is the people themselves who are filed away through the lack of creativity, transformation, and knowledge in this (at best) misguided system. For apart from inquiry, apart from the praxis, individuals cannot be truly human. Knowledge emerges only through invention and re-invention, through the restless, impatient, continuing, hopeful inquiry human beings pursue in the world, with the world, and with each other.[29]

●──●

Students, as they are increasingly posed with problems relating to themselves in the world and with the world, will feel increasingly challenged and obliged to respond to that challenge. Because they apprehend the challenge as interrelated to other problems within a total context, not as a theoretical question, the resulting comprehension tends to be increasingly critical and thus constantly less alienated. Their response to the challenge evokes new challenges, followed by new understandings; and gradually the students come to regard themselves as committed.[30]

Charlotte Danielson pulls together the idea that students should have experiences but be seen as *experienced* in her book, *Talk About Teaching: Leading Professional Conversation,* where she writes:

The most significant research finding is deceptively simple: Learning is done *by the learner.* That is, as teachers we tend to think that our students learn on account of what we do. But that is a mistake: Our students don't learn because of what *we* do; they learn because of what *they* do. Our challenge, then, is to design learning experiences for students that are interesting and that yield the learning we desire…The larger point is that school is, for students, more than hands-on; it is minds-on. For students, school is not a spectator sport.[31]

In short, while learning is accomplished through action by the student, students come to learning with existing knowledge and interests that inform what they are currently learning about. It is the job of the teacher to leverage what the students already know and can do in order for the students to learn what is taught.

If/Then

Here's what we already know about interest. Interest is a function of a willingness to do the task temporarily plus the desire for extrinsic consequences. We also know that if we're coming from the quadrant of compliance, the thing that has changed in order for us to shift to interest is the task. This is because vertical shifts are changes in motivation, but horizontal shifts, like those from compliance to interest, are shifts in the task.

This is of critical importance. When people are compliant, they do not want to do what they're doing, but they will do it anyway because of the extrinsic consequence for action. Think of a time when you were given an assignment, either at work or in school. The question that distinguishes whether or not you were compliant or interested is, "did you like doing what you were told to do?" If the answer is yes, then you are at least at the point of being interested. The follow-up question is, "would you still do it even if you were allowed to stop?" If the answer is no, then you were only interested and not absorbed. Interested people are engaged, but the engagement is not lasting. Interested people like what they are doing, but they do not love it enough to continue without compensation. That is why they are only interested (see Figure 10.1). As I've explained, interesting tasks have an extrinsic consequence that is needed, but since this is true for compliant tasks too, the difference between these is the desire to do the task. Interested people want to do the task.

Figure 10.1: Flowchart of Engagement

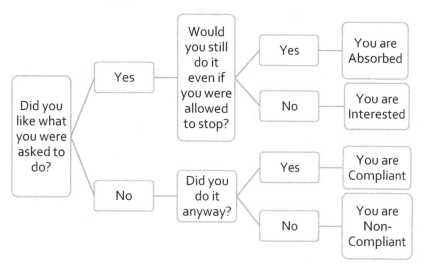

Make It Mindful

So what makes a task interesting? This is the question at the heart of any conversation about engagement. Conventional wisdom would tell us that people want to do tasks that are easy. We know better than that, though. Easy, like beauty, is relative. Walking is easy for me, but is not easy for infants. Speaking English is easy for me, but is not (initially) for those who are not native English speakers. Cooking at home is easy for me, but it would be difficult for me to learn how to cook in a fancy restaurant. What's more, I do not want someone to teach me (a) how to do things I already know how to do, (b) how to do things that I don't know the prerequisites for (don't teach me to conjugate verbs in Chinese if I don't even know the alphabet), and/or (c) mindless things where I am just expected to do something ad nauseam. Thus, it is not always easy to create tasks that create interest.

It is essential when thinking about engagement to be mindful of challenge within the Zone of Proximal Development (ZPD). Educational author and consultant, Candi B. McKay, explains that engagement is not the same for everyone because engagement requires "cognition; it is mental work."

Learning is a result of decisions teachers make in designing instruction to create opportunities that require students to think. This means thinking by all students, simultaneously and continuously, throughout the lesson. A classroom where three or four students are doing all of the mental work engages three or four students in learning. Students must be challenged to think at a level that is cognitively demanding and rigorous. When all students are required to complete the same task or assignment, the level of challenge will be appropriate for some, but not all. Student engagement requires pushing students to extend their thinking and to reach beyond their current capacities, to spend emotional, intellectual, and sometimes physical energy. Learning is work, mental work.[32]

McKay's point is that engagement is not a one-size-fits-all endeavor. No two students are alike, so the "mental work" for them will vary. But, if you want engagement, you must design tasks with those who will be doing it or that allows those who will do it choice and voice while doing it.

It's Time for an Adult Conversation

If we turn the tables towards the workplace and adults, there is an even greater expectation of voice and choice. Jim Knight, who was referenced earlier in the book, has found that there are "Five Simple Truths" connected to adult learning. The third of these is the belief that "When we do the thinking for other people, they resist."[33] This is just one important reason why choice and voice matter. I speak a lot about choice and voice throughout this book, so let me take a moment to clarify what I mean.

- **Choice refers to options.** Do I want the chicken or the fish? Do I want to do Problem Set One or Problem Set Two? Would I prefer the fall, winter, or spring date for the training? These are all the options that I can select.

- **Voice is the ability to give input regarding decisions.** This input might be on the design, implementation, or the product. It is allowing people to contribute their ideas and have a say in the design of the task.

Choice and voice are ideal, but they can also be a trap if they are not well presented. No one wants a false choice—I am allowed to choose, but the choices are too narrow or already decided. Nor do people want to be asked to weigh in only to have their voice be disregarded. These are just two examples of negative choice and voice scenarios that result in doing greater harm.

Several years ago, I was fortunate enough to be given a coach, Greg Speranza, to work with. One day, over lunch, he and I were talking and the topic of choice arose. He gave me advice that I use to this day.

There are three types of decisions: A-Level, B-Level, and C-Level. It is important that you are clear with those who you're working with about the level of the decision being made. Clarity leads to understanding, whereas confusion leads to hurt feelings and resentment.

- **A-Level Decisions**: These are decisions that others make *for* the leader. The leader will agree to whatever decision is made by the others.
  - *Example*: Mom asks the children what they want to eat tonight. She doesn't care which choice is made. The decision is left to the children.
- **B-Level Decisions:** These are decisions that others make *with* the leader. The leader works with others to make the decision together.
  - *Example*: Mom asks the children what they want to eat tonight. She and the children discuss the options, and they all agree with the decision. The decision is made jointly with the mom and the children.
- **C-Level Decisions**: These are decisions that the leader makes *for* others. The leader may ask others for input or recommendations, but the decision is ultimately the leader's to make.
  - *Example*: Mom decides what she wants to make for the children. Sometimes she asks them what they are in the mood for, but that doesn't mean she's obliged to agree.

I tell people that I'm working with about the three decision levels and what level decision I am asking them to make. When I do this, those with whom I work understand if it's a C-Level Decision that I am only asking for their advice or input but that I may not take it. This makes it easier for both of us no matter what I decide to do because there are no hard feelings if I go in a direction that they did not suggest.

> If I did not communicate the level of the decision upfront, I may have inadvertently created a false expectation that I was asking for them to make the decision.

Of course, there are times when choice and voice should not be possible. I would not want to be on the operating table and have the doctor ask me if I would prefer he use method X or Y for the incision. Though I am the patient, I will gladly rely on the doctor's expertise. Nevertheless, providing choice and voice when appropriate improves interest because people will be able to feel connected to the outcomes. After all, we should not be surprised that people could develop into problems if they were not a part of developing the solutions. Although some of the desire for choice and voice is generational (i.e., millennials are more likely than baby boomers to see a flatter hierarchy and assert their ideas even if/when they are not asked), it is human nature to have ideas and desire to contribute those ideas. When working with anyone, but especially adults, we need to seek ways to foster voice and choice so that they emerge in healthy and productive ways rather than in parking lot or side conversations.

> When working with anyone, but especially adults, we need to seek ways to foster voice and choice so that they emerge in healthy and productive ways rather than in side or parking lot conversations.

Creating Conflict

It's important to remember that healthy and productive communication means that conflict will arise. In *The Five Dysfunctions of a Team,* Patrick Lencioni identifies that conflict is critical to successful teamwork. He asks the question, "How many of you would rather go to a meeting than a movie?" I'm sure that you would be hard-pressed to find someone who wouldn't select a movie in response to this question. Yet, Lencioni writes,

Think about it this way. A movie, on average, runs anywhere from ninety minutes to two hours in length. Staff meetings are about the same…And yet meetings are interactive, whereas movies are not…And more importantly, movies have no real impact on our lives. They don't require us to act a certain way based on the outcome of the story. And yet meetings are both interactive and relevant. We get to have our say, and the outcome of any given discussion often has a very real impact on our lives. So why do we dread meetings?... Whether it is an action movie, a drama, a comedy, or an artsy French film, every movie worth watching must have one key ingredient. What is that ingredient?... Every great movie has conflict. Without it, we just don't care what happens to the characters.[34]

Participating in meetings where conflict arises does not mean that it is okay for people to be disagreeable—it means that it is okay for people to disagree.

Dale Carnegie said, "When two partners always agree, one of them is not necessary. If there is some point you haven't thought about, be thankful if it is brought to your attention." The purpose of collaboration is to create something that could not be created independently. Therefore, if one person could do the work independently, the team is irrelevant. This is why it is critical to ensure that the people working together can voice their thoughts, experiences, and ideas without fear even when the ideas brought forth run counter to other members of the team. This is true for adults and for children.

The idea of including everyone, even the voices of dissenters, can make people who have worked with disagreeable people who lacked strong leaders very uncomfortable. Disagreeable people seem like they want to argue about everything and hold everyone back. When this happens, I will be the first to say that it takes a very skillful leader to know (a) how to address these types of behaviors proactively (through meeting norms/commitments, for example) and (b) how to respond to these behaviors reactively when they arise. Nevertheless, when people of all perspectives are included in the planning of the work, the implementation of the work is universally stronger because the team was able to hear the things that needed to be said *during* the planning phase. As challenging as it can be to have a disagreeable team member who has an oppositional personal agenda, once the decision is made, that person is now linked to the decision and can be the best advocate for the work that was done. When working with teams, I always remind them that their names are attached to the work, and if they cannot support the decisions at the table when we're planning it, we need to know now so we can make decisions they can support.

What does conflict have to do with engagement? Everything. When there is a fear of conflict, i.e., people do not feel like they can share their ideas, the result is that people are compliant with the decisions during the meeting and exit the meeting without the commitment to the decision. This is Lencioni's third dysfunction—lack of commitment. This leads people to feel like they are hamsters in a wheel—attending meetings where, even if decisions are "made," they are not really made because there is no follow-through. Thus, a feeling of death by meetings happens as represented in Kaamran Hafeez's *New Yorker* cartoon pictured here.

"I know we didn't accomplish anything, but that's what meetings are for."

The Five Dysfunctions of a Team **are real and have a real impact on the work we do with our colleagues. When we avoid having honest conversations, we stymie the work we need to do because we are too afraid to say what needs to be said. Though conflict avoidance (also known as false harmony) seems like the lesser of two evils, it is not. It leads to compliance in the meeting and non-compliance afterward. Read below to see an excerpt from** *The Five Dysfunctions of a Team* **where Lencioni identifies teams that embrace or resist conflict.**[35]

But teams that engage in productive conflict know that the only purpose is to produce the best possible solution in the shortest period of time. They discuss and resolve issues more quickly and completely than others, and they emerge from heated debates with no residual feelings or collateral damage, but with an eagerness and readiness to take on the next important issue.

Ironically, teams that avoid ideological conflict often do so in order to avoid hurting team members' feelings, and then end up encouraging dangerous tension. When team members do not openly debate and disagree about important ideas, they often turn to back-channel personal attacks, which are far nastier and more harmful than any heated argument over issues.

It is also ironic that so many people avoid conflict in the name of efficiency, because healthy conflict is actually a time saver. Contrary to the notion that teams waste time and energy arguing, those that avoid conflict actually doom themselves to revisiting issues again and again without resolution. They often ask team members to take their issues "off-line," which seems to be a euphemism for avoiding dealing with an important topic, only to have it raised again at the next meeting.

Teams that fear conflict . . .

- Have boring meetings
- Create environments where back-channel politics and personal attacks thrive
- Ignore controversial topics that are critical to team success
- Fail to tap into all the opinions and perspectives of team members
- Waste time and energy with posturing and interpersonal risk management

Teams that engage in conflict . . .

- Have lively, interesting meetings
- Extract and exploit the ideas of all team members
- Solve real problems quickly
- Minimize politics
- Put critical topics on the table for discussion

All of this talk about healthy conflict and genuine commitments is critical when working with adults who are less likely to be supervised as directly as children. Students have homework that's due and come to class daily where the teacher (the supervisor) is required to be present. In the workplace, assignments are not graded and the boss may not often visit. So, what people do and say when the boss isn't there is the true measure of adult engagement or not. Consequently, the chances of people following through/completing the work that they were able to choose to do are greater than the chances of someone completing the work that someone else mandated. In other words, we do the work we choose to do because we chose that work and we avoid the work we were told to do because we didn't have a say in it. This is why engagement increases when voice and choice are present; I'm more likely to do the work when it was work I designed. Not only does this make it easier to supervise me, but it also makes my performance more effective.

Jim Knight has written extensively on working with adults. In his book, *Focus on Teaching,* he highlights the importance of accountability and autonomy where he reminds the reader that

> Giving people choices is important for other reasons than just reducing resistance. If we tell staff they must do what we, the principal, the central office, or the state say they must do, we are working from the assumption that there is only one answer and that we know what it is, or at least that we know better than them what they should do.
>
> In reality, however, those who work directly with students know a lot about what is best for those students. Teachers' knowledge should be embraced, not suppressed. When we give teachers choices, we ask them to think carefully about what they are implementing in light of what they know rather than simply implementing a one-size-fits-all plan. And when teachers' knowledge is a part of the process of planning and implementing, better teaching occurs.[36]

Thus, if you want something done, create clarity about the outcome expectations and clear the path to allow the person doing the work options in how to achieve the outcome. This is true not only for adults, but also for students.

From Engagement to Empowerment

Interest is fleeting engagement. So, it may be that most students do not continue learning X beyond the point that they could stop, but every once in a while, one will. Moreover, even those students who do not continue are likely to have engaged in the learning that what they studied will be retained. And, even if they forget the year that the Korean War ended, they will remember the way they felt during the learning and seek that feeling in

> **Helping people understand what engagement should feel like is important because it helps them become active participants in their work and teaches them to advocate for engagement.**

future learning experiences. In other words, the interest level of engagement allows people to advocate for themselves when they are in settings where compliance or non-compliance may feel like an option. Helping people understand what engagement should feel like is important because it helps them become active participants in their work and teaches them to advocate for engagement. This matters the most for students who struggle in school. I am not talking about healthy challenges for students who are ready for more, but students who have genuine difficulty with grade-level work. Students who have always struggled may falsely believe that disengagement is a part of learning and not understand that, at worst, we should find interest in the tasks that we are doing. On the other end of the spectrum, when students are able to recognize features of engagement, i.e., *I have to at least be motivated by the consequence/relationship and care about the task that I'm doing*, then they can start to see their work differently.

Chapter Summary

Interest is the starting point of engagement. You will know people are interested if they are enjoying the task in the moment but do not continue past the point that they can stop.

- There is confusion between standards, curriculum, and instruction. While the standards themselves are not negotiable, we should seek curriculum and instruction that are.

- Even more than children, adults expect voice and choice. Choice refers to options, and voice refers to input.

- It's important to remember that healthy and productive communication means that conflict will arise. When there is a fear of conflict, i.e., people do not feel like they can share their ideas, the result is that people appear compliant with the decisions during the meeting and exit the meeting without the commitment to the decision. This is not engagement.

- We do the work we choose to do because we chose that work and we avoid the work we are told to do because we don't have a say in it. This is why engagement increases when voice and choice are present; I'm more likely to do the work when it was work I designed. Not only does this make it easier to supervise me, but it also makes my performance more effective.

Reflection Questions

1. If all jobs paid the same, would you change jobs? Not including your current job, if all jobs paid the same, what jobs would you be interested in doing?

_____

_____

_____

2. Is the explanation of interested, as explained in this chapter, too low of a bar for engagement? Why or why not?

_____

_____

_____

3. Think of a time when you were not given voice and choice in a task. What impact did that have on your engagement? If you were asked for your voice and choice, what would have increased your engagement so that you would be interested?

_____

_____

_____

4. What is a task that you will assign in the future, and how can you inject choice and/or voice into the task?

_____

_____

_____

5. In your own words, what is the difference between standards and standardization?

_____

_____

_____

6. What are some ideas for managing the challenges associated with team conflict?

_____

_____

_____

Persistent Questions

1. What have you done so far regarding the three challenge questions from the Introduction?

   a. **Three:** Find at least three people with whom to share your learning.

   b. **Two:** Find at least two ideas that change you.

   c. **One:** Apply at least one idea from your reading.

_____

_____

_____

2. What have you learned so far, and how will you use it?

_____

_____

_____

Chapter 11

Absorbed: *So What*

"Working hard for something we don't care about is called stress;
working hard for something we love is called passion."
~Simon Sinek

Recognizing Your Thinking Before You Read...

- If absorbed is in the lower right-hand quadrant of The Engagement Matrix, what does this tell you about the connection to the external motivators and the assigned task?

_____

_____

_____

- Can you think of a time when you were absorbed in school?

_____

_____

_____

- With regard to absorption, what role does the teacher have in creating absorption for students? What is the role of students?

_____

_____

_____

- How does emotion impact absorption?

_____

_____

_____

Reflecting on Absorbed

As you recall, absorption is the highest form of engagement and is a sign that someone is interested in the task and intrinsically motivated. The truth is that when initially thinking about engagement, too many people do not delve into absorption. They falsely believe that doing what you're supposed to, rather than what you want to do, is the purpose of school. Therefore, misguided people believe engaged students are those who do what they're told, at worst. At best, they believe that engaged students are those who like doing what they're told to do. Hopefully, by this point in the book, you see the error of this belief. This chapter explains the importance of understanding absorption.

Emotional States

In the "Absorbed: *What*" chapter, I described three states of absorption: novice, enthusiast, and addict.

1. **Novice**: We feel smitten towards activities we are just "trying on" to see if we really like them; these can be a passing phase or may deepen into engrossment.

2. **Enthusiast:** We feel engrossed towards activities that are a long-term commitment of time and resources, fill our free time, and become a part of our identity.

3. **Addict:** We feel obsessed towards activities that result in the neglect of our responsibilities and other people.

These are important to understanding absorption.

School is a gateway to the discovery of things that one may not have any other opportunity to get exposed to. Becoming smitten is often something that happens as a result of school because school is a place where you get to interact with new people, ideas, and experiences. Through these interactions, you learn things from your peers and your teachers that you didn't know before. School is where many people get bitten by the acting bug, learn how to play a new sport, start to play an instrument, and learn new authors and genres. A window into previously unknown worlds is what school should be about.

> School is where many people get bitten by an acting bug, learn how to play a sport, start to play an instrument, and learn new authors and genres.

School should also be about providing mirrors that allow students to look at themselves. When looking at our reflections, we are able to tap into what we already know and expand on it—deepening what was into what can be. This is when schools allow students to take what they already know and can do and push them to the next best place and beyond. Providing students opportunities to do so means allowing them to access what they are already absorbed in and building on that. This is where engrossment happens in school.

The good news is that students rarely develop unhealthy obsessions with school-related content or activities. However, the bad news is that they may become obsessed with other things associated with school. Popularity and grades are just two school-related topics that can become obsessions for some students. Social media, which is not isolated to school, can be used as a tool for fueling obsessions when students use social media obsessively to communicate about school-related things.

Remember, each of these emotional states is a manifestation of absorption. Absorbed people differ from interested people in two important ways (see Figure 11.1). The first is that interested people need extrinsic motivation (a relationship with the person assigning the task and/or consequences), whereas absorbed people are intrinsically motivated. The second is that interested people will stop doing the task when given the chance and absorbed people will not.

Figure 11.1: Absorbed and the Engagement Matrix

	Compliant *Relationship to External Person and/or Payment: High* *Relationship to Task: Low*	**Interested** *Relationship to External Person and/or Payment: High* *Relationship to Task: High*
Relationship to the External Person/Payment →	**Non-Compliant** *Relationship to External Person and/or Payment: Low* *Relationship to Task: Low*	**Absorbed** *Relationship to External Person and/or Payment: Not Important* *Relationship to Task: High*

Relationship to the Task →

Why This Matters

I have to confess that when I was first thinking about engagement, absorption was not on my radar. When thinking about engagement, what I knew for sure was that compliance was not it, but was often mislabeled as "engagement." I knew this because I worked with administrators who, with compliance-based checklists in hand, would fan out into classrooms and scan the students to see who was "on-task." I also knew this because when I would talk with teachers after visiting their classrooms, I would ask them about whether or not they believed their students were engaged and ask them how they knew. More often than not, teachers would hand me the completed in-class assignment or exit tickets as evidence of students being engaged. Furthermore, if the students' behaviors were on-task, the students were deemed engaged, and everyone (teachers and administrators) celebrated.

Everyone, except maybe the students, who were often doing what they were told without any real opportunities or regard for their personal interests, lives, or choices to shape what they were doing. As teacher and staff developer, Daniel Wodarczak expressed to me in a conversation,

I think this is where a lot of secondary teachers struggle with students. They are enthusiasts or addicts in their particular subject area but have a hard time when students don't feel the same way. They don't teach in a way that is engaging for the student because they feel as though the material should be engaging enough. Put another way, the things being asked of the students depended on the adults in the room, **not** the students. The learning was designed by and for **adults**. Curricular or instructional choices depended on what the teacher found important, valuable, and/or liked. The systemic approach to teaching empowered and allowed teachers to exclude choice and voice because that's a lot of work, so the students do not get options. We design schools for the adults, and then we wonder why students are bored, checked-out, passive, or non-compliant.

> **We design schools for the adults and then we wonder why students are bored, checked-out, passive, or non-compliant.**

This happened to us when we were students, and this is why it is so hard for adults to answer the simple prompt of describing a time when they were absorbed as a student. At the same time, these adults are replicating experiences for students that do not invoke absorption. The message to students is clear, "Do what you're told." Imagine if rather than that directive, we asked students, "What do you like to do?" My desire is not to say that adults—either teachers or administrators—are bad. My desire in this chapter is to explain why it is so hard to create absorption in schools but to strongly advocate for why it is so important.

The highest form of engagement, which I call absorption, is a place where the task is so engaging that the motivation to do the task comes from within. This is when rather than coaxing someone to get started or to keep going, you have to coax them to stop. Rightly so. When you are absorbed, time passes differently—an hour can feel like ten minutes. There is also sufficient challenge that maintains the attention of the person doing the work. Absorbed people are plagued by the thought, "I just need another five minutes and then I'll…" finish my thought, solve this level, finish this chapter, perfect this skill, etc. Absorbed people are stretching themselves and feel like they are just within reach of success. Imagine having a classroom full of students who feel this way.

This gets back to the idea of engagement being a unicorn or a narwhal. When I speak about a classroom full of absorbed students, it sounds so mythical to some that they cannot imagine it. In Figure 11.2, I've put unicorn ideas of engagement next to narwhal ideas.

Figure 11.2: Examples of Engagement as a Unicorn Versus Engagement as a Narwhal

Engagement as a Unicorn	Engagement as a Narwhal
Students applaud and thank the teacher for the fantastic lesson	Students feel proud of their own work and learning
Teachers have endless amounts of resources to add bells and whistles to the lesson to entice students into learning	Teachers have some resources, but the students seek out and provide their own resources as part of the learning process
There is an infinite amount of learning time so the teachers can dig into the things they believe the students are interested in the most	Students make time outside of the classroom to continue digging into the things that they want to know more about
Students fall in love with what the teachers are having them study	Students are empowered to use what they know and care about to drive what they are studying
Parameters like standards, curriculum, and assessments are determined by the teacher	The teacher and students leverage the dictated parameters so that even if the teacher has boundaries, the students have high levels of freedom
Differentiation means that the teacher has created individualization for all students	Differentiation means that the students are trusted to create ways to personalize the task
Teachers can set aside the learning to get to know students	Everyone in the learning environment creates relationships through teaching and learning
All students always do their homework	Homework is learning practice meaning only those who need the practice need to do it
All students get perfect scores on all tests	Students who do not do well on assignments take advantage of the chance to re-do their work because they are focused on the learning
All students do what they're told	Students have a say in what they do
All students find even hard work easy	Students persevere even when the work is hard and seek out challenge

Notice that unicorn ideas can be both ideas of fancy such as "all students always do their homework," but it can also be a bar set too low like "students do what they're told." Absorbed people are not extrinsically motivated—they tell themselves what to do. Examples in the Unicorn column are adult-centered or have hopes for homogeneity. Conversely, the Narwhal column is student-driven and honors difference. If you try to achieve a classroom where "all students find even hard work easy," you will not only be disappointed, you will also think it's impossible. That's because it *is* impossible. Absorption is not about trying to make the impossible possible; it's about changing your idea of what's possible. Don't aim to make the work easy. That's the unicorn. Aim for promoting empowerment. That's the narwhal.

> **Absorption is not about trying to make the impossible possible, it's about changing your idea about what's possible.**

Before and After

Figure 11.3 shows a side-by-side photograph of a kindergartener on his first day before he left for school juxtaposed with the same child on the second day.[37] You may have seen this before. Notice the joy and anticipation are gone by Day Two. What's just as interesting to me is that if I showed you the photo and told you this child was a first-grader, you might say that the image on the left is from the *last* day of school for the year, not the first. What you're thinking, in that case, is that you expect that students do not want to be in school. Why are we surprised that a child would want to go to school but not surprised that they don't?

Figure 11.3: The First and Second Day of Kindergarten

In 2018, I heard Candi McKay say, "I've never met an intellectually lazy four-year-old." She specifically used the age of four because students typically enter kindergarten at five. Her point was twofold. First, humans are naturally curious. If you have ever spent any time around a child prior to the age of five, you will see perpetual motion, curiosity, a lack of fear to fail, and/or a zeal to try to do new things (except for maybe trying new foods to eat). As human beings, one of the most important traits that we have is the desire to learn. This is what allows us to learn how to speak and walk. This is why toddlers enjoy taking everyday objects and using them as toys—in fact, as most parents will attest, the first presents that your children probably enjoyed were the boxes that the toys came in, not the toys themselves. Humans are wired to enjoy learning. If this is true, then why is it also true that sometime between our first day of kindergarten and when we graduate from high school, we often forget that we once enjoyed learning? This is the second reason why McKay used the age of four. Something environmental about school has an adverse impact on our natural curiosity as humans. Rather than helping to foster our innate interest in learning, for far too many of us, school teaches us to stifle our curiosity and replace it with compliance.

> As human beings, one of the most important traits that we have is the desire to learn.

Never Give Up

When my youngest son, Oliver, was four, he would spend a lot of time playing *New Super Mario Bros. 2* on his sister's DS when she was distracted by something else. One day, I came home, and my husband showed me a video of Oliver playing the game. He recorded the video because he thought Oliver's reactions to the game were hilarious. When I watched the video, I saw something additional—I saw the highest form of engagement—absorption.

I show the video whenever I do Engagement Framework presentations because it is so powerful. You can watch part of the original video on YouTube, but I have edited it because no one wants to watch a four-year-old playing video games for more than a minute. That said, the rollercoaster of Oliver's absorption lasted far longer than the three minutes of the unedited video my husband recorded.

The video begins when, at four seconds in, Oliver "dies," and he screams, "No! No! Nooooo! Ahhhhhhh!!" The disappointment is immediately followed by returning to the game to start the process all over again. At about seventeen seconds, he exclaims, "I know. I get it. I get it! I know how. I get it! I know how! I get it! I get it! I know what to do now!" Several seconds pass, and he proudly states, "I did it!" After several more seconds, he dies again and says, "No! No! NO!!!!!" and then throws himself face down on the couch crying and slamming his fist into the cushion. He then immediately picks up the DS and starts playing again. The video ends here with Oliver repeating this cycle all over again. In fact, as I was writing this when Oliver was seven, he was ironically playing the game at a higher level (of course) and negotiating with his dad so that he could continue playing even though it was his bedtime.

Watch the video of Oliver absorbed in *New Super Mario Bros. 2* here and notice how he willingly returns to the game even after repeatedly losing https://cutt.ly/OliverAbsorbed.

I wish that I could take credit for Oliver's determination to persevere as though this was something that I instilled in him, but that would be a lie. Oliver's grit regarding this game (or any other) has nothing to do with some explicit expectations from my husband or me about not giving up. There are plenty of things in his life that we have wanted him to persevere in that he was more than willing to abandon. His persistence with this game had everything to do with the way that video games are structured.

Even if you are not a "gamer," most of us have played a video game at one time or another. If you are somewhere around my age, your first game was either *Super Mario Brothers* or *Duck Hunt* because they both came with the original Nintendo console. Maybe you are older than I am, and your first exposure to video games was by watching your children play, and you didn't play one until you had games on your smartphone, and you got sucked into *Candy Crush*. Maybe you are younger than I am, and you are a "digital native" who has always been around technology. You may have had several consoles in addition to an iPod, iPad, or other handheld gaming device. Whatever your experience or age, I have no doubt that you have either been drawn into a game or seen someone who has.

Why does this happen to so many? It's not the allure of the technology. It's the design of the process. Video games are designed to work within one's Zone of Proximal Development. The first level is often very easy, so you can see the basics of what you will need to do. Then, the game really starts. With that, you will almost certainly lose a few times before you progress to the next level. However, when you lose, you realize something about the game, and that fuels your desire to apply that learning immediately. It is that feedback loop of failure and learning that we find absorbing. We do not want to give up because we feel like we are just about to do what we haven't been able to do yet. As we are learning what will make us successful at this level, we are also being primed for skills that will be needed at the next level so that when we "level-up," we are sufficiently able to enter that level but insufficiently prepared to master that level. Indeed, we would not want to play a game where we could breeze through the levels the first time we played it; that would be too easy, and we would give up. No adult would want to play an alphabet game, but neither would a child who already knew the alphabet.

> It is that feedback loop of failure and learning that we find absorbing. We do not want to give up because we feel like we are just about to do what we haven't been able to do yet.

In truth, I do not really play many video games, and even the ones I do play, I don't play more than three to four times a year at most. However, on those occasions, the game that I'm playing is likely to be Tetris. I become uber absorbed in Tetris, a puzzle game where there are a limited number of shapes that are played one at a time to form a line. When you form a line, the line disappears (clears). As time passes, the shapes fall from the top of the screen quicker and quicker, making it more challenging to place them, particularly if you have several lines that have spaces making them difficult to clear.

In the version of Tetris I own, the players always start on "Level 1." This is great if you are not very skilled because you welcome the time to orient your piece and allow it to fall into place. I hate Level 1. It's too slow for me. I do not need that amount of time. I quickly turn the shape and then press the down button because I do not want or need to allow the shape to freely float into place. I actively drop it into place and move on to the next shape. The ability to quicken the placement of the piece is the differentiation I need to maintain my engagement until the pieces begin to fall faster on their own. As I'm playing, I can talk for the first few minutes, but once the game gets going, I can't. When/if I do, I become distracted and mis-position my pieces. At the end of the game, there is a summary of how long you played. Invariably, it feels to me like it has been no more than five minutes. In reality, it can be fifteen minutes or more.

Game On

Again, I am not a "gamer." Either way, though, my point is not that we should allow children (or adults) to play video games with abandon. My point is that it is worth exploring why video games are simultaneously challenging and engaging because I believe that there is something that can be learned from this that can improve what happens in schools. In fact, this is what is referred to as *gamification*, or applying video game elements or design to learning.

The first time I made this connection was when I heard Arizona State professor James Paul Gee speak. I was familiar with Gee's work around language and, specifically, discourse because of my background in literacy and English instruction. Yet, at this lecture, Gee spoke passionately about his entrée into the gaming world. In his book, *What Video Games have to Teach Us about Learning and Literacy*, he explains that his interest in this began when he watched his son playing a video game. Born in 1948, Gee did not grow up with access to the technology we have today, yet, he started to play his son's game so he could "coach" his son. "When I played the game," Gee writes:

> I was quite surprised to find out that it was fairly long and pretty challenging, even for an adult. Yet a very young child was willing to put in the time and face the challenge—and enjoy it, to boot. I thought, as someone who has spent the second half of his career working in education (the first half was devoted to theoretical linguistics): "Wouldn't it be great if kids were willing to put in this much time on task on challenging material in school and enjoy it so much?"[38]

Again, neither Gee nor I are advocating that video games are the end-all, be-all. The point being made is that if we took the time to examine why video games are so engaging, we could learn something important about how to infuse these features into instruction so that learning is more engaging.

In fact, Gee's book itemizes 36 "Learning Principles" that he found in video game play that could (should) be applied to the classroom. Gee's Principle 6, "Psychosocial Moratorium," states that "Learners can take risks in a space where real-world consequences are lowered."[39] Regardless of the reason for the risk-aversion, Gee says there are three strategies for designing opportunities to take risks with low-stakes:

1. The learner must be enticed to try, even if he or she already has good grounds to be afraid to try.

2. The learner must be enticed to *put in lots of effort* even if he or she begins with little motivation to do so.

3. The learner must *achieve some meaningful success* when he or she has expended this effort.

There are three principles here because people will not put in effort if they are not even willing to try in a domain; success without effort is not rewarding; and effort with little success is equally unrewarding.[40]

Gee's observation about effort and success seems self-evident, yet classrooms are

> **Gee's observation about effort and success seems self-evident yet classrooms are not always created with this in mind.**

not always created with this in mind. Still, classrooms that prepare students for failure, also prepare students for success. They do so by being forthcoming with the fact that, as Edison experienced with the lightbulb or anyone who plays a video game knows, there is much to learn when things don't work out the first or fiftieth time. They do so by stating that risk-taking will ultimately be rewarded, but risk-aversion will create stagnation and grow fear. They do so by fostering trust, both in the person who is the authority so that when the failure occurs, there is not a negative consequence, but also trust in the person, taking the risk to know that success *will* come with commitment and effort.

In the twenty-first century, technology abounds. The difficulty is in determining what to use, rather than not having things available. Technology for technology's sake is not the answer, nor is the idea that video games are the answer to getting students engaged in the classroom. Nevertheless, if we decontextualize the structures of video games, which are unquestionably engaging for people in ways that learning in the classroom generally is not, we can see that there is a lot that can be applied to classrooms to amp up levels of absorption for our students. This does not mean that it will be easy, particularly for those who teach in ways that position the adult as the sage on the stage and the students as consumers of the adult's knowledge. All the same, we cannot expect students to have different outcomes related to engagement if we are unwilling to attempt different approaches to our instruction.

Work Less

Here is a great place to pause and say that when we are aiming for absorption, we actually have less to do—at least when working directly with students. You read that sentence correctly. I said LESS to do. That's because we do not create absorption; we empower students to use what they like in order to connect with what they are learning about. You will have a much easier time designing opportunities for students to connect what they are absorbed in to the learning rather than trying to design ways to create absorption.

Finding ways to tap into things that students are absorbed in is rigorous because, at this level of engagement, other things must already be placed. It means that the teacher and student have a classroom environment that supports the students as producers, not just consumers, of learning. It means that the teacher has created tasks where the students have higher-than-expected levels of choice and voice. It means that the teacher and the students have created an innovative and empowering space that connects the curriculum and what the students already know and care about, which means that the teacher also has to be excited about the curriculum. This certainly sounds like a classroom I'd want to be in either as a student or as a teacher.

For those who are absorbed in the desire to create classrooms where students can be absorbed, I would offer Ellin Oliver Keene's guidance from her book *Engaging Children: Igniting a Drive for Deeper Learning K-8*. Keene writes, "In committing to a classroom that supports deep engagement, we must be determined to lead students towards independence and agency."[41] Her point is spot-on and reminds us that the job of the teacher is to create a space for students to link what they care about to what they are learning about.

When we confuse engagement narwhals for unicorns, we misguidedly feel responsible for motivating students to learn. This dynamic creates a paradigm where, as Keene shares, students are "dependent on an adult; you better wait for them to motivate you before you before you engage."[42] I have never met anyone, especially a child, who does not have an intense passion for something. Thus, perhaps rather than thinking we need to create the passion, we need to think about how we can provide ways for students to link their passions to the learning in the classroom.

Passion has many manifestations. It may be in relation to dinosaurs, dolls, dance, or the Dodgers. It can also be to an idea. In other words, while human beings are passionate about tangible things like people or places, they are also passionate about ideas like democracy, decency, discrimination, or dishonor. You could tap into their feelings like the feelings of duty or a feeling about an event like disaster relief. When you allow people to connect to the things they already care about, they are more likely to care about what you want them to connect to. While you may not be able to help someone who is passionate about dinosaurs find absorption in the French and Indian War, that does not mean that there are no other entry points for making connections. That same person may care a lot about colonization or North American conflicts or the plight of indigenous people. If we are only seeing absorption as an opportunity to connect to specific things like hobbies, we say things like, "Bella likes soccer, but there's no way to link soccer to what we're learning about" and give up too easily on finding ways to engage students at the highest levels. On the other hand, if we broaden our entry points to feelings and ideas, we exponentially increase the possibilities for absorption.

> **When you allow people to connect to the things they already care about, they are more likely to care about what you want them to connect to.**

I'm In It for Me

Keene writes at length about engagement and makes a strong case for what she calls the "Pillars of Engaged Learning." [43]   Specifically, the first two pillars are "Intellectual Urgency," or the notion that engaged people are hungry to "know more" about something and "Emotional Resonance," or the idea that engaged people have an emotional response to the thing(s) they find engaging. [v] In the "Absorbed: *What*" chapter, I wrote about the three levels of absorption being novice, enthusiast, and addict. These stages are really emotional states. Thus, we need to understand where our students already have intellectual urgency and emotional resonance as well as help them see how the things they're learning about can create new urgencies and resonance. Keene advocates for sharing examples from our own lives in order to model this for students and to explicitly teach them that these are responses they should be feeling and tapping into. Again, our job is not to motivate, but to empower, not to usurp, but to unleash.

In the June 2018 issue of "Education Update," Laura Varlas interviewed Mary Helen Immordino-Yang on "why emotions are essential to learning and how teachers can elicit and support emotional connections in the classroom." Immordino-Yang's research has found that reason and emotion are both needed—in fact,

> cognition happens *because of* emotion. There's really no such thing as thought that doesn't have an emotion attached to it or that doesn't have an emotion that follows it…It's literally neurobiologically impossible to remember or think about anything that you haven't felt emotion about. It just doesn't happen because it would be a waste of the brain's resources to think a lot about stuff that doesn't matter.[44]

Emotional responses to learning will happen regardless of whether or not we acknowledge that there are emotions to elicit. If we give credence to the need to foster and tap into the emotions that occur, we improve the chances for learning. If we disregard emotions, that doesn't make them go away. One of two possibilities can happen. First, students like what they're doing accidentally and not by design. Second, which is worse, negative or apathetic emotions creep in, including feelings of boredom, anger, and/or defeat.

The link between learning and emotion is also highlighted in Robert J. Marzano and Debra J. Pickering's book, *The Highly Engaged Classroom,* where they say that "to foster student engagement, classroom instruction decisions are based on four emblematic questions." These questions include:

---

[v] The other two pillars are "Perspective Bending" and "The Aesthetic World."

1. How do I feel?

2. Am I interested?

3. Is this important?

4. Can I do this?

The first two questions focus on the attention of the student, while the last two questions gauge the engagement of the students' interest in the topic. The attention questions deal with whether information from the outside world gets into working memory. If the information presented is not considered interesting, the working memory will not process it. Engagement is defined by importance; if the information is not deemed important, the working memory will not maintain it for long. If students do not believe they can perform the tasks, the brain will eventually reject it.[45]

> **The teacher's job is not to create *the* entry point for the student to join the work; it's the teacher's job to show the students that there are *multiple* entry points.**

In order for people to become absorbed, they need to be able to participate in work that matters to them and be able to contribute in ways that are sufficiently challenging for their abilities at that time. The teacher's job is not to create *the* entry point for the student to join the work; it's the teacher's job to show the students that there are *multiple* entry points.

Rigorous Or Ridiculous

In one of my former jobs, we used to ask the question, "Is this rigorous or ridiculous." This was around the time the Common Core was rolled out, and the term "rigorous" was tacked on to everything as though everything prior to the Common Core was a piece of cake. It's not that we didn't recognize the need for rigor; it's just that there were times when what was being described as "rigorous" was actually downright inappropriate or, as we said, "ridiculous." It is rigorous to ask me to run a mile in under ten minutes; it is ridiculous to ask me to run a mile in under two minutes. The first action I can do, but it will require dedicated training. The second would be like asking me to fly. I don't have wings. I am not a bird. It cannot be done. It wouldn't matter how much effort or preparation I had, the target is laughable. Rigorous is equivalent to narwhals, and ridiculous is a unicorn.

In her book, *Never Work Harder Than Your Students*, Robyn R. Jackson[46] explains the difference between expectations and standards. This is a key difference and should be considered when thinking about when something may be seen as ridiculous even if it is just rigorous.

Interestingly enough, most teachers believe that they have high expectations for their students, but when you examine what they are saying, what they really mean is that they have high standards. It's a subtle but important difference.

The difference between an expectation and a standard is that the standard is the bar and the expectation is our belief about whether students will ever reach the bar. Standards are the external criteria against which a product is evaluated. A standard does not tell us anything about the beliefs. What we believe about the standard, however, determines our expectations.

One common approach to raising teacher expectations is to impose or raise the standards by which students and teachers will be evaluated. Proponents of this approach argue that by adopting a common set of standards, teachers will be very clear about what students are expected to know and be able to do. They assume low expectations result from a poor understanding of what mastery is. This approach, however, is fundamentally flawed.

As Judith Lloyd Yero (2002) argues in her book *Teaching in Mind: How Teacher Thinking Shapes Education* and on her Web site at www.teachersmind.com/standards.htm, "It is possible to have extremely high expectations without any standards whatsoever. Conversely, it is possible to have very low expectations—even when the external standards are extremely high."

Raising standards is not the same thing as raising expectations. Holding students accountable for more and more information does not change what we believe about a particular student's ability to master that information.

There is no cause and effect relationship between raising standards and raising expectations. Just because you raise your standards does not mean that you have also altered your belief about whether your students will be able to meet your standards. In fact, the opposite may happen. If you do not believe that students are able to meet

> your prior standards, how can you believe that they will be able to meet your new, higher standards? Higher standards then may actually *lower* expectations.

Though I am the creator of The Engagement Framework, I do not want people to look at absorbed and think that I am suggesting that it is a rigorous (achievable) outcome to create the conditions for all students to be absorbed all day in all classes. That suggestion, even to me, is ridiculous. The reality of human nature is that there are things that are required that are not very engaging. What's more, some of these things are variable. I love writing, for example, but the person next to me may not. I do not want to play Pokémon, but the person next to me may be over the moon about it.

We do not have the luxury of homogeneously grouping students according to their abilities, interests, backgrounds, etc. Even if we did, that does not guarantee that they would be identically absorbed in all things. Thus, we have to be at peace with the fact that while every lesson can be of interest (not absorption) for every student every day, we need to rigorously strive to ensure that we know what every one of our students is absorbed in and find ways to allow them to link that to what they're learning. In other words, even though it is ridiculous to expect absorption for every student in everything we do in schools, it is rigorous to create opportunities for every student to be absorbed in something.

> In other words, even though it is ridiculous to expect absorption for every student in everything we do in schools, it is rigorous to create opportunities for every student to be absorbed in something.

Now, take all of these pieces I have just described and add on that absorbed is a state of engagement where you lose yourself in the task, and you do the task for the joy you feel of doing it. What I cannot help but feel at this point is that it is ridiculous to expect absorption to happen for every student in every lesson every day. I know this is a shocking and perhaps controversial statement for some.

Most of the time, absorption is a place we want students to visit often but recognize this is not going to be a place where they can live. There are too many requirements via the state, the district, and/or the school that make the high levels of choice and voice required to achieve absorption too difficult to maintain 100 percent of the time. This is not to say that absorption couldn't or shouldn't be a rigorous (achievable) goal for classrooms. This is not to say that the engagement level of interested isn't possible as the rigorous goal for all students all of the time. It's simply to shed light on why it is so difficult to have all absorbed students in every school every day.

Student-Centered or Student-Driven

Wolfgang Gerhardt, former leader of Germany's Free Democratic Party, is quoted as saying, "You are taking too much and giving too little in return." Though I'm sure he's thinking about this in a political fashion, I'm thinking of it in terms of what teachers and students do in traditional classrooms. Commonly, teachers are the ones who are breaking a sweat, which is why the title of Robyn R. Jackson's book *Never Work Harder Than Your Students* is so alluring. Let me say, I've never been to a practice where a coach is doing more physical exercise than the players—and if the coach is, the players are not very good. Why? Because the ones doing the work are the ones who are learning. I'm a big fan of things like read alouds with children. Yet, if all the children ever did was listen to the teacher read, how would the students become readers? In far too many classrooms, though, teachers are literally *doing* the work for students who are likely to be passive observers.

As we progress, we begin to elicit student input and create student-centered classrooms. These are classrooms where students are not just the audience to the teacher, but where the teacher seeks student contributions from the students by giving students a seat at the table. In settings like this, the role of teacher is shared with the students. This is certainly progress and will spark and fuel student interest.

But this chapter isn't about interest, it's about absorption. Absorption is not about shared billing between the teacher and the student, it's about positioning the student as the expert. Education consultant and leadership coach David E. Goldberg writes that "The kind of education that really unleashes students as confident lifelong learners who have the courage to take initiative depends, in part, on the ability of faculty members who can relinquish control and really trust students with a central role, a leadership role, in their own educations."[47] Again, this is not mythical or impossible; it's just not typical. One of the best resources I have found to frame the difference between teacher-driven, student-centered, and student-driven education is Barbara Bray and Kathleen

Figure 11.4: Bray and McClaskey's Stages of Personalized Learning Environments (version 5)[48]

Stage One Teacher-Centered	Stage Two Learner-Centered	Stage Three Learner-Driven
The teacher...	**The learner...**	**The learner...**
understands how each learner learns based on Learner Profile (LP) and data.	with teacher guidance updates LP by recognizing how learning changes.	monitors and adjusts LP as he or she learns with teacher as a partner in learning.
makes instructional decisions on methods and materials based on four diverse learners' LPs to create a Class Learning Snapshot (CLS).	identifies learning strategies and skills with teacher to create action steps for learning goals in PLP.	is an expert learner with agency who applies innovative strategies and skills to redesign and achieve learning goals in PLP.
refers to CLS to redesign learning environment by changing physical layout of classroom.	co-designs the learning environment with multiple learning zones with teacher.	expands the learning environment in and outside of school to include the local and global community.
universally designs instructional methods and materials and guides learners to establish learning goals in Personal Learning Plan (PLP).	with teacher decides how he or she accesses information, engages with content, and expresses what they know using learning goals in PLP.	self-directs how, when, and where he or she achieves, monitors, and adjusts learning goals in PLP.
revises lessons and projects that encourage learner voice and choice.	and teacher are transforming lessons and projects together to include learner voice and choice.	designs challenging learning experiences based on interests, aspirations, passion, and talents.
designs activities to include tools and strategies that effectively instruct and engage all learners in the classroom.	with teacher acquires skills to choose and use the appropriate tools and strategies to access information, engage with content, and express what he or she knows and understands.	independently applies tools and strategies so he or she can explore deeper and challenging experiences that extend learning and thinking.
is introduced to competency-based learning. Learning may be part of a standards-driven, time-based grade level system.	demonstrates mastery of learning standards that may or may not be in a grade-level system transitioning to or are in a competency-based system.	learns at his or her own pace and demonstrates mastery with evidence of learning in a competency-based system.
or counselor suggests after-school and extra-curricular activities to learners based on learning goals in PLPs.	and teacher work together to determine extended learning opportunities (ELOs) based on college, career, personal, and citizenship goals in PLP.	self-selects ELOs based on college, career, personal and citizenship goals as well as his or her interests, aspirations, passion, and purpose.
uses or adapts existing formative and summative assessment strategies and leads learner conferences with parents.	contributes to design of peer and self-assessment strategies, reflects on learning, and leads conferences with parents, teachers, and peers.	designs assessment and showcases evidence of learning through exhibitions that involve parents, peers, teachers, and community.

McClaskey's "Stages of Personalized Learning Environments (version 5)." Both experienced educators and authors, Bray and McClaskey's "Stages" (see Figure 11.4) does a terrific job stretching the reader's thinking beyond what is familiar to what is possible.

When Were YOU Absorbed in School

In my presentations on engagement, towards the end, I ask participants to talk to the person next to them and "Share an example of when you were absorbed in the learning as a student. What made that experience more than just interesting for you?" As you are reading this book, I'd like to ask you the same prompt. Think about this for yourself. Really. Please take a moment before you read any further and reflect on a time when you were academically absorbed as a student.

No, for real. Stop. When you were academically absorbed as a student?

Was this prompt easy or hard for you? If you're anything like the people who I have presented to, this prompt proved to be exceedingly difficult. It's not because the prompt is difficult. It's very straightforward.

The difficulty is not in the question, but in identifying even one example of a time when most of us were absorbed as students. This is because, by this point in the presentation, as is the case for this book, you have already been exposed to the definition of absorption—doing something challenging that you want to do and being so immersed in it that you lose track of all other things including time. As well, you would do it even if you didn't have to. As a student, unless you went to school or had a teacher who used something like project-based learning (PBL) opportunities or maybe you were in a vocational or advanced pathway, there were probably only a small handful of academic experiences you had in school that were absorbing. Why? Because most of us were in classes where the expectation was to do what you were told to do rather than to apply what you were learning to something that you wanted to do.

Remember, that absorption is on the bottom right side of the Engagement Matrix. As such, the person who you're doing the task for is YOU, and the rewards for doing the task come from WITHIN. When you read "Bringing the Lessons to Life" at the end of this chapter, you will see how I respond to this prompt.

When Are You Absorbed at Work

I'm betting that some of you reading this chapter are thinking something along the lines of what I wrote in the Introduction of this book…

> The challenge is that it is not easy to design lessons about things that students *have to learn* in ways that students *want to learn*. Indeed, there seems to be a paradox that suggests that if students have to learn X, they won't want to learn it AND what they want to learn about is Y.

You may also be thinking that you are not absorbed in your work because of all of the real and perceived restrictions you have. So, you wonder, *When is someone going to ask me what I want to do in my classroom?*

With all due respect, unless you literally have a scripted curriculum that tells you exactly what to say and do, you probably have a great deal of choice and voice with how to teach the students you have. Though it can be more difficult at times to exercise your choices and voice, difficult is not the same as impossible. Indeed, one of the most important choices you have is how much choice you will choose. It *is* easier to pull out old lessons or to use the lessons the program provides without modification(s). But, easier doesn't mean engaging. I suspect that teachers who choose to work in this way are actually less engaged. If this chapter clarifies nothing else, let it be stated that to get to absorption—either as a student or as a teacher—is not a passive act; absorption is an active pursuit of personal challenge.

Bringing the Lessons to Life:
When Was I Academically Absorbed as a Student?

Truth be told, when I think about how I would answer this question, it's not easy for me. We had annual public speaking contests in my district growing up that began in the seventh grade. I excelled in this and vaguely recall spending a great deal of time on my speech in the seventh grade to make it perfect. I'm sure one of the aspects that I enjoyed the most was being able to talk about whatever I wanted to. When I was a senior in high school I had to do a research project. I cannot remember what course it was in, but I have memories of feeling really proud of myself for the work that I did, particularly in my choice to design and administer a survey as a part of that work. Even so, I would have stopped writing the speech and quit doing my research project if I wasn't being graded. Thus, those tasks were only interesting to me. While I can think about the positive relationships that I had with countless teachers as a student and I can recall feeling rewarded or disappointed in various assignments, for the most part, absorption as a student has been elusive for me.

When given time to think of an example of when I was academically absorbed as a student, I point to my undergraduate work when I took a pottery course as my art credit. Though I had no prior experience using a pottery wheel, I genuinely loved creating pottery (also known as "throwing"). In fact, to this day, I tell people that if I didn't have to make money, I would love to be a potter. Unfortunately, my pottery was ridiculously bad. In that semester, I was unable to truly accomplish the task of making my pottery the proper thickness. As a result, all of my pottery was dense and heavy even after it was fired and all the water was removed. That didn't stop me from relishing the process of wedging (kneading) the clay, throwing it on the manual wheel, and kicking frantically so that the wheel would spin. I would press my hands into the clay as it fought back against my desire to turn it into anything more than the weighty, shapeless mass that it was.

It was through this process that I looked differently at all the other creations in my life. As an English Major, I churned out essay after essay, either analyzing someone else's writing or trying to create my own masterpieces. There were times when I would submit something I wrote that I thought was easily worthy of the highest marks and receive something less than what I expected. There were other times when I would submit something that I thought was lackluster (at best), and I would receive glowing grades. When I would get back the assignment, I would allow the external evaluation to not just influence, but overshadow, my intrinsic beliefs about the quality of that work. If the professor said it was good, it was good. If the professor said it was bad, it was bad.

The pottery class changed my life. I knew the pottery was not objectively good. It was heavy and lopsided and imperfect. Subjectively, to me, I was so proud of my work! I loved it because of the effort I put into it. Not all of it was lovable…maybe the glazing didn't turn out as I wanted it to. Maybe the lid didn't fit as I had hoped. Maybe I had to scrap it entirely and start over. It wasn't that I could not see clearly; it was that I shifted the power from the external evaluator to my internal voice. Through that,

> It wasn't that I could not see clearly, it was that I shifted the power from the external evaluator to my internal voice.

I saw my writing differently. I would embrace the feedback I received, but I was no longer going to let the feedback determine the value of my work. This was a wonderful and unexpected side effect of being absorbed in pottery and shows how absorption in something can change the absorbed person beyond the thing that they are currently absorbed in. It's not that I no longer cared about the grades that I received; it's that the grades were no longer the motivation. I wanted to do it. Not just my pottery, although that was true, but also my writing. I was liberated.

Chapter Summary

Absorption is the highest level of engagement. You will know people are absorbed if they lose themselves in the task even when the work is hard and they could stop. When thinking about absorption, here are additional points this chapter included.

- Engagement is a function of emotional connections. Schools should be places where we learn things we didn't know before that build on our emotions about what we already cared about.

- Too often, we mistake what engagement should look like in schools and think that engagement means all students want to and will do the same things. Absorption is not about trying to make the impossible possible; it's about changing your idea of what's possible. Don't aim to make the work easy. That's the unicorn. Aim for promoting empowerment. That's the narwhal.

- Humans are wired to be curious and seek learning.

- Video games use the Zone of Proximal Development to teach skills at certain times and build on what you already can do. Failure is expected and appreciated because it provides important, real-time feedback.

- Adults do not create absorption. We empower students to use what they like in order to connect with what they are learning about. This is student-driven education.

- Absorption is not the goal for every student in every lesson every day. That's ridiculous. The rigorous goal is to target the interested level for all kids and to provide all students with the opportunity to find absorption some of the time.

- You were probably not academically absorbed very often, if ever, as a student. But, you have the ability to choose to be absorbed in your work as a teacher and to create absorption opportunities and mindsets with your students.

Reflection Questions

1. Share an example of when you were absorbed in the learning as a student. What made that experience more than just interesting for you?

    _____

    _____

    _____

2. This chapter said that absorption is a choice. Do you agree or disagree? Why?

    _____

    _____

    _____

3. In what ways are your students able to connect what they are absorbed into your content?

    _____

    _____

    _____

4. Think of a task that you have your students doing that is interesting to them. What are some alterations that you could make that could foster absorption?

    _____

    _____

    _____

5. In your own words, why is absorption important?

    _____

    _____

    _____

Persistent Questions

1. What have you done so far regarding the three challenge questions from the Introduction?

   a. **Three:** Find at least three people with whom to share your learning.

   b. **Two:** Find at least two ideas that change you.

   c. **One:** Apply at least one idea from your reading.

   _____

   _____

   _____

2. What have you learned so far, and how will you use it?

   _____

   _____

   _____

Section IV: Now What

*T*he next three chapters will provide numerous next steps, including books, websites, and strategies on how to shift from one level in *The Engagement Continuum* to the next highest level. These suggestions are meant to be launching pads because there are countless books, websites, and resources available on engagement. The value of these chapters is that they are categorized by *The Engagement Continuum* and thus can help build engagement based on the current level. By the end of Section IV, you will be able to identify actionable steps to take to shift from one level on *The Engagement Continuum* to the next.

Chapter 12

Non-Compliant: *Now What*

"Make no mistake between my personality and my attitude.
My personality is who I am.
My attitude depends on who you are."
~Unknown

Recognizing Your Thinking Before You Read…

• When thinking about non-compliance, what behaviors are you dealing with now that you would want to change?

_____

_____

_____

• What resources have you learned from and/or used in the past to help you build relationships with others?

_____

_____

_____

• What resources have you learned from and/or used in the past to create consequences to avoid non-compliance?

_____

_____

_____

From Non-Compliant to Compliant

So now we know what being non-compliant is all about. We know that, assuming the task is within the Zone of Proximal Development (ZPD), there are generally three (3) different reasons why people would be non-compliant:

1. ***Low Regard for the Extrinsic Relationship:*** They do not care about you
2. ***Low Regard for the Extrinsic Consequence:*** They do not care about the consequence
3. ***Low Regard for the Task:*** They do not care about the task

We also know that people who are non-compliant fall into three different categories known as (1) rebels, (2) normalizers, and (3) activists. Now that we know all of this, what can we do when we are working with someone who is non-compliant? That is what this chapter is all about—moving someone from the point of non-compliance to compliance[vi] through changing the relationship and/or the consequence.

It's Not Rocket Science

Regardless of the motivation for the non-compliance, the best and first way to approach moving into compliance is to improve your understanding of the other person. What does he like? What motivates her? What do they like to do when given choice? etc. This isn't rocket science. In many ways, it's harder because humans are complex, unique, and unpredictable. At the same time, the cliché, *I don't care what you know until I know that you care* encapsulates the value of relationships to motivation. Improving your understanding is a first step to building a relationship. As a result of the relationship, there is a chance that the person will comply because that person cares about you and does not want to disappoint or disrespect you by not doing what you want. The second option you have if someone is being non-compliant is to focus on the external reward for completing the task. Again, this can take the form of carrots (make

---

[vi] Though it is also possible to move someone from compliance to absorption, doing so does not lead to compliance; it leads to absorption because the task has changed. This is hard since, in reality, you would change a belief system(s). It is possible, for example, that someone could convert to a different religion, register with a different political party, or have once been a racist but now believe in racial equality. Making changes like these are drastic because these people are more likely to see themselves as "absorbed" in their behaviors rather than "non-compliant." This was explained throughout this book. In truth, what you would be trying to do is to have activists disengage with their beliefs. This would be an abandonment of something they intrinsically believe to be not just true, but absolute, and that is a hard sell.

the reward more appealing) or sticks (make the consequence of not doing the task more severe). Finally, if the non-compliance is due to the task not falling within the ZPD, you could change the task that is required. With regard to shifting from non-compliance to compliance, there is only so much to the task that you can change because this is more about making a vertical move rather than a horizontal move (the next chapter will provide many strategies for changing the task).

One final reminder. Rebels are the stereotype for non-compliance. However, most of the time, those who are non-compliant are normalizers. If you were a child who had negative feelings towards school, it is not surprising that when you grow up and still have those negative feelings about school that you pass on those feelings to your own children. The normalized behavior of distancing yourself from teachers and principals by not attending conferences or approaching home-school connections as home-school indictments is quite common and often culturally reinforced. Thus, what appears as non-compliance can be taken personally as rebellious indifference even though it is really normalized trauma. Normalized non-compliance explains why children need to be repeatedly asked to do things by their parents even if they have a fantastic relationship. The problem is not with the relationship, per se, but with the normalized patterns of non-compliant behaviors.

> Rebels are the stereotype for non-compliance. However, most of the time those who are non-compliant are normalizers.

The point of normalized non-compliance is that this is more common than rebellious non-compliance, but because it is so ordinary, it gets overlooked. We all triage and want solutions for rebellion. The price we pay for this prioritization is that we disregard normalized bad behaviors. Rebellion is death by suicide bombs; normalization is death by 1,000 cuts. Both are acts of terrorism, but only one does so with shock and awe.

> Rebellion is death by suicide bombs; normalization is death by 1,000 cuts. Both are acts of terrorism but only one does so with shock and awe.

When thinking about the shift from non-compliance to compliance, it is important to simultaneously hold two contradictory truths in mind. The first is that compliance is better than non-compliance, and it will feel like a victory when the formerly non-compliant person makes the leap to compliance. The second is that compliance is still disengagement and should only be a stop on the engagement journey, but not the final destination. Accordingly, the goal of this chapter is to share strategies that can help shift others from non-compliance to compliance, to yield an improvement, but not to appear as the ultimate goal.

Making Homework Work

Actress Lily Tomlin said, "I like a teacher who gives you something to take home to think about besides homework." I do too. Nevertheless, homework is as much a part of school as anything else. It is also one of the most ubiquitous tasks that produces non-compliance. There are entire books that are written about how to improve the learning and completion of homework, so what I share below is the tip of a very big iceberg. All the same, it's important to note that many of us are thinking about homework incorrectly.

To illustrate the misunderstanding of homework, I will use two non-academic examples. The first is with sports. If you were ever an athlete or the parent of an athlete, my guess is there were practices. At the practices, the players did warm-ups and drills that allowed them to hone specific skills they were working on. Sometimes, but rarely, was there time to actually scrimmage at practice because the point of the practice was to focus intensely on isolated skill(s). For this reason, practices are more frequent than games in the beginning and generally less fun. After all, who wants to do endless fielding drills or burpees? Yet, parents do not balk at their child attending practice. Those who opt-out of practice are removed from the team.

Not an athlete? Then try this second homework analogy on for size. If you were ever a musician or the parent of a musician, my guess is there were practices and lessons. In the beginning, these practices came in the form of playing independently at home to rehearse the music or parts of the music. A common feature of home rehearsal for new musicians is a practice log that the musician completes throughout the week and has a parent sign to confirm the authenticity of the practice. The expectation of home practice for musicians is commonplace, and parents do not flinch at this expectation. Those who opt-out of practice are those who do not improve their talents and get left behind or are demoted to a lesser chair position.

Even the greatest professional athletes and musicians have required practices. This is, in part, how they got so good and maintain their greatness. If professional athletes miss practice, they can be fined (a negative consequence to generate compliance). So if practice is so important for new and master athletes and musicians (not to mention other fields), why are there debates about practice related to academic learning?

I would argue that one reason is that we do not think about homework as practice of academic learning. This is why we have students who can pass tests but fail courses due to homework incompletion. Think about that for a moment. If homework is practice of learning, but the students know it already, is the homework necessary? You could argue that even with students who know the material already, there could be homework to enrich what they know. I would agree. That's not the homework I'm talking about. The homework I'm talking about is the one-size-fits-all kind that everyone has to do regardless of if the students have already demonstrated proficiency.

In fact, too many do not understand that the intention of homework should be to reinforce what was taught not to use it as an introductory teaching tool; i.e., it hasn't yet been taught, but the students are asked to demonstrate their knowledge. If this introductory work is presented as diagnostic (see Figure 12.1), then that's okay. If it's not, this can quickly create a feeling of being overwhelmed for students who are working outside of their Zone of Proximal Development.

Figure 12.1: The Types of Assessment

Assessment Level	Meaning	Examples	Parallel Example
Diagnostic	Assessment *before* learning	• Pre-tests • Fall benchmarks	Bloodwork
Formative	Assessment *for* learning	• Exit tickets • Homework • Journal entries • Models	Physical
Summative	Assessment *of* learning	• Unit tests • Final exams • Culminating projects • State exams	Autopsy

For all the reasons described above, the purpose of homework is to see what the child is able to do independently with the learning to inform the teacher of the gap between teaching and learning. More concretely, Figure 12.1 reinforces that homework should be *formative* and provide the teacher with information s/he can use to change the instruction if needed. Moreover, since homework is formative practice of what the students are learning, they need feedback to let them know how they're doing; otherwise, they are just practicing how to do something incorrectly.

Unfortunately, formative assignments can become lethal weapons that obliterate any student intrinsic motivation and reduce it to compliance. But, the compliance target can be overshot and lead to nothing remaining but non-compliance. If the purpose of homework, which should be formative, is to practice what was taught, then it should receive feedback and be reviewed by the teacher so the teacher can learn what the students know. But, it should **not** be graded. Athletes don't lose runs in baseball or touchdowns in football for a mistake during practice.

One of the best books I've read about homework is Myron Dueck's *Grading Smarter, Not Harder: Assessment Strategies that Motivate Kids and Help Them Learn.*[vii] This practical and straightforward book provides a solid underpinning about why our traditional approaches to assigning work and giving grades actually demotivate learning and create more work for teachers. While I would strongly recommend every educator read this book, because grading and homework draw ever more attention from teachers and parents as students progress through school, Dueck's chapter on grading is one all secondary teachers should be required to read. This is because there are beliefs around homework that go something like this, "'I have to grade it, or my students will not do it.'"[49] Yet, grading homework can actually communicate messages that undermine the messages that we want to send. Not sure what that could look like? Homework for a grade booster is an example. The avoidance of a negative grade is another example. A third example is when we assign homework that requires all students to complete the same work, what Dueck refers to as "uniform

---

[vii] Anyone who is an ASCD member has access to the one-hour recording of a webinar (https://cutt.ly/GradingSmarter) by the same name he gave in January 2015. Trust me, it's worth watching!

homework." In all of these cases, we create an environment where there are high stakes around low-interest tasks.

Students who are compliant with the expectation of homework completion and have a low interest in the tasks they must complete are concerned about getting the tasks done, not about the learning the tasks are meant to reinforce. As such, we should not be surprised that students in this teacher-created situation are likely to cheat—a non-compliant behavior. In summarizing his chapter on homework, Dueck writes:

> Homework can be the key to academic success for one student, and seemingly a waste of time for another. To understand the role of homework, it is critical first to determine the extent to which it is needed for each student, and then to ensure that students are completing the work themselves. Homework assignments should provide students with an opportunity to practice what they're learning in the classroom. It is a tool in the learning process, not an instrument to measure understanding.[50]

Neither Dueck nor I am advocating that we eliminate homework; we are advocating for a different approach to homework. Included here are a handful of suggestions for how to approach homework differently.

1. **Begin at the End:** I recently heard a high school math teacher tell me that she uses her homework assignment as the "Do Now" for the start of the next day's class. Students do not need to do the homework, but if they do it, it will help them be successful in the "Do Now."

2. **Show What You Don't Know:** Many times, students have some gaps in their knowledge, so when they do their independent practice on their homework, they ask for help. How is a teacher to know that the student needed help and that the work that they think was independently completed was actually done with assistance? Without this important information, the teacher incorrectly assumes the students are proficient with their knowledge when, in fact, the students are developing. Thus, teachers should make one or both of these things clear to students and their families:

a. When working independently, the students should do what they can, but do it *on their own*. It's important for the teacher to know what the students don't know.

b. If the student asks for help, note that this was something the student got help with. If possible, note what help was given so that the teacher knows that with X support, the student was (or was not) able to demonstrate proficiency.

3. **Entry and Exit Tickets:** If you are working in a setting where the culture does not support homework completion (in other words, either homework is taboo or students just do not do homework), then do not assign it. There is no point in fighting this battle because everyone will lose. Instead, use entry or exit tickets to get a sense of what the students are able to do or need more instruction with.

4. **Thoughtful Homework:** If students are assigned the exact same task in the form of questions/problems, worksheet, or other "uniform homework" assignment, then we should expect there will be those who cheat because the outcome is completion, not learning. If learning is the outcome, then create ways for the students to determine what they need to practice. Therefore, you can say something like, "Based on the work we did today and your exit ticket, those who were not successful independently may want to consider doing this tonight for practice." This level of communication, trust, and independence sounds much more like the type of decision-making students will have to make in college and their careers. After all, a boss (or college professor) is more likely to expect and respect their employees' (or students') initiative rather than wait for someone to tell them they need to put in more time to improve.

5. **Puzzle Pieces:** What if the homework was in service to a larger product rather than an isolated task? Then, doing the homework becomes purposeful. I need to do this so that I can get to Y. I need to do X, Y, and Z because they are all connected to the project. Again, this is how higher-level learning institutions and careers work. When I wrote my dissertation, I had to complete a series of smaller tasks to feed into the dissertation. At work, I need to process assessment data in order to analyze it so that I can share the analysis with the board.

Give It A Try

Over the next several pages are some strategies that you can use when trying to shift from non-compliance to compliance. Again, the way to do this is through changing consequences and/or changing the relationship. Changing relationships is a lot harder than building relationships, so there are some strategies here on how to proactively build relationships so that you could avoid non-compliance altogether. For those strategies, you may think, "Where's the non-compliance?" Remember, you don't need to wait for non-compliance and could take the mindset that the best offense is a good defense and prevent problems before they start.

Getting to Compliance Strategy 1: Equity Sticks

We've all been there. We asked a question, and some students volunteer to answer the question by raising their hands. Do you know what volunteers aren't? Non-compliant. If I ask a question and students raise their hands, those students are willing to participate. And, you know what most teachers do when they ask a question, and they have students who raise their hands? They call on a student whose hand was raised, and they ignore the students who didn't. This is the game of school, and we all did it as students and as teachers.

We need to change the game by telling students to put their hands down. Do not use student volunteers to select who will answer the question—use equity sticks. The equity stick strategy is the best and easiest strategy for improving cognitive compliance that I know of. In fact, if you only tried one strategy, this would be the one I would recommend. Equity sticks are numbered popsicle sticks (or have the students' names written on them) that are in a jar. Each student in the class has a corresponding number, so when the stick with the number three, for example, is pulled, Aiden knows that he's three so he will answer the question. Numbering the sticks works well if you have multiple classes like special area teachers (art or music in an elementary school) or if you are a secondary teacher who sees multiple classes. If you are in an elementary class or another setting where you have the same students all day, I would encourage you to personalize the sticks by writing the students' names on them.

With equity sticks, the teacher asks the question *first* before drawing a stick to identify which student will answer the question. This is key. Why? If you ask the question after you announce who will answer the question, then you allow the students who are not answering the question a greater opportunity to opt-out of the thinking needed to answer the question. When you ask the question first, all students need to formulate a possible response (it keeps them on their toes).

I have also seen it where once the stick is pulled, the stick is not replaced in the jar. While you could do that, I would advise against it. If I was the first person to answer a question and the stick with my name/number didn't go back into the jar, I know that

Want to see equity sticks being used in a real classroom? Watch this video at https://cutt.ly/Equity Stick.

I will not have to answer the rest of the questions, and I can again opt-out. The purpose of this strategy is to help all students do the thinking. Not replacing the stick undermines the intended purpose.

If there are times when you are concerned about a student being put-on-the-spot, you can do some magic behind-the-scenes to ensure that doesn't happen. You can pull a stick and intentionally say that student's name even if that was not the name on the stick. No one will know. I have seen classrooms where it was a student's job to be the stick-puller. There is nothing wrong with having student roles in the classroom. If you do this, you can still use a wrong name by taking over briefly or by saying something like, "Lucas, what do you think about this question?"

Getting to Compliance Strategy 2: Chart It

When my children were younger, we used to have a sticker chart to make our invisible expectations about good behavior visible. In 2011, I wrote about it in my weekly letter to my staff at the time. When you read it, you will see that my goal was to move my son from non-compliance to compliance through positive consequences.

Hello Friends!

For the record, I'm writing this on Monday night. I'm saying that because in truth I'd really rather watch TV right now or surf the internet or thumb through my new Pottery Barn catalog (not that I'd buy anything, but I like looking). Instead of doing any of that, however, I am writing my letter. When I finish, I'm going to reward myself with a sticker. That's right. You heard me. A sticker.

Before I tell you about my sticker, let me tell you that prior to my work at Pinnacle, I'm not sure that I really had much experience with behavior mods. I was a Gen Ed ELA teacher with no true SPED background. Interestingly, my Master's degree as a Reading Specialist provided me with the opportunity to become certified in Special Education, but I was honest enough with myself and any potential employers to know that my training in reading did not provide me with the wealth of knowledge necessary to do justice to any Special Education students with whom I would have been charged to work. My education training as an undergrad did not offer me much in the way of classroom management knowledge either, considering at the time, to get my secondary certification required a minor with 18 credit hours of work—most of which was consumed in the student teaching credits. That said, I'm fairly certain that I never created one for a student, nor do I recall having to sign off on another teacher's mod for a student.

At Pinnacle, however, creating behavior mods for students who need something above and beyond the general system that works for the bulk of the class is an important step in working with students. As has been said before, one of the interview questions that you all answered dealt with *what you would do if you had a student who continually spoke out in class, and despite your attempts to contact home, nothing has changed.* The response that receives the highest score to this question includes getting to the root of the student's issue by speaking with the student, creating an individual behavior plan with specifics of what the student will work on (possibly involving others in the school), implementing the plan, and finally weaning the student off of the plan and back to the whole-class behavior plan. This strategy of providing the student with the ability to think about what s/he is doing, therefore empowering the child to recognize unfavorable behaviors and create favorable ones, when done well and repeatedly, is extremely effective.

Just like I feel like I didn't get much training in B-Mods for teaching, I didn't get any training in parenting. So, when Nolan's temper tantrums—which are age-appropriate—began escalating, Howard and I helplessly tried doing more of what we had already been doing. We're "time-out"ers. So, we'd go through the steps: (1) give a warning, (2) give a time-out, (3) send him to his room, (4) threaten to take away toys, and (5) take away toys. This process generally included raised voices (both Nolan's and ours). Ultimately, if steps 1-3 didn't work, steps 4 and 5 were nails in a coffin. Instead of deescalating the situation, as a parent is supposed to, we aggravated the problem; we felt helpless in doing the right thing because what came naturally wasn't working.

On the way home from Thanksgiving (we were at Howard's family who lives a couple hours away), I took advantage of the time to try to talk through our dilemma with Howard. "I think Nolan needs a behavior modification plan," I told him. "What we're doing right now isn't working. We need to have a strategy for what's going to happen when Nolan doesn't do what he's supposed to, and we need to be on the same page with that." We talked about this in detail. "We also need to reward him when he does what he's supposed to. We spend so much time focused on what he's doing wrong, and I think he needs to *see* when he does something well. Besides that, he has a sense of entitlement because he just gets things and never has to earn them. We should get him a sticker chart, and he should get a sticker when he's done something that he's supposed to incentivize making good choices. Then we can give him something that we would have otherwise given him once he's earned a set amount of stickers."

After getting the sticker chart for Nolan, it didn't take long for him to catch on. Every behavior he made that was positive gets rewarded with a sticker. You got ready in the morning without whining? You get a sticker! You played well with Lilia while mommy put Oliver to bed? You get a sticker! You ate your dinner without complaint? You get a sticker! You've earned a row of stickers? You get a special treat!!! I can motivate Nolan now to do just about anything with the promise of a sticker on his chart. He's putty in my hands.

Judge me all you want. Tell me that I am not creating intrinsic motivation. Call me out for bribing my child. I can take it because it is working. For nearly two months, my son has earned, rather than been given, things that he would have received anyway (aside from his Christmas presents). For now, it has had a positive effect on Nolan's life as well as ours since his negative behaviors have decreased because we are transparent about what good behavior is, and we reward him for it.

All of which got me to thinking that a little extrinsic motivation might be nice for me. I like special treats too. There are quite a few things that I know I should do but do not do often enough. Exercise, eat right, clean the house, organize the basement, read, etc. What if I earned a sticker every time I did something that I should have done but may not have been motivated enough to do in a more timely manner? Voila! A carrot on a string. So, I'm exercising more, doing household chores more, etc., because, in addition to the reward of doing it, I'm earning my way to special treats! I figure writing this letter on Monday night instead of procrastinating until Thursday night has to be worth something, right? Why not a simple little sticker?

Charts work well when tracking progress is general. That is the premise behind chore charts. The chart displays both what is supposed to get done and if it was done. It is the combination of both of these things that lead to success. Why? Because it not only displays what needs to happen, but it also creates a way to quickly and easily see if the task was done. After all, most of the time, there is not confusion about what is needed, there is neglect in doing it. Charts, therefore, create accountability.

The more visible and accessible the chart is for the person doing the task and the person who assigned the task, the better. This is because it allows both people to know what still needs to be done and what has been completed. In school settings, public displays of progress can sometimes be controversial. If you work in a setting that frowns on public displays of students' progress, then find ways for students to have

private access to their progress and build in ways to check in with them privately. Certainly given, there are countless ways to use technology to do this. Students could have a shared Google Sheet with you where they mark off what is done; there could be a Trello Board (a free online platform that organizes and tracks progress), Chorepad.com, etc. You could also give students an old-school, hardcopy chart that they keep in a binder or folder that they share with you during a conference or quick check.

Visit https://cutt.ly/Chore App to see some suggested chore apps

No matter if you use a new- or old-school method of charting, it's important that you do more than check the chart—you will also need to inspect the work. We have all fudged checklists or charts when we've realized that no one is really checking the quality of the work. You do not want to create compliance to the chart; you want to create compliance to the task. To do this, you have to check the task since the chart is just a way to let you know that the task is ready to be checked.

Getting to Compliance Strategy 3: Make the Learning Visible

When I was about twelve, I got in trouble for "slamming" the toilet lid down too hard one too many times. As a consequence, my mom made me go into the bathroom and open and close the lid to the toilet 100 times quietly. My mom left me to do this task without supervision. Since the task was intended to be noiseless, and since she wasn't standing there watching me, I simply stood in the bathroom for what seemed like an appropriate amount of time and left. I did not touch the toilet lid once, but she never knew. I was compliant with the noise level expectations but not compliant with the task.

According to the website www.phrases.org.uk, the proverb, "While the cat's away the mice will play," was originally a Latin phrase that was adopted by the French in the early 1300s. The English version that we know today traces back to around 1470. In many classrooms in this century, one can see this proverb in action when students are compliant with the behavioral expectations but non-compliant with the learning. Creating accountability through deliverables that document the learning increases the likelihood that students will learn. For example, if you have ever walked into a classroom where students are supposed to read for an extended period of time, like with Drop Everything and Read (D.E.A.R.) or to watch a movie without needing to take notes or any other product, there is a high chance that there are students who are not doing the learning even if they are being quiet.

When students are working without supervision, there *must* be a deliverable, meaning a product that cannot be produced without doing the work. Certainly, the easiest thing to have them do is complete a worksheet, and if you really are only hoping for compliance, then that will achieve this outcome. Here are some other easy ideas for how to achieve visible learning that are likely to be more engaging than completing a worksheet. The goal here is to ensure that the task leads to an outcome that the teacher can use to determine what the student *learned*.

1. **Response Journals:** When students write down their thinking, it not only gives the teacher insight into the students' schema, it provides a record of their thinking for the student to be able to refer to later. This is why I would advocate for a response journal over any other method of documentation (e.g., post-it notes, worksheets, etc.). The other suggestions shared below could all integrate or be done using a response journal. The response journal becomes the storeroom of thinking—all neatly held in one location.

2. **Double Column Entries:** Have the student create a T-Chart with one side that is twice as wide as the other. On the narrow-side, the student will write a quote with the page number of what they read, and on the wide-side, the student will write their thinking about that quote. Set a minimum number of entries that are required. The same could be done with a movie. On the narrow-side, write what was happening or what was said. On the wide-side, write an analysis of that event.

3. **Text Tagging:** If students are reading something they can write on, have them "tag" the text with specific symbols to indicate they have a question (?), or they made a connection (C), or they had an idea (!). You can work with the students to determine the tags or create them yourself. Since it is easy to tag a text without actually even reading it, you will want to have a complimentary task that they need to complete. For example, write a brief explanation for each question, connection, idea, etc. Here again, you will want to create a minimum number of tags.

4. **What I'm Thinking:** In 2000, I heard Roger Farr, a professor and speaker on reading, talk about the relationship between reading, writing, and thinking. He would say, "Good thinkers make good readers make good writers." Farr encouraged having students frequently have to report on their thinking as they're reading. To accomplish, this I took the text that the students were reading and inserted blank text boxes where they were required to stop and jot down their thinking. Before allowing students to do this independently, I modeled my own thinking by doing a read aloud and stopping at different points to do think alouds. I created a lot of work for myself in the process of recreating the text in Word, so I could insert the text boxes. You could accomplish this through post-its or reading journals. Where the students put their thinking is not important; it's important that they do the thinking. An important caveat is that the students were not allowed to use the thinking blocks to summarize what they read. Farr cautioned that students should be able to summarize, and the thinking we needed them to do was more than summary. Summary, he said, was the foundation, and we needed to move them beyond that point.

   Another piece that was added to this was to have students recognize the types of thinking that they could do other than summarize. I had the students work in groups to compare their thinking blocks and see if they could cluster them into categories. We then created labels for the categories. For example, the categories included:

   - Predictions
   - Text-To-Self/World/Text/Media Connections
   - Inferences
   - Visualizations

- Questions for the Author
- Author's Purpose
- Surprises

We would give each category a number, and I would then have students identify their boxes with the numbers to see the trends in the types of thinking they did, and we did as a class. I would challenge them to choose a category to try that was outside of their comfort zone and/or assign them a specific category to try.

5. **Mental Models:** When the Common Core Math Standards came out, math practices were also unveiled. One of the practices is "Model with Mathematics." Developing and using models is also a practice found in the Next Generation Science Standards (NGSS). In this case, modeling is not meant to be a manipulative like the model of atoms; it's meant to be a representation created by the student to demonstrate understanding of their thinking at the time. Indeed, with every training in the NGSS that I have attended, the idea that students should have consistent access to their original models to be able to revise them as their learning grows is a stressed feature. This is something that could be done in any content area and would be very engaging to students who are inclined to draw. For those who consider themselves to be less artistic, it is not the artistry, but the ability to convey thinking that matters.

6. **Keeping Score:** Many times, particularly in elementary classrooms, I have seen students playing content-based games in centers. This opportunity to build social skills and academics is important. Unfortunately, if there is nothing that keeps track of the process, it is reasonable to expect that the students are not on-task or inaccurate. To monitor this without being present with the students, ensure that the students note the scores throughout the game. If the game, for example, has the students roll two dice and add up the scores, have them write the number on each dice and the total each time.

7. **How to Get Groups to Work:** It is extremely difficult to determine in a group who has done what. The purpose of group work is to provide students with the opportunity to do something that *cannot* be achieved without the group. If it can be done independently, then there is no need to do it as a group except to have everyone

do less than they would have had to do independently. If that's the case, then go for it. If not, then do not do group work.

When doing group work, ensure that all members of the group have to produce and are accountable. That does not mean that you have to assign the tasks to the students, just that there needs to be a task for each member to do at all times throughout the duration of the process. Idle time leads to opting-out. In other words, while the end-product is a deliverable, each member of the group should have to explain what they learned from his/her contribution and what they learned from the others in their group.

A word of caution. There are three levels of learning.

- Independent: I do not need the teacher's help to do this.
- Instructional: I can do this as long as the teacher is guiding me.
- Grade Level: I am expected to do this for this grade level with the teacher's assistance and then on my own.

Ideally, the student's instructional level is their grade-level instruction. The truth is, for many, the grade level instruction is beyond their initial reach even with teacher assistance. This means that if the teacher is asking the students to do grade-level work independently, the students will be outside of their Zone of Proximal Development. If this is the case, it will also be the case that the students will be non-compliant with the learning because they need help. Thus, when assigning independent work, be sure that it is at the student's independent level. This will safeguard against non-compliance due to the challenge level of the task.

Getting to Compliance Strategy 4: Creating a Classroom the Students Own

We know that Monday through Friday, students spend as much or more time in school awake than they do at home. In other words, their classroom is like a second home. Given this, rather than decorate the classroom for the students, have the students decorate the classroom for themselves. In elementary classrooms, this is especially easy given that there are not a hundred or more students who use the space on any given day. I love what @GregoryMichie did with his students by having them go through his "posters, photos, and art to decide what they wanted to display + why." It's not just a great way for him to get to know his students, but for them to get to know each other.

Getting to Compliance Strategy 5: #Startingtheyearoffright

Kerry Smith (@micdropmrssmith) is a fourth-grade teacher at Hoover Elementary School in the Kenmore-Town of Tonawanda School District who wanted to get to know her students before they even stepped foot in her classroom. To do this, she wrote a letter to her incoming students, which was sent out with the placement letters. The letter was a chance to introduce herself and explain that she wanted to have a little fun before school began by creating videos of the students introducing themselves. She gave the students detailed directions in the letter for how to log into Flipgrid and asked that parents email her so that she could give the parents their child's school password. Kerry only told the students how to log in and how to open the area where they would make the video. She wanted them to be able to explore the app and video capabilities on their own and self-discover. The students were excited and proud of their videos and to come back to school. An added bonus from doing this is that because the parents had to email Kerry to get information, she was able to build relationships with the parents even before school started.

Though not all the students may do the activity, those who do are likely to go above and beyond by navigating the program, figuring out how to edit it, adding pictures, drawings, and more. Also, the tool that Kerry used was Flipgrid, but it didn't have to be. It could have been that students were asked to send a postcard or letter. It could have been that there was an Instagram page or just texting the teacher via Remind with photos of things you like. The medium is not what's important—it's taking the time to get to know your students and their families, that is.

Getting to Compliance Strategy 6: Parents As Partners

At my oldest son's third-grade Open House, his teacher had posters out with markers for parents to share with her answers to questions about themselves. One of the questions asked parents to write down what they read that day. The answers surprised me because though some parents wrote down things like "the newspaper," most wrote down things like "texts," "emails," or "Facebook." I thought this was such a great way to get to know the students through the parents. She also asked the parents to respond to the question, "When I think about the 3rd-grade state assessments, I feel…" The responses were so telling. Many of the parents indicated feelings like anxiety and annoyance.

Going back to the idea of modeling from chapter 9, "Compliant: So What," you'll remember that parents' feelings can impact their child. This is why we should ask important questions of parents to learn how they felt when they were in school or how they feel about school now. Below are a list of possible topics to consider and some sample questions to go with each. The point is not to ask all of these questions, but to improve your understanding of the child through better understanding the parent—both how the parent connected with school as a student and how the parent connects with school now.

Topics	Sample Questions
Associations they had with school as a child and/or an adult	1. How did you feel about school when you were a student? 2. How do you feel about school now? 3. Who was your favorite teacher, and why? 4. If you could change one thing about your time in school, what would it have been? 5. What was your favorite subject in school, and why?
Concerns and expectations about school for their child	1. Do you have any concerns about school this year for your child? If so, what are you concerned about? 2. What expectations do you have for me as I work with your child this year? 3. What expectations do you have for your child this year in school?

Areas that the parent feels (un)able to support learning at home if the child needs help	1. When your child has homework, what subject do you feel the most confident in supporting your child if s/he needs help and why? 2. When your child has homework, are there any subjects that you feel like you might not be able to support him/her with should s/he need help? Please let me know what those are. 3. How often does your child ask for help? How often do you offer it?
Feelings about testing and grading	1. How do you feel about the state assessments? 2. What questions do you have about how your child is graded? 3. On a scale of 1-10 (with 1 being low and 10 being high), how important do you think grades are?
The parents' time demands after school	1. Many children have afterschool activities or responsibilities. What types of afterschool things take place in your family, and how frequent are they? 2. Many parents have to juggle responsibilities after school, like getting kids to practices, doing work at home, maintaining the house, working another job. What types of demands do you have of your time after your child's school day ends?
Goals for their child	1. At the end of this school year, what do you hope your child is able to do that s/he cannot do yet? 2. What does success for your child look like to you?
Best way to communicate	1. I want to make sure that you and I have the opportunity to communicate regularly about your child. What is the best way (phone, text, email, etc.) and time to reach you? 2. I like to use social media to communicate with parents what the students are learning about and doing. What social media sites do you visit?
Feelings about homework	1. How did you feel about homework when you were in school? 2. What routines does your child have at home for doing homework?

Getting to Compliance Strategy 7: Do a Home Visit

It is far easier to change a consequence or a task than it is to change a relationship because building relationships takes time. Nevertheless, building relationships is the surest way to avoid non-compliance altogether. Building relationships can start even before the first day of school. How? Home visits are a great example of connecting with families before they even start.

The slogan for Head and Shoulders shampoo used to be, "You never get a second chance to make a first impression." Of course, they were referring to how you look, but the sentiment holds as much, if not greater, weight with regard to how you treat people.

If your first interaction with someone is negative, then you have a steeper hill to climb to demonstrate that you are someone who is kind and wants to have a positive relationship. There are some students who have had experiences in school that have caused them to believe that schools and the people in them are unwelcoming, injurious, and off-putting. These are students who tend to approach all school-related people with skepticism that can manifest as non-compliance.

Many families have had experiences with school—either when they were students themselves or with their own students—that have left the families with strong negative associations with schools. In the book *101 Ways to Create Real Family Engagement,* author Steven M. Constantino shares advice that educators do not often try. "There is a very simple rule to engage families who have traditionally been or have become disengaged: *before they will come to you, you must go to* them."[51] Home visits provide an easy way to "go to them." What's more, the National Education Association reports:

> programs that provide time and funding for teachers to visit students and parents on their own turf are a way for teachers to learn more about their students, get the parents more involved in their child's education, and bridge cultural gaps that might occur between student and teacher. Most teachers report their home visits have a lasting effect on the child, the parent, and parent-teacher communication.[52]

A traditional time for face-to-face meetings with families is during open houses or parent/teacher conferences. The problem with most open houses is that they are not a time to have dialogue about a particular student or family. This is a chance for the family to visit the classroom and learn about the learning. Though parent/teacher conferences are one-on-one opportunities for communication, they tend to occur after learning has happened and tend to be a time for the parents to learn about how their child is doing in school. In other words, both open houses and parent/teacher conferences are primarily designed to be opportunities for families to learn about things taking place in school. Home visits, however, are a chance for the school to learn about things taking place in the home.

See what a home visit can look like by visiting https://cutt.ly/HomeVisitsing.

It's obvious that visiting the home is the best way to achieve this despite the fact that this is not a common expectation or practice. I think people think that it's going to be hard to do the visits, or they are concerned about going to specific neighborhoods. First of all, this is not a solo act, and no matter what neighborhood you go to, you should go with at least one other person. While a visit later in the year would be a fine idea too, the point of this particular strategy is to do this *before* the start of school so you can start a relationship with the students/families. A very user-friendly "Guide to Team Home Visits" can be found by visiting this link: https://cutt.ly/HomeVisitForms.

Ron Clark, Disney's 2000 Teacher of the Year award winner, author, former Survivor contestant, and founder of the Ron Clark Academy, is known for home visits. This is a something that teachers at the Ron Clark Academy (RCA) do. This Facebook post tells the story.

Getting to Compliance Strategy 8: The 5 Questions

Granted, home visits are a large scale, labor-intensive approach to building relationships. Looking for something a little easier? How about asking George Couros' "5 Questions to Ask our Students to Start the School Year?"[53] These questions are not only ones that you could ask your students, but ones that you could modify and ask their parents.

1. What are the qualities that you look for in a teacher?

2. What are you passionate about?

3. What is 1 big question you have for this year?

4. What are your strengths, and how can we utilize them?

5. What does success at the end of the year look like to you?

What these questions have in common is that they ask the students to reflect how they see themselves.

Alternate Use: Imagine asking students these questions before setting up class making class sections and using this information to form the classes. Students could be paired with other students who have similar styles or, conversely, intentionally placed with students with complementary styles. This is akin to how college students are assigned dorm mates. As well, students could be matched by the teacher's style.

How Engaged Are You In Learning More?

Looking for even more strategies to use to get your students compliant with what they're learning? Please visit my website, www.LyonsLetters.com, for lists and links. In the meantime, here are some that I would recommend.

Further Reading

- *A Repair Kit for Grading: 15 Fixes for Broken Grades* by Ken O'Connor

  This book is very short but answers any question you can think of as to what is wrong with traditional grading systems and how to fix it, even giving example language for grading policies. The book uses real students and teachers as examples of grading problems and solutions.

- *Grading Smarter Not Harder: Assessment Strategies That Motivate Kids and Help Them Learn* by Myron Dueck

  This is also a very quick and straightforward read. I mentioned earlier in this chapter that I would recommend that any secondary teacher read this book because of how clearly it explains the challenges with homework and very learner-centered approaches to how to address these challenges. There are great personal stories that bring the text to life as well as sample documents to use for increasing student learning through homework.

- *Classroom Assessment and Grading that Work* by Robert Marzano

  This book explains how grading on a 0-100 scale is flawed and provides methods to shift to a grading approach that isn't. What's more, it explains how assessments should be configured to be able to determine what students actually know and do not know and how that can more appropriately be translated into an evaluation of their learning.

- **"The Case Against the Zero" by Douglas B. Reeves**

  This *Phi Delta Kappan* article from December 2004 (https://cutt.ly/AgainstZero) explains in two pages the obliterating impact a zero can have on a child's grade and provides suggestions on how to grade without using zeros.

- ***101 Ways to Create Real Family Engagement* by Steven M. Constantino**
  The book delivers on its title giving the reader dozens of ideas that are grouped under four categories: (1) Creating a Welcoming Environment at Your School, (2) Two-Way Communication Between Home and School, (3) Increased Degree of Engagement, and (4) School Support for Home Learning.

- ***Teaching to Strengths: Supporting Students Living with Trauma, Violence, and Chronic Stress* by Debbie Zacarian, Lourdes Alvarez-Ortiz, and Judie Haynes**
  Students and families who have large issues outside of school can bring those issues into school and appear to be disengaged with learning when, in fact, they are just distracted. *Teaching to Strengths* helps those who work in schools to rethink and reframe what they see from students and families. When thinking is reframed, school staff are better able to understand and better support the needs of students and families even their needs are ones that arise outside of school since the home impacts what happens in schools.

- ***The 5 Love Languages of Teenagers: The Secret to Loving Teens Effectively* by Gary Chapman**
  Want to better understand a teenager and what makes them tick? This book provides a framework for how to best communicate with teens and how to interpret how they communicate with you as well as ideas on how to establish boundaries and create independence.

Digital Resources

- **Video "The Myth of Average" Todd Rose at TEDx Sonoma County**
  https://cutt.ly/average
  Todd Rose explains that an average may work in a mathematical sense, but in life, may not really give us the answer that we're looking for. Instead, Rose advocates for "designing to the edges" to make sure that everyone who needs to participate can do so to their fullest potential.

- **Video: "Every Kids Needs a Champion" Rita Pierson TedTalks Education**

  https://cutt.ly/Rita_Pierson

  Rita Pierson, an educator with over forty years of experience, talks about the value and importance of relationships.

- **Video: "Kid President Pep Talk about Teamwork and Leadership 1"**

  https://cutt.ly/KPTeamwork

  Honestly, I think I love every Kid President video, but this one, in particular, expresses that we are all on the same team. This sentiment is designed to foster relationships.

- **Video: "Cultivating Collaboration: Don't Be So Defensive!" Jim Tamm TEDx SantaCruz**

  https://cutt.ly/Jim_Tamm

  Jim Tamm, a lawyer who worked for decades on contract negotiations, explains that defensiveness is the number one inhibitor of collaboration. He then shares ideas on how to improve collaboration in order to achieve mutual outcomes.

- **Podcast: *The Brian Mendler Show***

  https://cutt.ly/Mendler

  Author, consultant, speaker, and former teacher, Brian Mendler shares advice on how to effectively respond to even your most difficult students. Brian is funny, straightforward, and kid-centered.

- **App: ClassDojo**

  www.classdojo.com

  Looking for a way to keep track of who is doing what in your classroom? Want to reward kids in the moment? Would you like to communicate a students' behavior with a parent easily? The ClassDojo app can help you do this.

Chapter Summary

This chapter was about moving someone from the point of non-compliance to compliance. There were a variety of topics addressed, including how to tackle homework, how to build relationships, and how to create accountability. A myriad of strategies and extension opportunities were provided as well. Since humans are complex, unique, and unpredictable, not every strategy would be appropriate for every situation. First, you have to determine what the cause for the non-compliance is so you can determine if you need to focus on the relationship and/or the extrinsic consequence.

Reflection Prompts

1. Think of a time when you worked with someone who was non-compliant. What idea from this chapter would have assisted in preventing that dynamic or would have facilitated a shift towards compliance?

    _____

    _____

    _____

2. What is a strategy that you have used to effectively shift someone from non-compliance to compliance that wasn't included in this chapter? Was that a strategy that focused on the relationship or the consequence?

    _____

    _____

    _____

3. Name one thing you could do tomorrow based on what you learned from this chapter.

    _____

    _____

    _____

4. Of all of the extension suggestions provided, which one intrigued you the most, and why?

    _____

    _____

    _____

5. Tweet me @LyonsLetters to share an idea for a future reading or digital resource I should look into that would help someone who is non-compliant become compliant.

Persistent Questions

1. What have you done so far regarding the three challenge questions from the Introduction?

    a. **Three:** Find at least three people with whom to share your learning.

    b. **Two:** Find at least two ideas that change you.

    c. **One:** Apply at least one idea from your reading.

    _____

    _____

    _____

2. What have you learned so far, and how will you use it?

    _____

    _____

    _____

Chapter 13

Compliant: *Now What*

"In a nutshell, the problem with compliance is that it is just another form of disengagement—of students not being invested in their own learning."
~ Allison Zmuda and Robyn R. Jackson

Recognizing Your Thinking Before You Read...

- With regard to the Engagement Matrix, what would need to happen to get someone to move from *compliance* to *interested*?

  _____

  _____

  _____

- In your experience, how have you helped move people from being compliant to being interested?

  _____

  _____

  _____

- In your own experience, think of a time when you shifted from being compliant to being interested. What change(s) occurred that accounted for this shift?

  _____

  _____

  _____

From Compliant to Interested

So now we know what being compliant is all about. People who are compliant do not want to do the task any more than those who are non-compliant, but they are willing to do it based on the extrinsic relationship to the person or the consequence.

In order to move from non-compliance to compliance, there needed to be a change in the external relationship or consequences.

- I did not like you so I would not do what you wanted me to do, but now I do like you so I'll do it.

- The consequence was not enticing enough before, so I would not do what you wanted me to do, but now it is so I will do it.

- The consequence was not revolting enough before, so I would not do what you wanted me to do, but now it is so I will do it.

The change is to the motivator even though the task has remained the same.

The good news is that compliant people will do the work. The bad news is that they don't want to do it. So, now that we know all of this, what can we do when we are working with someone who is compliant? That is what this chapter is all about—moving someone from the point of compliance to interested through changing the task.

It's All About the Task

Now that we are talking about compliance, we need to think about how we shift people from being compliant to actually being interested in what they are doing. What is needed, then, is a change in the task. People will not move from being compliant to being interested unless and until you change what they are being asked to do. This is because compliance means that they are doing the task because they have to. As we shift towards being interested, people do the task because they want to. As was discussed earlier in the "What" and "So What" sections on Engagement, this is the first step into being engaged.

There are countless books, websites, curriculum, lessons, etc. that will all say that they will engage students. When you look at these, remember that the goal for getting students to the interested level of engagement is to create a desire to do the work when asked because they like what they're doing. Hopefully, this work will involve a level of challenge that is differentiated to operate within groups of students' Zone of

Proximal Development. The more homogenous the task is, the less likely you are to ensure that it will be all of your students interested. So, if every student needs to…

- Read, is it possible to have them read different books? No? What about having at least choice between two books on the same theme or topic?

- Show that they know the math concept? Is it possible that they each have to create one or more math problems that demonstrate the concept and ask another student to solve it? No? What about giving them the choice between doing the problems or giving them the wrong answers and ask them to determine why it's wrong?

- Do the science lab, is there a chance that the students have two different labs to choose from—both of which align to the concept that is being taught? No? What about some students looking over the lab results and designing a process that would yield that outcome?

- Are you learning about a certain historical event? Can the students work in teams where they find a primary source and create a "primary source" that would complement the primary source? No? What about creating a pro and con debate to defend the historical significance of the event being studied?

I could go on, and, as you can see, these are just examples using the "Four Core." The difficulty is not in thinking up different ideas; the difficulty is in putting ideas into practice and trusting that things will work out. In reality, you don't have anything to lose. Your compliant students will likely do what you want them to regardless. On the upside, you could shift students to a higher level of engagement, and that is the whole point.

Give It A Try

Over the next several pages are some strategies that you can use when trying to shift from compliance to interested. Compliance was really about behaviors—are you doing what you are expected to do. Interest is really about connecting the behaviors with someone's heart and mind. These strategies are designed to make the task as appealing as (a) the relationship with the person assigning the task and/or (b) as appealing as the consequence for doing the task. As well, remember that these tasks get students to the point where they enjoy doing the task in the moment; do not mistake momentary engagement for absorption. You will know that the students are interested because while doing the task, they're into it, but when given the chance to stop, they do.

Getting to Interest Strategy 1: Earning Your Pay

As I have said repeatedly throughout this book, choice and voice are critical pieces to engagement regardless of where one is on the Engagement Continuum. One of the easiest ways to offer choice and voice is in the task that is completed. Often the work we have students do is identical. Rather than having a one-size-fits-all approach to the tasks, create a menu of options for the students and design a way that the students have to sample different tasks but not do all of them.

When I facilitate workshops on engagement, I provide the participants with a Tic-Tac-Toe board of possible tasks they need to complete in order to learn more about engagement. I tell them, "I don't care which of these nine tasks you do, but you need to do at least three of them that form a line either vertically, horizontally, or diagonally." As an alternative to the Tic-Tac-Toe board, I then show them that there is an approach I call "Earning Your Pay." Using the same nine tasks, I assign the tasks each a point value; the easier/shorter/less complex the task, the lower the value and the harder/lengthier/more complex the task, the higher the value. I tell the participants that they need to earn a minimum number of points total. The participant decides which tasks they choose to do (see Figure 13.1 to see the Tic-Tac-Toe Board and "Earn Your Pay" Samples, Rubrics, and Possible Alternatives). It took me time to think about the tasks, but since I took that time prior to the workshop, I can spend my time during the workshop with the participants to answer questions or provide support.

If they were actual students whom I worked with daily, I would know that some of them didn't do well on the last test so I could pull them aside in a small group or individually to work with them for remediation. I would also know that there were some students who were really interested in football, so I could incorporate football into some of the options, etc. You get the picture. When I give the students/participants the opportunity to choose what they do, their interest in the work increases, and that increases my ability to focus on groups or individuals. While teaching is important, formatively assessing what is understood to inform who needs what next is equally important.

As well, since these are tasks that are asynchronous and do not require my direct instruction, I could easily pull groups or individual students to work with on something they may have been struggling with that is not directly connected with their tasks but is directly connected with the learning for the course.

Figure 13.1: Tic-Tac-Toe Board and "Earn Your Pay" Samples, Rubrics, and Possible Alternatives

Directions: Do any three activities below so that you form a vertical, horizontal, or diagonal line. The expectation is that everyone is at least Proficient.

Read and Reflect	I Know You	Back to the Start
Read the text "Have to Learn Vs. Want to Learn." Jot down (with words or pictures) how this paradox is impacted by an improved understanding of engagement.	Read over Danielson 1b at each level of the Framework. 1. How are engagement and demonstrating knowledge of students linked? 2. Given your response to question 1, how can you use this link in your classroom? Be able to support your response	Knowing what you know now, with a partner discuss the questions from the start 1. What do you do for fun? 2. How do YOU define *engagement*? **Be sure to note the changes from the initial responses and now.**
Navigating the 3 Cs	**The Matching Game**	**Time to Act**
Read over Danielson 3c at each level of the Framework. Then take the given example and: 1. Determine what this has to do with engagement. 2. Determine the level of that example. 3. Rewrite the example so that it's either one level higher OR one level lower. Be able to support your response	In a Group, attempt to match the "Dutiful Learner" traits with the corresponding "Engaged Learner" traits. Discuss: 1. How these traits may be surprising. 2. List 5 or more conditions needed for learners to become engaged in the classroom.	Read over "4 Practices for Increasing Student Engagement." Create a brief skit to teach others about one of the 4 Practices.
What Do You Think	**Working the Plan**	**2b or Not 2b**
If the highest form of engagement is akin to being absorbed in a task, is it necessary for a student to be engaged in all classes at all times? If so, what would be required? If not, what is an acceptable expectation?	Think about a lesson you have coming up. Using the knowledge gained from this presentation, rework the lesson so you can make at least one change that will lead to increased engagement for your students. What is/are the change(s) and why will this increase engagement for your students?	Read over Danielson 2b at each level of the Framework. Then take the given example and: 1. Determine what this has to do with engagement. 2. Determine the level of that example. 3. Rewrite the example so that it's either one level higher OR one level lower. Be able to support your response.

Directions: Do any the activities below so that you "earn" points. The expectation is that everyone is at least Proficient.

	Tasks	Point Value	Your Points
1.	Back to the Start: Knowing what you know now, with a partner discuss the questions from the start • What do you do for fun? • How do YOU define *engagement*? **Be sure to note the changes from the initial responses and now.**	5 points	
2.	Read and Reflect: Read the text "Have to Learn Vs. Want to Learn." Jot down (with words or pictures) how this paradox is impacted by an improved understanding of engagement.	5 points	
3.	What Do You Think: If the highest form of engagement is akin to being absorbed in a task, is it necessary for a student to be engaged in all classes at all times? If so, what would be required? If not, what is an acceptable expectation?	10 points	
4.	I Know You: Read over Danielson 1b at each level of the Framework. • Determine what this has to do with engagement. • How are engagement and demonstrating knowledge of students linked? • Given your response to question 1, how can you use this link in your classroom? Be able to support your response.	15 points	
5.	Navigating the 3 Cs: Read over Danielson 3c at each level of the Framework. Then take the given example and: • Determine the level of that example. • Rewrite the example so that it's either one level higher OR one level lower. Be able to support your response.	15 points	
6.	Two B or Not Two B: Read over Danielson 2b at each level of the Framework. Then take the given example and: • Determine what this has to do with engagement. • Determine the level of that example. • Rewrite the example so that it's either one level higher OR one level lower. Be able to support your response.	15 points	
7.	The Matching Game: In a Group, attempt to match the "Dutiful Learner" traits with the corresponding "Engaged Learner" traits. Discuss: • How these traits may be surprising. • List at least 5 conditions needed for learners to become engaged in the classroom.	20 points	
8.	Working the Plan: Think about a lesson you have coming up. Using the knowledge gained from this presentation, rework the lesson so you can make at least one change that will lead to increased engagement for your students? What is/are the change(s) and why will this increase engagement for your students?	20 points	
9.	Time to Act: Read over "4 Practices for Increasing Student Engagement." Create a brief skit to teach others about one of the 4 Practices.	30 points	
10.	Choice: I will develop my own task with corresponding point value—I must have this approved before I move ahead.	TBD	
		Your Total	

Tic Tac Toe

Assessment Rubric

Criteria	Struggling	Developing	Proficient	Highly Proficient
1. *Independence*	Even with support, I am not able to do the tasks	Only with support am I able to do the tasks	I am able to do the tasks without support	I am able to do the tasks without support and create and complete my own rigorous task
2. *Accuracy*	Work is completely inaccurate or illegible	Work is mostly inaccurate and/or illegible	Work is mostly accurate and legible	Work is completely accurate and legible
3. *Squares Completed*	0-1	2	3	More than 3

Options to consider if you use this with your students:
1. Leave a space blank and say "Create your own task."
2. Consider ways to integrate multiple intelligences into the options.
3. Allow students the option of modifying any of the tasks to meet their needs/interests/abilities.
4. Put the easiest tasks in the same column or row and the hardest ones in a different column or row so that the tasks are tiered.
5. Have students "play" with each other in pairs.
6. Include an expectation of reflection on learning for each student no matter which options s/he selected.
7. Other

Earning Your Pay

Assessment Rubric

Criteria	Struggling	Developing	Proficient	Highly Proficient
1. *Independence*	Even with support, I am not able to do the tasks	Only with support am I able to do the tasks	I am able to do the tasks without support	I am able to do the tasks without support and create and complete my own rigorous task
2. *Accuracy*	Work is completely inaccurate or illegible	Work is mostly inaccurate and/or illegible	Work is mostly accurate and legible	Work is completely accurate and legible
3. *Points Earned*	0-10	15-30	35 points	More than 35 points

Options to consider if you use this with your students:
1. Have them assign the point values.
2. Consider ways to integrate multiple intelligences into the options.
3. Allow students the option of modifying any of the tasks to meet their needs/interests/abilities.
4. Include an expectation of reflection on learning for each student no matter which options s/he selected.
5. Other

This can be done while the other students are working on their tasks. With this approach, the products from the students are differentiated, but the interventions the students receive are also differentiated.

If I wasn't pulling small groups or individual students, I would be walking around taking anecdotal records on my observations of the students' application of their learning while completing the tasks. This information would guide my future instruction.

Getting to Interest Strategy 2: Make Me an Offer I Can't Refuse

In June 2011, former Target Vice President of Merchandising and Apple Senior Vice President of Retail Operations, Ron Johnson became the C.E.O. of struggling J.C. Penney's. One of his first moves was to drop the prices of the merchandise and discontinue the use of coupons. He was of the belief that it is deceitful to falsely inflate prices so that you can offer a coupon, sale, or other discount later. As Brad Tutle wrote in an article for *Time* magazine's website:

> Johnson thought it made sense to cut to the chase by listing realistic prices from the get-go and foregoing nonstop sales. It does make logical sense, after all. But shoppers aren't purely logical creatures. They're often drawn to stores not by the promise of fair pricing, but by the lure of hunting for deals via coupons and price markdowns. It's all a game, and a contrived one at that. But it's a game that shoppers are accustomed to playing, and that many — consciously or not — like playing, with the "How Much You Saved" line at the bottom of the receipt serving as a score.[54]

In Johnson's approach, rather than the customer needing to game a system, he preferred an approach he called "fair and square." This would allow the shopper to pay the same amount without a coupon that they had paid before when they used a coupon. The amount the shoppers paid was no different without the coupon than it used to be with the coupon. This exemplifies the impact of psychology on why we do what we do. People like feeling like they have come out ahead even if the person in power gets the same result either way.

I learned this strategy from Brian Mendler, a well-known author of books like *Tips for Teachers* and *That One Kid* and presenter on working with difficult children. Brian is now a personal friend of mine, and I have heard him speak numerous times. One of the first times I heard him speak, he shared that when he was a teacher how he would trick the students into doing work. He recognized that most of the time, he did not need the students to answer every question on the worksheet or complete all the questions at the end of the section in the textbook, etc. He also knew that there was power in keeping that secret to himself. Instead, he would say, "There are ten questions on the homework tonight. If it were up to me, I'd have you do all ten. If it's up to you, how many would you assign?" He had a number in his head that he would not go under, but as long as the students said at least the number he had set in his head (or more), he would go along with it.

The students, like the J.C. Penney's shoppers using coupons, felt like they won, and Brian knew all along that he won. If the students did not share a number that was high enough, he would say something like, "Come on, guys! If you're going to throw out numbers like that, then I think I'm going to have to have you do all of them." Most of the time, Brian said, the students would select a number larger than his internal target.

If that is not clever enough, here is the genius twist! Imagine the agreed-upon number of questions the students now need to do is five out of ten. Brian would tell the students to "Choose whichever questions are easiest and do those five." This is not any more work for him to do. He has already given them ten questions to do and looked like a hero because they actually only need to complete half of the questions. Now he is The Best Teacher Ever because he's told his students to do the five ***easiest***.

Here is the con…how will they know which ones are the easiest unless they actually review the questions and metacognitively evaluate each question to determine which ones are more difficult than the others? Of course, you could always tell students to choose the hardest questions. This would be a great way to foster a growth mindset, for example. They could be the trickiest, the shortest, the newest, the best, the quickest, etc. It doesn't matter. Moreover, if you ask the students to explain why they thought those were the _____-est or why they did not choose certain questions, you are obtaining great information to help you help them. This is differentiation at its easiest and best!

Sometimes when I share this idea with some teachers, I am asked, "I have some lazy students who will just do the first five even if I tell them to do the easiest. Now what?" In channeling Brian, I say, "Who cares? You wanted them to do five, and they did. If they decide that they don't care enough to take the time to consider which five would really be the easiest for them, it doesn't matter. They still did the work. It happens choosing the first five was the easiest for those students."

> *Alternate Use:* This concept can be used with adults too. For example, set a meeting time for longer than you will need and end early. Or ask the adults to make parent contacts with the students who are the five _____-est.

Getting to Interest Strategy 3: Choose Your Adventure

Often there are long-term projects that students have to complete. Less often, but not any more difficult, is to provide students with choice in the project they complete that will demonstrate their learning.

An example of a long-term project that has various options to demonstrate learning can be seen from when I taught a seventh-grade poetry unit. Throughout the unit, there were lessons that everyone experienced to establish a consistent foundation, but the project at the end was student-selected (see Figure 13.2). In order to do this, I created seven different project choices. All projects required the students to create a proposal describing what the student wanted to do and their plan for completing the project. There were three deadlines over the course of the project.

There was a deadline for submitting

1. The proposal so I could approve it
2. A rough draft for feedback
3. The final project for a grade

At the end of the unit, each student completed a reflection on the project they did. These were the consistent pieces, but everything else about the project was influenced by their interests. Doing the task was required; what they did was optional.

Assigning long-term projects was something I did commonly, particularly as a way to end the unit. With this, I always included the option for students to create their own task that allowed the students to propose an idea that I did not think to offer. In fact, there were not often students who selected this option, but those who did were generally the most engaged in learning because they felt they had the most voice and choice in the project.

If I did this now, I would have been explicit about the learning standards that were aligned to each project to be sure that even if they were not identical, that both the students and I were aware of what the intended learning was.

Figure 13.2: Differentiated Poetry Unit Project Example

Directions: Create a project of at least three typed pages, double spaced, with one inch margins on all sides using the project choices below. Each project must have the proper heading and be free of grammatical and spelling errors.

PROJECT CHOICES

1.   (a) Write a poem <u>and</u> (b) analyze the poem using as many literature terms as possible (a minimum of <u>5</u>). Then, write a paper telling (c) what inspired you to write that poem, (d) why you chose that poem to analyze, <u>and</u> (e) what you learned by doing this project. Be sure to include a copy of your poem in your paper.

2.   (a) Select a poem by any author <u>or</u> a song by any artist <u>and</u> (b) analyze it using as many literature terms as possible (a minimum of <u>5</u>). Then, (c) write a description of why you chose that poem or song, (d) what you think the meaning of the poem is, <u>and</u> (e) what you learned by doing this project. Be sure to include a copy of the poem or song in your paper.

3.   (a) Memorize a poem <u>or</u> at least 10 lines of a poem. Then, write a paper stating (b) why you chose to memorize that poem or those lines, (c) what you did to learn your lines, (d) what you think the meaning of the poem is, <u>and</u> (e) what you learned by doing this project. Be sure to include a copy of the poem in your paper. You must (f) recite the poem to the class.

4.   (a) Research a poet <u>and</u> (b) write a paper on his/her life <u>and</u> poetry. Then write a paper stating (c) why you chose to research that person, (d) what about the poet's life surprised you, <u>and</u> (e) what you learned by doing this project. Be sure to include two of the poet's poems in your paper.

5.   (a) Write a song to help you learn at least <u>**6**</u> literature terms <u>and</u> write a paper stating (c) how you created the song, (d) what songs and poems have in common, (e) why you chose to sing about those literature terms, <u>and</u> what you learned by doing this project. You must (e) perform your song for the class.

6.   (a) Create an illustrated book of at least <u>**3**</u> poems that have the same theme. Then, write a paper (b) stating why you chose those poems, (c) the relationship of the poems to the pictures, <u>and</u> (d) what you learned by doing this project. Be sure to include a copy of all the poems in your paper.

7.   (a) Create a form of prose (a story) based on a poem (include the poem in your paper). Then, write a paper (a) stating what you think the meaning of the poem is, (b) why you chose the poem on which you based your story, <u>and</u> what you learned by doing this project.

8.   Propose a project not listed above.

Getting to Interest Strategy 4: Vote With Your Feet

Plato said, "Opinion is the medium between knowledge and ignorance." Not everyone is comfortable sharing their opinions, but most people have them. As I'm sure you know, some students love to share their opinions and will be the first kids to raise their hands, and there are those students who sit back and are more observant.

This strategy is one in which students share their opinions through their movement from one end of the room to another. Here, one end of the room is labeled as "Strongly Agree," while the other end is labeled as "Strongly Disagree." At the center point would be "Neutral." In this way, the room becomes a continuum. Someone—it could be the teacher or a student—poses a question or statement that requires people to move to a location on the continuum. The closer they move to the poles of the continuum, the more they agree or disagree with the statement.

Once participants move, the facilitator opens the discussion up so that people can talk about why they selected their position. This can be accomplished in a variety of ways. For example:

- You can have them turn and talk to the person/people closest to them to explain their thinking. In most cases, due to proximity, these conversations tend to be validating. *I'm here, you're right next to me, we pretty much agree or we are identical in our thinking.*

- You can count up the number of participants you have and divide that number in half. Then have the participants count off by half so that they each have a partner that is not like-minded. *I have twenty participants. Half of twenty is ten. Participants will count off by ten and find each other to talk about why they chose their place on the line.*

- You can have the participants make pairs with their reflective counterpart. This means that some of them will have validating conversations because they will be close to each other, and some will have conversations about their differences in opinions. *There are twenty people in the line. The person closest to the Strongly Agree end says, "One," and the person closest to the Strongly Disagree end says, "One." The person next to each of them becomes "two," etc.*

Figure 13.3: Vote With Your Feet Documentation

Directions: I will read you a statement that you will write down. Then you will mark where on the continuum you fall and why. You will have the chance to share your thinking with someone else. Be sure to write down your partner's opinion in the box next to yours.

1. Statement 1:	
Strong Agree---|--Strongly Disagree	
I chose this point on the continuum because...	My partner chose this point on the continuum because...

2. Statement 1:	
Strong Agree---|--Strongly Disagree	
I chose this point on the continuum because...	My partner chose this point on the continuum because...

3. Statement 1:	
Strong Agree---|--Strongly Disagree	
I chose this point on the continuum because...	My partner chose this point on the continuum because...

4. Statement 1:	
Strong Agree---|--Strongly Disagree	
I chose this point on the continuum because...	My partner chose this point on the continuum because...

I would encourage having the students position themselves on the continuum on paper *before* you have them move their feet. This provides think time and reduces groupthink. I would also suggest increasing student accountability by having the students write down what their partner said to them about why s/he selected that point on the continuum. You could also have the students include what their opinion was. Either way, this documentation of their thinking and conversation would be something that the students would turn in (see Figure 13. 3 for a sample of what this could look like). This strategy is best accomplished when you give the students a reasonable amount of time to talk and record thinking but not so much time that they start to have conversations that are unrelated to the topic. I'd give about two to three minutes per partnership. Do not forget to have the students vote with their feet silently as they become human scatterplots, which is one of the most interesting components of the strategy. You can always have the students verbally report out on their conversations. It's also fun to give participants the chance to change their position after speaking with others.

The first time I did this, I remember that one of the statements was, "I believe that if there are unused snow days at the end of the winter, they should be tacked on to Spring Break." If you are from a state that snows, you can appreciate this. If you are not, let me just say that, at least where I'm from, districts have to build in extra days into the school calendar in the event that school needs to close due to inclement weather. Most winters the days are exhausted, but, every so often, there is a day or two that was unused. It is up to the discretion of the superintendent to decide if the schools will remain open for extra days that school year or to use those days in other ways and allow "bonus" holidays. You can imagine that the statement, "I believe that if there are unused snow days at the end of the winter, they should be tacked on to Spring Break," evoked strong opinions. What are statements or questions that would evoke strong opinions in your class?

Generally speaking, this strategy elicits high interest from most students. Here are some additional variations to consider:

- Ask a question as a diagnostic assessment at the start of a lesson or unit to see what the students think before instruction. Provide the students something to read or watch or do that will inform their understanding and then ask the initial question again. Have students note how their opinions changed based on their learning.

- Have students vote with their feet based on how they believe a character or a person in history might respond to the question. For example, if you're studying the American Civil War, make the statement, "If you a Georgian during the Civil War, how would you position yourself on this continuum related to the statement, 'I believe that state's rights were not important to Abraham Lincoln when he was president.'"

- Have students develop questions/statements and use the ones they created.

- Use this as a way to get to know students at the beginning of the year by asking questions about their interests, hobbies, and preferences.

Getting to Interest Strategy 5: My Favorite No

This strategy is inspired by the video of the same name on www.TeachingChannel.org. In the video secondary math teacher, Leah Alcala, uses this strategy as her regular warm-up activity. Before you think that this is a strategy that is only applicable to math, please keep reading as I have no doubt that this strategy can be modified to use at any grade level in any subject.

Alcala explains that this strategy is called "My Favorite No" because she "want[s] the kids to recognize that, first of all, what they're about to see is wrong, and I want them to recognize that there is something good in the problem." There are just a handful of steps.

1. The teacher gives the students a warm-up question and passes out index cards. (You would not need to use index cards—the students could use a sheet of paper or the teacher might even have the problem written out for them on a worksheet or in a virtual platform.)

2. The students do the problem within the set time. (Alcala uses about four minutes.)

3. When the time is up, the students pass in their index cards, and the teacher immediately sorts the answers into two piles—one with the correct answers and one with the wrong answers.

4. Of the wrong answers, the teacher selects one of them to share with the class.

5.   The teacher asks the students to explain what is good about the wrong answer. Then the teacher asks the students to explain why the answer is wrong.

For the record, Alcala shows the students the problem in her own handwriting using a doc cam (although she could also have written it on the board), and then they start by talking about what is good about the math first.

One of the best aspects of this strategy is the timeliness of the feedback to students. "A mistake is your opportunity to share with me how much you understand," Alcala says about her students. "I need to teach you before the test. The test is too late." This is formative assessment at its best, and it is a great way to get students interested in learning.

Watch Leah Alcala model "My Favorite No" at https://cutt.ly/FavoriteNo

If you're not a math teacher, you could still use this strategy. Think of any concept the students are learning. Perhaps in art class, the concept is on gradation. You could ask students to draw shade in four consecutive boxes from light to dark. In chemistry, it could be drawing a molecule. In elementary school, it could be punctuation, spelling, or grammar. The only thing you would not want to do is ask the students questions that require a yes/no or right/wrong answer because then you cannot diagnose why the answer is wrong.

Getting to Interest Strategy 6: Socratic Circles

In most classrooms, if there are discussions between and among students, they are limited to strategies like turn and talk. I am a fan of turn and talk as an easy way to ensure that all students have both the opportunity and accountability to respond to a question/prompt and share their thinking. Nevertheless, turn and talk discussions tend to be brief and, therefore, superficial.

If you're looking for a way to have deeper, extended discussions, consider Socratic Circles (SCs). SCs are a strategy to evoke student discussions that hold students accountable and get students involved as the students talk "long and strong" in response to a topic or prompt. As described by high school teacher Jessica Lander in the article, "Can We Talk,"

> A Socratic circle is not a debate. There are no right answers or winners. No one raises a hand. The learning happens in the ebb and flow of conversation among students, in the process of collaborative thinking. It is a type of discussion that can cultivate the kind of deeper learning…learning that pushes students to sink into material, think critically, and direct their own academic exploration. These are the essential skills students will need for college seminars and study groups, as well as the skills they will need in business and in their roles as engaged citizens.[55]

The goal then is to help students learn how to have evidence-based conversations with others who may not agree with you. If this isn't a skill-set that people need in the 21st Century, I don't know what is.

The most common SCs have a concentric circle configuration (see figure 13.4) with a smaller subset of students arranged in an inside circle with the rest of the students in a circle on the outside. The inside circle students actively participate in the discussion, and the outside circle students act as active observers who monitor the discussion—purposely listening for specific points or conversation behaviors of those in the inner circle (like paraphrasing the speaker, rephrasing the question, providing an alternative point, etc.). Thus, only a portion of the students is actually permitted to speak, thereby giving the remaining students models of what discussion should and should not look like. Ultimately, all students sit in both the inner and outer circle so that they have the ability to be a participant and an observer.

As you can see in Figure 13.4, there are other variations of how SCs can be arranged. There is the large group discussion, which might work well if you have a smaller total number of students. There is also the simultaneous circle configuration, which is good for getting people to share information before a larger SC or when you might have more adults in the room who can help monitor the conversations. I quite like the triad configuration because it creates small teams of students. In this set-up, "the goal of the lesson is to maximize both inquiry and collaboration among all classroom students. Similar in structure to the Inner/Outer Circle variation, the Triad model allows for greater interaction and mobility between the outer circle of students and those in the inner circle."[56]

Figure 13.4: Examples of Socratic Circle Configurations[57]

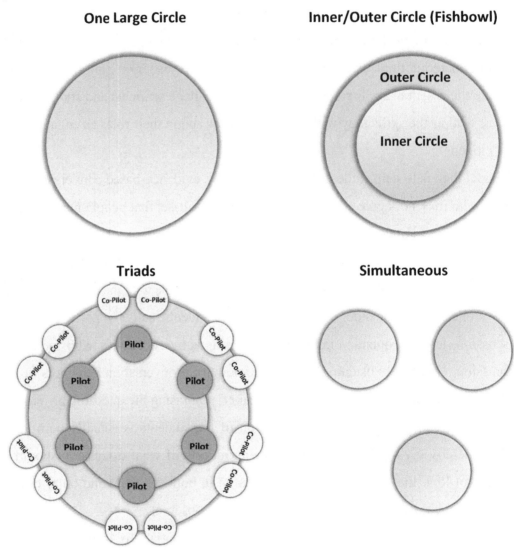

What is the teacher's role in this process? In the beginning, the teacher frontloads a great deal. For example, if the students have never done this before, the teacher would need to explain the roles and responsibilities of the students before the SC even begins. That means helping students to select and assemble what they believe to be the strongest evidence to use during the SC. Also, students may not know how to question each other, or how to do so appropriately. Taking the time to explicitly teach these desired behaviors will be critical to the success of the SCs. The teacher would also want to show the students the graphic organizers that they will use while listening as the outer circle and the scoring approach the teacher will use for the students. I would also encourage reflections from the students after the SC was completed, giving them an opportunity to share (a) globally and (b) personally what they observed, heard, and learned. For the teacher, perhaps the hardest part will be remaining silent and not joining the SC and not rescuing the students when there are awkward silences, lulls, or weaker examples of true conversation. If the teacher is doing the work, the students are not.

At the end of this chapter, please see additional resources, including great examples of student graphic organizers, videos of SCs in action at the elementary, middle, and high school levels, and links to further explanations of SCs.

Getting to Interest Strategy 7: Authentic Audience

In most instances, children don't run home to tell their parents about how they wrote an essay or did a project for their teacher. This is because, more often than not, in these cases, the work is done compliantly for a grade. Even if the learning is meant to be persuasive or informational, the most likely person looking at the final product is the teacher because the product is artificial. Artificial work rarely generates engagement.

I supposed it is not uncommon for students to write a letter to the principal to try to get more recess time or use of cell phones in the cafeteria, etc. This is certainly better than writing for the teacher exclusively. Nevertheless, if you are working on learning something in science or social studies, art or physical education, it might make sense to include professional scientists, historians, artists, or athletes as a possible audience member. Making connections to people outside of the walls of the school ups the ante for the purpose of the task and for putting true effort into doing the task. It's even better if there is the possibility that the person will respond.

Imagine if students wrote to authors of books they are reading rather than writing a book summary or review exclusively for a grade from a teacher? What if, while studying space, students wrote to someone at NASA, tweeted to the International Space Station, or to Elon Musk? When studying conflicts and the country's involvement, ask a veteran to come in to speak and then invite that person back to listen to and participate in a discussion with the students where the students share what they have learned? What about asking students at the end of the unit to create videos that you will share with

Watch "How to Age Gracefully" at https://cutt.ly/CBCAge.

next year's class in which this year's students give advice to next year's kids? This idea is inspired by a video called, "How to Age Gracefully" produced by CBC Radio. This video starts with a 7-year-old child giving advice to a 6-year-old. Then an 8-year-old gives advice to the 7-year-old. The video shows approximately fifteen people who get progressively older until the last person, a 93-year-old, gives advice. It's really inspiring and might be something that your students find great interest in.

I can't talk about an authentic audience without talking about recording videos for YouTube. A July 2019 post on *Business Insider* shared that a survey of 3,000 kids aged 8 to 12 showed that being a YouTuber was more popular for kids in the US and the UK than the other options of being an astronaut, musician, professional athlete, or teacher.[58] If that's the case, why not ask students to demonstrate their learning via YouTube by creating and uploading videos? If they are willing to do it, then your work is not in teaching them how to navigate video production and editing (unless that is your content). Your job is to help them master the content that they will ultimately include in the video. In the same way that children who want to be a musician need to learn how to play an instrument, if a child wants to be a social-media entrepreneur, then they need to have the drive to learn how we can tap into that to create interest in learning.

How Engaged Are You In Learning More?

Looking for even more strategies to use to get your students interested in what they're learning? Please visit my website, www.LyonsLetters.com, for lists and links. In the meantime, here are some that I would recommend.

Further Reading

- ***17,000 Classroom Visits Can't Be Wrong: Strategies that Engage Students, Promote Active Learning, and Boost Achievement* by John V. Antonetti and James R. Garver**

  After doing over 17,000 classroom visits, the authors wrote this book to share strategies that they have seen yield both high levels of interest in students and high levels of student outcomes. This book does an excellent job focusing on learning rather than teaching.

- ***Never Work Harder Than Your Students and Other Great Principles of Teaching* by Robyn R. Jackson**

  Jackson asserts that there are seven principles that "master" teachers have. She explains what these are and then explains how they are used to shift a classroom from teacher- to student-centered. Her point is that the students should be doing the work in the classroom because the work should be done by the one doing the learning.

- ***Teach Like a Champion 2.0: 62 Techniques that Put Students on the Path to College* by Doug Lemov**

  Teach Like a Champion is like a reference book for teaching "techniques" (though others may use the word strategy) that is clearly categorized according to different types of outcomes the teacher may be hoping for. Even better, the book comes with a DVD so that the reader could see most of them in action by real teachers with real students. A word of caution…there are techniques in the book that will generate compliance, not interest. Those tend to be ones under the heading, "Systems and Routines" and "High Behavioral Expectations." Having now read *Engagement is Not a Unicorn (It's a Narwhal)*, you will be able to read through these techniques and spot the ones that are about the relationship/consequence and ones that are about the task.

- *Leaders of Their Own Learning: Transforming Schools Through Student-Engaged Assessment by Ron Berger, Leah Rugen, and Libby Woodfin*

  This book is similar to *Teach Like a Champion* in that it too has a DVD with videos of real teachers with real students using the strategies. I am particularly fond of the chapters "Models, Critique, and Descriptive Feedback" and "Student-Led Conferences." These are relatively easy but under-utilized strategies in schools.

- *AVID Critical Thinking and Engagement: A Schoolwide Approach* **by Paul Bendall, Adam Bollhoefer, and Vijay Koilpillai**

  This book has dozens of engagement strategies, including probably the best descriptions and resources for conducting Socratic Circles. In fact, most information about Socratic Circles referenced in this chapter can be found in Bendall, Bollhoefer, and Koilpillai's book.

- **"Raising Student 'Voice and Choice' is the Mantra. But is it a Good Idea?" by Michelle R. Davis**

  This article explains that too much choice or voice can actually be harmful. Yet, the article contends that appropriate input and options can push students to learn things they need to while helping them do it in ways they want to.

Digital Resources

- **Video: "Socratic Seminar Strategies for the Second Grade Classroom"**

  https://cutt.ly/Socratic

  In this video, Kristi Leader conducts a Socratic Circle with her second-grade students.

- **Video: "Best Practices: Socratic Seminar for Critical Thinking"**

  https://cutt.ly/FairFax_Socratic

  This video, produced by Fairfax Network (Fairfax County Public Schools), highlights upper elementary students participating in a Socratic Circle.

- **Video: "A Socratic Seminar with Brian West of East Hall High School"**

  https://cutt.ly/BrianWest

  This video, shared by EHHSVikingChannel, demonstrates how the room is set-up for the Socratic Circle, including the routines and procedures Brian West uses with his high school students who are seen participating in a Socratic Circle.

- **Video: "Seniors teach Brazilian students how to speak English" by the Chicago Tribune**

  https://cutt.ly/SeniorsTeach

  Karen Larson, Executive Director of Windsor Park Retirement Community in Chicago, is interviewed in this video. The senior citizens in Windsor Park Retirement Community are communicating via the internet with students in Brazil who are learning English. This is a fine example of what an authentic audience can look like.

- **Blog Post: "How to Promote Critical Thinking with Socratic Seminars" by Mari Venturino**

  https://cutt.ly/Mari_Socratic

  In this post, Mari Venturino concisely explains how she has used Socratic Circles with her middle school students. What I like about this post, in particular, is that she includes her prep work and jobs for students during the circle. She also shares a guideline for time buckets, which is really helpful when thinking about doing this for the first time. She uses an approach that is similar to the triad model.

- **Blog Post: "Four Socratic Seminars to Engage High School Students" by Jacque Decker**

  https://cutt.ly/4Socratic

  In this post, Jacque Decker shares with nice explanations how to do a fishbowl, philosophical chairs, simultaneous, and whole-class circle. For each, she describes the process so that teachers could immediately give it a try with their students.

Chapter Summary

This chapter was about moving someone from the point of compliance to interested through a myriad of strategies. Since humans are complex, unique, and unpredictable, not every strategy would be appropriate for every situation. Getting to interested involves higher levels of voice and choice by those who are doing the work. This is because to shift from compliance to interested, a change in the task is needed.

Reflection Prompts

1. Think of a time when you worked with someone who was interested. What idea from this chapter would have assisted attaining this level of engagement?

_____

_____

_____

2. What is a strategy that you have used effectively to shift someone from compliance to interested that wasn't included in this chapter? How was the task altered to achieve that shift?

_____

_____

_____

3. Name one thing you could do tomorrow based on what you learned from this chapter.

_____

_____

_____

4. Of all of the extension suggestions provided, which one intrigued you the most, and why?

_____

_____

_____

5. Tweet me @LyonsLetters to share an idea for a future reading or digital resource I should look into that would help someone who is compliant become interested.

Persistent Questions

1. What have you done so far regarding the three challenge questions from the Introduction?

    a. **Three:** Find at least three people with whom to share your learning.

    b. **Two:** Find at least two ideas that change you.

    c. **One:** Apply at least one idea from your reading.

    _____

    _____

    _____

2. What have you learned so far, and how will you use it?

    _____

    _____

    _____

Chapter 14

Interested: *Now What*

"There's a difference between interest and commitment.
When you're interested in doing something, you do it only when it's convenient.
When you're committed to doing something, you accept no excuses; only results."
~Ken Blanchard

Recognizing Your Thinking Before You Read...

- When thinking about absorption, what behaviors are you hoping to see from students?

  _____

  _____

  _____

- What strategies do you use to foster absorption currently?

  _____

  _____

  _____

- How do you foster a culture of failing forward?

  _____

  _____

  _____

- What is the difference between having a student-centered class and a student-driven class?

  _____

  _____

  _____

From Compliant to Interested

In the "Non-Compliance: *Now What*" chapter, the emphasis was on taking the time to build relationships. By strengthening a relationship, you will consequently discover what motivates those with whom you work. This emphasis was important because shifting from non-compliance to compliance required improving the relationship and/or improving the impact of the external consequence.

When we shift from compliant to interested, we are able to focus our attention on the task. This is why the "Compliance: *Now What*" chapter highlighted ways to increase enjoyment from the task. Much was noted about finding ways to elicit opportunities for options or personalization in the task. The goal of the previous chapter was to create at least momentary engagement in the task so that even though the person doing the task would stop if given the choice, they are enjoying the process and/or task that they have been assigned.

As we think about "Interested: *Now What*" things become difficult to create because, at this level, we are looking to help others do tasks that they do not want to stop doing. This is an extremely tall order. Think of the things that you do not want to stop doing. How many of them were introduced to you without your initiation? Probably not many. Therefore, rather than thinking about creating tasks that people crave, this chapter will focus on how to nurture the state of and foster the traits that lead to absorption. This means that students are participating in learning that they would not need grades for; they would "pay" to do this work, and they will work on it even if they didn't have to. Doing this task would be challenging for students, and yet they will persist. If that's what we want from our students, then we owe it to them to persist in creating the space for this to happen.

The Light at the End of the Tunnel

If you think about the "What" and "So What" chapters on absorption, you will recall there was a great deal written about hobbies. This is because our hobbies are things that we make time for and find resources to support. Rather than an expectation of compensation for the hobby, there is an expectation of a cost to do it. It is reasonable to question how that would work with what you're trying to do with students in a school if you teach a core content area, for example. In this case, you might be thinking, *what am I supposed to do to create a more hobby-like environment in my classroom? My course/class is required and has standards that I need to teach.* Fair enough. Some things are "must-dos." Nevertheless, there are also ways to make "must-dos" as engaging as possible.

That said, for most of us, making "must-dos" interesting is the best we can do. This is why those things that are not "core" but are "above and beyond," like art, music, physical education, clubs, athletics, technology integration, school plays, student council, and the like are so important. These non-core items can be the reason why some of our students come to school. Even for students who are interested in school, things like recess, band, reading with younger students, internships, and so forth are not just things they are willing to do, but things they seek out and want to do.

Schools should be interesting places where our students see themselves as willing participants, professionals, or strategists in their learning. We also want schools to be absorbing places where students can cross the threshold and become a novice in something they're really passionate about or even find a new identity because they now see themselves as an actor, an athlete, or a musician. What's more, even scientists, mathematicians, historians, and writers all have things they do on-the-side that have nothing to do with their profession that give them joy. The takeaway here is that we must find ways for schools to allow students to explore things that are not tested, that do not have grades, and tap into curiosity that feeds the human desire to find flow.

The book, *Unbroken: A World War II Story of Survival, Resilience, and Redemption* by Laura Hillenbrand is a biography about Louie Zamperini, an Olympic distance runner and a prisoner of war during World War II. Zamperini was not just a good runner, he was a great runner who set a national collegiate record for the mile in 1938 with a time of 4 minutes 8.3 seconds—a record that stood for fifteen years. What's just as fascinating is that his behaviors in and out of school were not great. At fourteen, he figured out that his house key could also get him into the back door of his high school's gym. He used this knowledge to allow his friends to sneak into basketball games without paying. When he was caught, his principal banned him from being able to

participate in afterschool activities, including social and athletic events. Though he had not previously participated in these things regularly, his brother, Pete, recognized Louie's talents and saw athletics as a way to improve Louie's focus. In the excerpt below, you can see how Pete confronted the principal. How many Louie's do you have in your class or school? What are the things that are taken away in the pursuit of compliance that could be championed in pursuit of engagement?

When Pete learned what had happened, he headed straight to the principal's office. Though his mother didn't yet speak much English, he towed her along to give his presentation weight. He told the principal that Louie craved attention but had never won it in the form of praise, so he sought it in the form of punishment. If Louie were recognized for doing something right, Pete argued, he'd turn his life around. He asked the principal to allow Louie to join a sport. When the principal balked, Pete asked him if he could live with allowing Louie to fail. It was a cheeky thing for a sixteen-year-old to say to his principal, but Pete was the one kid in Torrance who could get away with such a remark, and make it persuasive. Louie was made eligible for athletics for 1932.[59]

Managing Expectations

By far, this chapter was the hardest to conceptualize, and I got to a point when I thought that my work on engagement was bogus because I started to question if absorption in schools was indeed a unicorn. I'm sure that there are those who are reading this even now and wondering the same thing. If you're one of these people, you may be expecting to find strategies in this chapter that you have never even dreamed of before that will blow your mind. Let me manage your expectations and tell you that this is probably not going to happen. These strategies are not mind-blowing; they're student empowering. These are strategies that will challenge you to do what George Couros and Katie Novak refer to as "innovate inside the box," in their book by the same name.

We all want to feel a sense of purpose in our work, but we can't count on others to create that for us. We can't even always count on people or policies to support us in our efforts to do what best serves our individual learners. The most natural response to a roadblock is to stop and turn around. I want to challenge you to *Innovate Inside the Box* instead. Rather than backing up or stalling out, look for another way around the problem. Your final solution may look very little like your original idea, but that's okay! I always lead with my purpose of doing what's best of each learner to drive decisions.[60]

Couros and Novak are trying to get readers of their book to think about what they can do given the parameters in which they work. In the same vein, the real goal of my book is not to share mind-blowing strategies, but to share mind-*changing* understandings about what engagement really is so that you can think differently about what you're doing and what you want your students to do.

In talking to others about absorption, I am often asked if I think that absorption is the expected level of engagement for every student for every lesson every day. You may be wondering the same thing. If you've read the "Absorbed: So What" section of this book, you already know my answer. Nevertheless, let's reframe this question. Rather than is it possible for every student…ask, would it be possible for you? If you went back to school, would it be possible for you to lose yourself in every lesson every day if you were the student? Would you do the work if you knew that you didn't get a grade or that not doing it wouldn't negatively impact your grade?

Though I am very curious and love learning, I am not intrinsically compelled to learn about everything, nor have I met anyone who would be. That's because we all have things that we are more captivated by than others, even in the best situations. Since being absorbed requires a desire to do the task for the intrinsic joy of doing the task— not the grade, not avoiding the punitive consequence, and not to please someone else— I do not believe that we should aim for absorption for every student for every lesson every day. That doesn't mean that we should lessen our expectations of the interested level for every student for every lesson every day, but we need to manage our expectations around absorption.

Thus, if you are reading this chapter because you want to increase absorption in your classroom, I think that's great! However, as you dive into these waters, I ask you to reflect on your classroom as it is right now. Are all of your students at the interested level yet, or do you have some students who are still non-compliant and compliant? The Engagement Continuum is just that, a progression from one level of engagement to another. As I have repeatedly said, we should expect that we move from one level to the next highest and celebrate that as a victory. Nevertheless, trying any of these strategies will benefit all students and may have some students leap from lower levels of engagement to the highest, but do not be discouraged with yourself or them if they do not make it all the way to *absorbed*. Be happy that they are on their way!

Given this, I like to use what Dave Burgess calls "TWO QUESTIONS FOR RAISING THE BAR" in his book, *Teach Like a Pirate* to best understand absorption.

> **Question one: If your students didn't have to be there, would you be teaching to an empty room? Question Two: do you have any lessons you could sell tickets for?**[61] (emphasis in original)

The power in these questions is that it reminds us that absorption means that students will keep going even if they didn't have to and even when told to stop. It means doing the task is the compensation because they are intrinsically compelled to do it. It means that someone would spend their own resources (time, money, etc.) doing the task even when they could be doing something else instead. If this is the expectation for absorption, what are you going to do to get the students to achieve that bar? The answer is not in a single strategy or even a combination of strategies, but in your beliefs about your students and yourself.

Give It A Try

Over the next several pages are some strategies that you can use when trying to shift from *interested* to *absorbed*. *Interested* was about doing the task for another person while getting temporary enjoyment. *Absorbed* is about doing the task for me because I enjoy it on my own time. These strategies are designed to make doing the task the compensation. You will know that the students are absorbed because they will continue doing the work even when they can stop and even if there was no grade.

Before we get to the strategies, though, I need to point out that in the prior two "Now What" chapters, the strategies were fairly straightforward in that they asked the teacher to more or less *do* something different. This chapter, however, is premised on more than just actions, but thoughts; this chapter requires the teacher to *think* differently. You cannot create a classroom where absorption happens just by building relationships or increasing accountability, and you can't get there by having some interesting discussions or by choice or voice alone. Absorption means someone is compelled to do the work, and that means that this is something they want to do, they get to do, and they will do even when told they can stop. Absorption is a really high bar to establish and reach. This is why the strategies below are not really ones that you can try tomorrow. Even if you already have a student-centered environment where students are taken into account, the goal would be to create a student-driven environment where students take the lead. Elements like the following create an environment and culture that promote absorption:

- Celebrate failure

- Believe that the one doing the talking is the one doing the learning

- Find ways for authenticity

- Create flexibility in process, product, or content

This is why the first "strategy" below is more about helping the teacher establish a mindset for absorption rather than the traditional strategies found in previous chapters or other books.

Getting to Absorbed Strategy 1: Authentic Learning

When I was in the fifth grade, and we did our science fair projects, we were able to choose to create a project around anything we wanted. I chose to do something about the layers of the earth. Honestly, I didn't care what I learned about; for me, it was about the chance to make a model using clay. When we read our word problems in math, the problems were directly from the textbook and were just a means to practice the application of the math. Though there's nothing inherently wrong with either of these things, they were missed opportunities.

In school, many students wonder the proverbial question, "When will I use this anyway?" This is parodied in the comic below from the *Divergent Learning* article, "Real World Learning."[62] I can't imagine anyone being okay with the idea that students

would leave school without practical skills. Yet, schools so often look like sit-and-get places where assessment is almost exclusively paper-pencil.

When we seek answers to authentic problems, i.e., problems that exist in the world and not from the textbook—we can see the learning from the text and other resources as a means to solve problems. This orientation is the opposite of how traditional instruction happens. In traditional instruction, students are told the information and then presented with problems which have them apply the learning. If we start with authentic problems, we present the problem and learn through the pursuit of understanding the problem.

"Another principle of authentic learning is that it mirrors the complexities and ambiguities of real life," as explained under the "Authentic Learning" entry from EdGlossary.org.[63] The entry continues, "On a multiple-choice science test there are 'right' answers and 'wrong' answers determined by teachers and test developers. But when it comes to actual scientific theories and findings, for example, there are often many potentially correct answers that may be extremely difficult, or even impossible, to unequivocally prove or disprove."

Figure 14.1: Benefits of Authentic Learning[64]

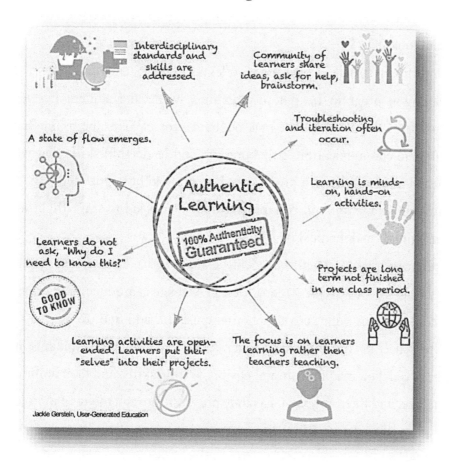

The crux of authentic learning[viii] is to set up and step back—or the notion that the teacher's job is to create the conditions for the students to discover the learning that will help them understand what is unknown. Though this is not common in schools, the benefits are numerous (see Figure 14.1). One of the best outcomes of authentic learning is initiative. Rather than students waiting to do tasks assigned by the teacher, the students are active agents looking for answers to questions they have.

[viii] I want to make a critical point here before diving into how to use authentic learning with students. Notice that I'm choosing to use the term "authentic" and not the phrase "real world" (although you can find information about both "authentic learning" and "real world learning" that is identical). Though some may say that these terms are synonymous, for me, authentic suggests that this is what happens in a professional setting or outside of a controlled classroom environment. Real world, on the other hand, can be insulting to students because it can be (and often is) used to minimize the experiences that students have. Strictly speaking, the opposite of real is fake, and what happens in our students' lives is certainly real, and what they do in school should be too.

Since authentic learning can take many forms, and there is no one right way to approach it, below are several verbatim examples from Wikipedia of what authentic learning can look like.[65]

- **Simulation-Based Learning:** Students engage in simulations and role-playing in order to be put in situations where the student has to actively participate in the decision making of a project. This helps in "developing valuable communication, collaboration, and leadership skills that would help the student succeed as a professional in the field he/she is studying." Learning through simulation and role-playing has been used to train flight attendants, firefighters, and medical personnel, to name a few.

- **Student-Created Media:** Student-created media focuses on using various technologies to "create videos, design websites, produce animations, virtual reconstructions, and create photographs." In addition to gaining valuable experience in working with a range of technologies, "students have also improved their reading comprehension, writing skills, and their abilities to plan, analyze, and interpret results as they progress through the media project."

- **Inquiry-Based Learning:** Inquiry-based learning starts by posing questions, problems, or scenarios rather than simply presenting material to students. Students identify and research issues and questions to develop their knowledge or solutions. Inquiry-based learning is generally used in field-work, case studies, investigations, individual and group projects, and research projects.

- **Peer-Based Evaluation:** In peer-based evaluation, students are given the opportunity to analyze, critique, and provide constructive feedback on the assignments of their peers. Through this process, they are exposed to different perspectives on the topic being studied, giving them a deeper understanding.

- **Working with Research Data:** Students collect their own data or use data collected from researchers to conduct their own investigations.

- **Reflecting and Documenting Achievements:** The importance of metacognition in the learning process is well-documented. Giving students the opportunity to reflect upon and monitor their learning is essential. Journals, portfolios, and electronic portfolios are examples of authentic learning tasks designed to showcase the student's work as well as give the student a means to reflect back on his/her learning over time.

Authentic learning is not the only approach that positions the learners as the doers. Examples of other approaches include:

- **Personalized Learning**: Katrina Stevens, former Deputy Director and Senior Advisor for the Office of Educational Technology in the United States Department of Education, defined personalized learning as "instruction in which the pace of learning and the instructional approach are optimized for the needs of each learner. Learning objectives, instructional approaches, and instructional content (and its sequencing) may all vary based on learner needs. In addition, learning activities are made available that are meaningful and relevant to learners, driven by their interests and often self-initiated."[66]

- **Experiential Learning**: Rhodes Wellness College described experiential learning as "the process of learning through participation rather than by listening to a lecture or reading about a topic."[67]

- **Activity-Based Learning**: In the Dictionary for 21st Century Teachers, activity-based learning is listed as learning where "'students do public service, fieldwork, community-based research and internships in conjunction with in-class work. ABL pedagogy aims to enrich students' academic experience and learning outcomes by connecting theory with practice, and concepts with methods, using data and insight they obtain through engagement with the larger world.'"[68]

- **Challenge Based Learning:** According to The Challenge Institute, challenge-based learning is "collaborative and hands-on, asking all participants (students, teachers, families, and community members) to identify Big Ideas, ask good questions, identify and solve Challenges, gain in-depth subject area knowledge, develop 21st-century skills, and share their thoughts with the world. The Challenge Based Learning framework emerged from the 'Apple Classrooms of Tomorrow— Today' (ACOT2) project initiated to identify the essential design principles of the 21st-century learning environment."[69]

(Please see the end of this chapter for further reading and resources to learn more about these different approaches).

Regardless of the name of the approach, the purpose is quite similar—to ensure that the students are active agents in both what they are learning and how to demonstrate what they have learned. This is more than just student-centered; it's student-driven, meaning there is relevance to the students for their work.

Finally, I want to share Steve Revinton's list of observable behaviors (see Figure 14.2) that result from student-driven learning experiences. His list specifically mentions authentic learning, but these would be applicable to any learning in which absorption was occurring. As well, this list is not all-inclusive but a great compass to know if you're headed in the right direction.

Figure 14.2: "Student Behaviours When Immersed in Authentic Learning"[70]

When your class is engaged in a properly designed authentic learning event see if these behaviours are occurring.

- Are the students deliberately engaged because they are immersed in meaningful activities that provides major connections to their world?

- Is there a sense of freedom and creation in their individual pursuits?

- Is there a heightened pride in the collective team event goal?

- Is your student's genuine curiosity peeked and are you observing prolonged bouts of concentration.

- Are you seeing tendencies in students, who are normally disorganized and disconnected to school papers, now being more concerned for them?

- Are the students engaged in dialogue that refer to outside world?

- Is there a spark of excitement or urgency in your student's questioning?

- Do you have to remind your students that it's time to go for recess, lunch or home?

- Do you find that certain students with absentee problems are starting to show up more regularly?

- Are you experiencing less behaviour problems?

These are some of the signs that your students are significantly engaged in activities of relevant, authentic learning.

Getting to Absorbed Strategy 2: Create a Safe Place to Try (and Fail)

Since absorbing tasks have a high challenge before there is success, there will be failure. The easiest way to kill the possibility of absorption in a classroom is to punish failure. Why? If failure is penalized, then that means that risk and challenge need to be eliminated or at least minimized. After all, if I have to be perfect, then the work I do has to be easy since perfection doesn't happen right away (if ever) with things that are difficult. Remember what I said earlier about video games? We get bored playing a game we always win since it's too easy. We expect to fail a level several times before we can move on. The same should be true in a classroom.

> I once worked with a leader who gave a great deal of lip service to growth mindset and criticized teachers who were not allowing their students to do more than sit and listen to lectures. At the same time, this leader was someone who was quick to condemn teachers who tried something new and struggled. The talk about having a growth mindset was just that, talk. The reality was that risk was only rewarded if you could guarantee success. That translates to avoiding risk, not taking it. In order to truly foster risk-taking, the environment must focus as much or more on the process and the learning; the product is secondary.

Creating an environment that honors learning and creates safety to take risks is actually easy. What's hard is living that yourself. Here are some tips from the 2016 Colorado Teacher of the Year Leticia Guzman Ingram's Edutopia post, "A Classroom Full of Risk Takers."[71]

- CELEBRATE PERSEVERANCE
  Jean Russell, an elementary school teacher from Indiana, said her class puts a marble in a jar when students persevere. That includes trying different strategies to read a new work, solve a math problem, rewrite a sentence, or work out a difference with a friend. The marbles mean that when each student sticks with learning, the whole class benefits. "When the jar gets full, we have a perseverance party!" Russell said.

- SHARE YOUR MISTAKES

  Several teachers lead by example. Arizona's Christine Porter Marsh admits her own mistakes and talks about them. "I'll say, 'You were right. I was wrong.'" She also tells her classes that it's OK to be wrong during discussions: "I'd rather have you contribute and be wrong than not contribute." Topher Kandic of Washington, DC, demystifies the role of the teacher as an all-knowing sage by reading new texts with students and predicting how stories will turn out—often getting it wrong, but showing students that it's OK to make mistakes.

- ALLOW RETAKES

  To encourage thinking and exploring ideas, Ernie Lee of Georgia says he allows retakes of assignments and tests. "The grade is important, but the main goal is for them to be able to think and to know the material." And he makes sure that whether students agree or disagree with him, they back up their comments with well-thought-out ideas to support their answers.

- DISCOVER 'THE POWER OF YET'

  Teachers can model desired behaviors in all aspects of teaching, including how to handle a mistake and move forward, says Natalie DiFusco-Funk of Virginia. Most important, teachers can communicate how to learn from mistakes and do things differently next time. As a teacher, she says, "I use the phrase 'the power of yet.'" It means—for her personally and for her students—that just because they can't do something yet doesn't mean they can't do it.

- FAILURE FRIDAYS

  That's right. Failure Fridays. This idea comes from Diane McKee of Florida. Each Friday, McKee shows movie clips of famous people like J.K. Rowling, Michael Jordan, or Oprah Winfrey sharing stories about how they experienced failure before going on to succeed. It's one of her students' favorite activities.

In addition to these suggestions, I also find Patricia Calton Buoncristiani's use of the phrase "Have a go," to support risk. She writes, "In my classroom there was no shame in 'having a go' and getting it wrong. In fact, most times the child didn't get it entirely wrong. Almost always some part was right and I would highlight that so the child would be confident to take a risk next time."[72] When a child in her classroom says, "I need help" or "I can't do this," Buoncristiani responds with, "Have a go." My guess is that as a result, she eventually has more students saying, "I've had a go of this, and I'd like some feedback on my attempt" than students who say, "I can't do this."

Alternate Use: These same strategies would be valuable if used by an administrator. Imagine if teachers were told, "Have a go," or if the administrator sent out video clips or quotes about risk-taking and failure? What impact would that have on the culture in the building/district?

Getting to Absorbed Strategy 3: Innovation Experience

Even though we're already one-fifth of the way through the 21st Century, we are still working on integrating 21st Century skills into our classrooms. There are twelve skills that are associated with this, as shown in Figure 14.3. Being able to identify these skills is one thing; being able to teach them in such a way that creates absorption is something else. This is where the Innovation Experience comes in.

Figure 14.3: The Twelve 21st Century Skills[73]

Learning Skills	Literacy Skills	Life Skills
1. Critical Thinking 2. Creativity 3. Collaboration 4. Communication	5. Information Literacy 6. Media Literacy 7. Technology Literacy	8. Flexibility 9. Leadership 10. Initiative 11. Productivity 12. Social Skills

Lewiston Porter Middle School teacher and adjunct college professor, Nina Calarco, collaborated with her then-principal, Dr. Dean Ramirez, to design an integrated, ungraded, full-year elective for their eighth-grade students that would create ways to engage students in their preparation for high school and beyond. Figure 14. 4 shows the five major components around which the IE is built. As you can see, the 21st Century Skills are embedded into the work.

Figure 14.4: The Innovation Experience Components

Component	21st Century Skills	Example
Book Study	1, 4, 5	Texts read or considered for future reading include: • Donald T. Phillips' *Lincoln on Leadership* • Ryan Hyde's *Pay it Forward* • Carol Dweck's *Mindset: The New Psychology of Success* • John C. Maxwell's *The Maxwell Daily Reader*
Community Photo Essay	1-2, 4-12	Students independently chose a community that they were able to visit over the summer and then researched that community's history and culture then presented as if they were real estate agents
Honing Problem-Solving Skills	1-5, 8-9	Students visited a real escape room and used kits from Breakout EDU kits (www.breakoutedu.com)
Research Project	1-12	Students chose a topic on their own that had some purpose in their lives, formulated a research question, and found a way to present their findings
Capstone Presentation	4, 8-9, 12	Students presented their research projects at a local university to their families, college students, professors, and administrators

In the spring of their seventh-grade year, students are formally told about the possibility of participating in IE with a small presentation about what it is. Parents are then invited to an informational parent meeting. The IE begins over the summer with the students reading that year's book independently. Students meet in person one or two days before the start of the year to discuss the book using a workshop approach in addition to the virtual interactions using Google Classroom. During this time, there is a very strong focus on trying to create a culture of curiosity and responsible risk-taking. It is also over the summer that the Community Photo Essay is assigned. This allows the students to do their visitations and start their research.

When school starts in the fall, students meet once per week with the teacher, generally in groups of eight to ten. The teacher is given some flexibility in her schedule by the principal but also uses her planning periods to accommodate these small groups. The teacher and students provide feedback to each other on their photo essays. By mid-fall, students present their work to their groups, and the students evaluate their success and select one member of their group to present to the other groups. All IE students come together for an afternoon to hear the selected group members present and give feedback and reflect on their learning.

In the winter, students go to a local university to see college students present. The students debrief their observations and discuss takeaways to apply to their own presentations. This is also the time when they begin working on their Genius Hour projects that expose students to a variety of new technologies that they can use in their projects. These have included Scratch (coding), Makey-Makey, Hummingbird Robotics, and green screen video editing. All of the technology is introduced through mini-lessons with the goal of purposeful integration into the work rather than for isolated novelty.

From mid-winter through early spring, students spend several months on their research projects—selecting a topic, formulating a question, working on their pitch, reflection blogging, and revising their work. At the end of the year, students go back to the local university to showcase their work.

One of the most fascinating features of the Innovation Experience is that it is optional and ungraded. IE students do more work than their non-IE peers, yet they value the work they are doing. In fact, over the history of the IE, each year, more and more students elect to participate.

Though the Innovation Experience (IE) was designed for eighth-grade students, it is not limited to any one grade level. You are certainly able to replicate it as described here. You are also able to customize the project for your own setting. If possible, see if there are other schools or teachers who are willing to collaborate with you in this endeavor, which has been an evolution of Calarco's work, having now extended to multiple districts creating a consortium around the IE.

Getting to Absorbed Strategy 4: Competition for Learning

Have you ever played a game but, before you had a chance to finish, time ran out? How did you feel? If you were into the game, I'm going to bet that you didn't respond with, "That's okay" and quietly walked away without protesting. In fact, you were probably frustrated and wished that you could finish what you started.

If you're already thinking that competition breeds haves and have-nots or winners and losers, you are actually twisting the intention. As Ashley Merryman, co-author of the book *NurtureShock* clarified in an interview, "How Competition Affects Your Brain," competition originally meant cooperation. Merryman explains, "the benefit of competition isn't the win. The benefit of competition is improvement…In the moment, competition improves your performance because if you see what someone else does, it's not about tearing them down, it's about saying, 'Is there more I can do that I didn't even realize?'"[74]

This explains why the students in the PBS documentary video *Inventing Tomorrow* were so driven. This documentary showed students from around the world as they prepared for and competed in the annual Intel International Science and Engineering Fair. Participants commit to a year researching and creating a project—one that requires them to use resources outside of the school day and curriculum. Rather than being annoyed by this, the students are absorbed. Their learning has relevance, is rigorous, and provides an intrinsic return on their investment.

Certainly, you can create a competition within your own classroom, school, or district. The more the competition is student-driven, the more likely the students are to become absorbed. In other words, a small competition like creating a jeopardy game will probably lead most students to be interested. On the other hand, a larger competition like a debate can create higher levels of engagement—particularly if the students have to prepare for the debate over time and are permitted to select what the debate topics could be. There are also innumerable competitions that already exist, so you would not have to create your own. The website, studentcompetitions.com, is a one-stop resource to find existing competitions (see the end of this chapter for more student competition resources). Rather than selecting one *for* your students, you could consider having students find and select a competition they would be interested in.

Now-college student, Miguel Bautista, competed in the International Student Science Fair (ISSF) his senior year of high school. He explains the impact this had on him—both in terms of what he learned and how this opportunity impacted how he saw learning.

During my senior year, I had the opportunity to participate in the ISSF in Singapore. ISSF is a competition where students, in various areas of scientific studies, bring together the culmination of their research into a presentation and research paper. In essence, ISSF is a platform to share discoveries while competing with other likeminded students. I had never done anything like it and initially, the very thought made me queasy. I mean, I had barely been outside the country much less flying over 24 hours away to present to brilliant professors and peers.

Under the supervision of my science teacher, Michelle Hinchliffe, my team decided to research the use of green leafy vegetables for the natural abatement of nitrate and phosphate. What struck me soon after starting was that the success or failure of the project was completely on us; this was not like chemistry or physics class, where the labs were structured and the results were certain. We had to gather our own data in a quantitative way that is uncommon for your typical science lab in order to extrapolate accurate conclusions. While the inherent uncertainty of it all was disconcerting at first, I grew to love the idea of it. The multi-faceted nature of the experiment was alluring; there were seemingly endless questions to answer. How would changing surface area affect absorption? What are the correlations between these variables? What if we grew the samples in the contaminated water? It was this very pursuit of answering these questions that drove me to work harder on the project. As opposed to working hard just for the sake of getting a good grade, like in my high school coursework, this research allowed for a breadth of creativity. Combined with the inherent competition between others presenting their environmental research, my ambition and drive to do the best I possibly could was fueled.

In a general sense, the analytical, research, and public speaking skills I gained through my participation in ISSF have permeated into my collegiate experiences as well. As someone who aspires to be an entrepreneur or a successful businessman, being able to present your ideas clearly and concisely is essential. Furthermore, my experiences researching and hearing brilliant people at ISSF, while being at the forefront of scientific exploration and discovery, stands above all my other memories and I would jump to have another opportunity like that.

Getting to Absorbed Strategy 5: Goals (Not Grades)

Imagine that you go to the doctor, and s/he notices that there is an issue that you should be working on. For the sake of this analogy, let's say it's your weight. Your doctor, using the guidelines generated by the Center for Disease Control, identifies that you need to lose twenty pounds. Here's the hitch—the doctor never tells you the goal. What's more, the doctor's goal for you is enough to get you from the most dangerous category ("Morbidly Obese") to the next category ("Obese"). But, if you had known this information, you would have set a different goal because, you figure, if you were going to go to the trouble of developing a better lifestyle, you would want to get to a healthy weight category ("Normal").

It seems absurd that a doctor would create a goal for a patient without communicating the goal, how it was identified, and/or including the patient in the process. Yet, this is exactly what happens in classrooms daily where teachers do this for students. The teacher has in mind goals for the students but does not tell the students what the goal is and, even when the teacher does, the students are rarely involved in the goal-setting process. However, which are you going to care more about, a goal that someone else has created for you or a goal that you created for yourself? The answer is easy.

When talking about student-developed learning goals (SDLGs), I want to be explicit that I am not talking about grades. Grades are not learning. "Unfortunately, grades are generally an account of points earned through various activities that are influenced by artificial deadlines, grade inflation, extra credit, and subjectivity," wrote Brad Kuntz, the 2011 ASCD Outstanding Young Educator winner. He continues, "It's time for us to change the student mind-set currently focused on reaching a particular percentage and instead empower them to take charge of their learning and measure their own success."[75] Think about it. If a student can earn a higher grade by bringing in a box of tissues or turning in an assignment early, what does that show about the learning of the content? Thus, when talking about SDLGs, we must steer students towards goals that are rooted in what they hope to learn and how they will be able to demonstrate that learning.

In truth, though it is easy to find information on goal setting outside of the classroom, it is not easy to find examples of what it looks like for students inside the classroom. In fact, much of what you can find about goal setting in the classroom is simply having students be able to interpret the teacher-created learning targets in the students' own words. While that is important, that is also not what I'm talking about since what I'm referring to would be a goal developed *by* the student—not a goal developed *for* the student.

So if SDLGs are not goals about getting certain/better grades and they are not translations of the learning targets, what are they? SDLGs are goals that students create for themselves about the upcoming learning based on data about their previous learning successes and struggles.

This process starts with the teacher identifying the major learnings for the upcoming unit or lesson. After all, if the students are not given some upfront information about what to expect from the content, their goals could not connect to the content they are studying. During this step, the teacher's job is to preview the learning and present some possible SDLGs, ideally categorized by the types of successes and struggles observed from the students in their prior learning and/or by anticipating possibilities based on the teacher's (a) knowledge of the content or (b) experiences in teaching this to students in the past.

Once students have a sense of what the unit or lesson will be about, the students should have a chance to review their successes and struggles from prior learning experiences. Students can do this one-on-one with the teacher, independently, and/or by partnering students in order to push each other's thinking.

Based on the data and the upcoming learning, students should be able to develop their own learning goals. This will require explicit coaching from the teacher initially because this will be new for the students. Many people use the "S.M.A.R.T. Goal" format to do this. S.M.A.R.T. stands for Specific, Measurable, Attainable, Realistic (or Reasonable), and Time-Bound. The problem I have found with S.M.A.R.T. Goals is that even adults struggle to respond with clarity to these categories. What's the difference between attainable and realistic, for example.

I prefer Jim Knight's "P.E.E.R.S Goal" format, which is actually designed for use with a teacher but can be easily adapted for use with students, as shown in Figure 14.5. You can see the differences between the original and adapted by noting the underlined words. Knight emphasizes the importance of the goal being emotionally compelling because if someone isn't moved to do the work, the work won't get done. This is certainly linked to Keene's research on the impact of emotional resonance on engagement mentioned in the Absorbed: *So What* chapter.

Figure 14.5: Original and Adapted P.E.E.R.S. Goal

Components	Original P.E.E.R.S. Goal[76]	Adapted P.E.E.R. Goal
Powerful	Makes a big difference <u>in children's lives</u>.	Makes a big difference <u>in current and future learning</u>.
Easy	Simple, clear, and easy to understand.	Simple, clear, and easy to understand.
Emotionally Compelling	Matters a lot to the <u>teacher</u>.	Matters a lot to the <u>student</u>.
Reachable	Identifies a measurable outcome and <u>strategy</u>.	Identifies a measurable outcome and <u>plan</u>.
Student-Focused	Addresses a student achievement, behavior, or attitude outcome.	N/A

With the P.E.E.R. goal format I've outlined in the right column of Figure 14.5, students create an outcome and identify a plan to use in order to achieve that outcome. This is part of the goal-planning process. In other words, it is not enough for the student to say, "I want to get better in math." The "R" (Reachable) portion of the goal means the student has to identify what "better" means and how they will attempt to improve. To assist students in thinking through this, a teacher could ask questions like these that were created by Jen Bradshaw, author of the blog TeacherKarma.com and the inspiration for the goal-setting steps outlined for this strategy:[77]

- Why did you choose that particular goal?

- What can you do to achieve your goals?

- Is there anything you can do during class to learn better?

- Is there anything you can do at home?

- Have you learned any strategies in class that could help?

- What do you notice about other students that are doing well?

- What skills are you already good at doing?

In the book, *The 4 Disciplines of Execution*, authors McChesney, Huling, and Covey, write about the law of diminishing returns, stating that the fewer goals one has, the more likely one is to achieve those goals. "Your chances of achieving 2 to 3 goals with excellence are high, but the more goals you try to juggle at once, the less likely you will be to reach them."[78] For this reason, it is best to have one to three powerful goals instead of multiple goals that cannot be achieved.

Now that the student has data-based learning goals with measurable outcomes and a plan to achieve the goals, the student needs a way to track progress. This should provide the student with a means to visually see improvement, stagnation, or regression. Also, progress monitoring is best when it is simple to do and simple to interpret. *The 4 Disciplines of Execution* use the concept of a scoreboard in a sport. At-a-glance, the players can peek at the scoreboard and know a wealth of information—how much time is left, who's ahead, possible penalties, etc. The purpose of the tracker is to provide information relevant to the progress that can be gleaned in an instant.

Visit https://cutt.ly/7best to see seven different goal setting apps students can use

Finally, it is important to celebrate the progress and ultimate attainment of the goal. While it is fine to receive a tangible acknowledgment in the form of a certificate, for example, for accomplishing the goal, the celebration should reinforce intrinsic motivators and minimize or avoid extrinsic rewards like class parties. In fact, the student could identify how they would like to be celebrated as part of the goal-setting process. Suggestions for possible intrinsically-aligned celebrations could include things like the chance to call their parents to tell them about their accomplishments, additional responsibilities, additional complexity of a future task, and/or additional independence.

 ***Getting to Absorbed Strategy 6: Genius Bar***

If you are someone with an Apple device, what happens if you need to have your device serviced? You go to the Apple Store's Genius Bar. It's a tech support site within an Apple Store. Now imagine you're a student in a school that provides you with a device. Where do you go if you need support? In most schools, you probably have to find an adult who will create some type of service ticket where another adult will provide the IT support.

Burlington High School in Massachusetts is not most schools. Rather than adults providing the tech support, students do it. In the article, "Student-Run Genius Bar: The Facilitator's Guide," Wong, Aher, and Scheffer explain how students and staff work together to position students as experts while they gain transferable and practical skills they can use in the moment and beyond. Students who work in the school's "Genius Bar," also known as the BHS Help Desk, are actually enrolled in a 2.5 credit-bearing, semester-long course. For one period a day, the students report to the BHS Help Desk and learn how to provide tech support, as well as, develop an "individualized learning endeavor" and learn how to "leverage social media and blogging platforms. They explain:

> Read the article about the BHS Help Desk at https://cutt.ly/BHShelpdesk

> We expect students to be self-driven, independent, and capable of managing multiple projects, just as they would be if they were in the workplace. We encourage them to take initiative and devise an independent learning path centered on technology. Help desk students do this by developing an individual learning endeavor (ILE), our version of a 20-percent time Genius Hour project.

> One such ILE project was the artificial intelligence (AI) chatbot pilot program that we implemented in the spring and summer of 2018. ISTE had

approached us about our interest in participating in this program, which covered the basics of using Amazon Web Service's Lex and Lambda tools to create a chatbot. Lex is essentially the "intelligence" behind the Alexa smart speaker, and Lambda allows you to create and run additional code that uses Amazon's servers and integrates with your chatbot.

During help desk, senior Gati Aher headed a team that researched and developed a chatbot that could assist users with basic tech support questions. She presented her work at ISTE 2018 in Chicago.[79]

The BHS Help Desk is a win-win. Students who participate are absorbed in the learning because it is contextualized and immediate. As well, the school community benefits because the devices in need of support can be addressed on-site in a timely fashion.

How Engaged Are You In Learning More?

Looking for even more strategies to use to get your students absorbed in what they're learning? Please visit my website, www.LyonsLetters.com, for lists and links. In the meantime, here are some that I would recommend.

Further Reading

- *Teach Like a Pirate* **by Dave Burgess**

  This book doesn't just share ideas and strategies related to creating absorbing classrooms and lessons, it underscores the importance of doing so. Burgess, a former secondary social studies teacher, describes things he did when he was in the classroom that will make you wish you were in his room and wonder, "why didn't I think of that."

- *Innovate Inside the Box: Empowering Learners Through UDL and the Innovator's Mindset* **by George Couros and Katie Novak**

  If you feel like you'd love to try something that you've read or heard about but also feel like you're unable to do it because of external constraints, this book will challenge you to rethink your obstacles. Couros and Novak will push your thinking without pushing you away, giving you great ideas and inspiration to take into your school today.

- *How to Personalize Learning: A Practical Guide for Getting Started and Going Deeper* **by Barbara Bray and Kathleen McClaskey**

  Personalized learning can definitely feel like a unicorn if you're unsure of what you need to do in order to help each of your students achieve their highest potential. This book is exactly what it says it is…a how-to that helps teachers understand personalized learning and how to create the conditions for students.

- *The Relevant Classroom* **by Eric Hardie**

  Curious about some user-friendly ways to make your classroom more relevant and find ways to integrate authentic learning? This book shares six "steps" to help you achieve that goal. I appreciate that Hardie acknowledges that his book is not a panacea, but a recourse for achieving deeper learning.

- **"Moving from Education 1.0 Through Education 2.0 Towards Education 3.0" by Jackie Gerstein**

  This sixteen-page chapter originally published in *Experiences in Self-Determined Learning* does a fantastic job of talking about the evolution of education—specifically with an eye on the shift from teacher-driven (1.0) to student-centered (2.0) to student-driven (3.0) education. There are also helpful visuals to support the text.

Digital Resources

- **Article: "How to Make Your Teaching More Engaging" by Joyce Hesselberth**

  https://cutt.ly/MoreEngaging

  This article, published on *The Chronicle of Higher Education* website, gives support to why engagement matters, four principles of engagement, and suggestions on how to put those principles into practice.

- **Website: "Make Learning Personal"**

  http://kathleenmcclaskey.com/

  This website has countless resources for creating personalized learning for students.

- **Website: "Authentic Learning"**

  http://authenticlearning.weebly.com

  If you want to learn more about authentic learning, Steve Revington's website is an outstanding place to look. This website is not just vast, but user-friendly and chocked-full of great ideas, visuals, and samples of student work.

- **Blog Post: "Modern Trends in Education: 50 Different Approaches to Learning"**

  https://cutt.ly/50Approaches

  This post on the TeachThought blog not only delivers on its title, but it also provides links to additional explanations with many of the fifty approaches it lists. There are probably at least one to two things listed here that you may not have heard of.

- **Blog Post: "The Big List of Student Contests and Competitions" by Ruth Lyons**

  https://cutt.ly/contests

  In this post, on weareteachers.com, there are over fifty student contests for students of all ages and additional links to find even more contests and competitions.

- **Post: "Experiential Learning Definitions" by Mohawk College**

  https://cutt.ly/Experiential

  This post on the Mohawk College website explains six guiding principles and provides definitions related to experiential learning. There is also a strong visual of examples of experiential learning and work-integrated learning. Also on this website, there is a video that quickly summarizes the why, how, and benefits of experiential learning.

- **Post: "Experiential Learning" by The University of Tennessee Health Science Center**

  https://cutt.ly/THSC

  This website does a nice job explaining what experiential learning is with a helpful visual to show how experiential learning cycles through concrete experiences, reflective observations, abstract conceptualization, and active experimentation.

- **Infographic: "The Value of Experiential Learning" by Rhodes Wellness College**

  https://cutt.ly/RWC

  If you are a visual learner or work with those who are, "The Value of Experiential Learning" infographic is made for you. This infographic explains experiential learning with benefits, how it works, etc.

- **Infographic: "What is Experiential Education" by The Association for Experiential Education**

  https://www.aee.org/what-is-ee

  The infographic, "What is Experiential Education," concisely summarizes the four key components of experiential education, including (1) adventure and challenge, (2) observation and reflection, (3) abstract thinking, and (4) application to life.

- **Video: "Authentic Learning" by Shakipee Digital Learning**

  https://cutt.ly/SDL

  This video shows teachers and students talking about what authentic learning is and what the students gain from this process.

- **Video: "School Should Take Place in the Real World" by Trevor Muir TEDx San Antonio**

  https://cutt.ly/Muir

  Muir explains how his school has found ways to offer students opportunities to link the learning that takes place in the school with the things taking place outside of the school. Muir gives specific examples of how some of his students have done this and challenges the viewer to do the same.

- **Video: "Solving Real-World Problems: Bringing Authentic Context to Learning" by Edutopia**

  https://cutt.ly/TRPCS

  In this video, students in Two Rivers Public Charter School that serves students in grades kindergarten through eighth grade are highlighted as they speak about how the authentic problem-solving approach enhances their learning and their engagement in learning.

Chapter Summary

This chapter was about moving someone from the point of interested to absorbed through a myriad of strategies. Since humans are complex, unique, and unpredictable, not every strategy would be appropriate for every situation. Getting to absorbed involves the time and space to lose yourself in the work. This also necessitates a shift from extrinsic consequences to internal; a shift from teacher-centered to student-driven.

Reflection Prompts

1. Think of a time when you worked with someone who was absorbed. What role did the authority play in this? What role did the individual play?

_____

_____

_____

2. What is a strategy that you have used effectively to shift someone from interested to absorbed that wasn't included in this chapter? Were there consequences for doing or not doing the task?

_____

_____

_____

3. Name one thing you could do tomorrow based on what you learned from this chapter.

_____

_____

_____

4. Of all of the extension suggestions provided, which one intrigued you the most, and why?

_____

_____

_____

5. Tweet me @LyonsLetters to share an idea for a future reading or digital resource that I should look into that would help someone who is interested become absorbed.

Persistent Questions

1. What have you done so far regarding the three challenge questions from the Introduction?

    a. **Three:** Find at least three people with whom to share your learning.

    b. **Two:** Find at least two ideas that change you.

    c. **One:** Apply at least one idea from your reading.

_____

_____

_____

2. What have you learned so far, and how will you use it?

_____

_____

_____

Section V: Conclusion

*T*his is the last chapter and brings to a close Engagement is Not a Unicorn (It's a Narwhal). It has been a long journey from the beginning to end, and the hope is that not only was the journey worth it, but that you are changed as a result. What's more, that you're ready, willing, and able to take what you have read and see what it looks like in your school.

Chapter 15

Do It

"If you want something you can have it, but only if you want everything that goes with it, including all the hard work and the despair, and only if you're willing to risk failure."
~ Philip Pullman

Recognizing Your Thinking Before You Read...

- In your own words, what does it mean to be a unicorn versus a narwhal?

  _____

  _____

  _____

- How has your understanding of engagement changed as a result of reading this book?

  _____

  _____

  _____

- Now that all is said and done, what have you learned? What will you do?

  _____

  _____

  _____

What?

This book started with the idea that there was a lack of agreement on what engagement in the classroom was. One person identified on-task students as engaged while another person might have said that on-task students were not engaged. The range of what qualified as "engaged" was vast, and disagreement abounded.

Even worse, some people are so disengaged with learning that they can't imagine that being absorbed in school is possible. When told that not only is there a way to uniformly identify engagement, but that there is a level of engagement that is so high that students are compelled to learn (and have to be told to stop), skeptics think that this is a mythical state—the engagement unicorn. Their experiences, either as a student or a teacher, were those that honored compliance and so there was no joy of learning.

I disagree, and I hope you do too. Engagement is not abstract or out-of-reach. It's a narwhal. Very much real and very possible if you know what to look for and how to create the conditions. The Engagement Framework lays out the four distinct markers of engagement so that once you understand where someone is on The Engagement Continuum, you can help create a rightward shift by understanding the Engagement Matrix variables. And, with that, now you understand the what, so what, and now what regarding engagement.

So What?

In Chapter 3, "The Engagement Framework: Now What," I invited you to read with a purpose. As a reminder, there were three action-oriented purposes:

- **THREE**: Before you read, identify at least three people with whom you will share ideas you're having as a result of your reading. It doesn't matter who you will share your ideas; it just matters that you will share.

- **TWO**: As you're reading, find at least two ideas that change you…it may be because you are surprised or unsure or validated. It doesn't matter why you change; you're just noting the change.

- **ONE**: When you're done reading, apply at least one idea. Don't limit yourself to a professional application; it could just as easily be a personal one. The point is that you do more than just read and think about engagement—it's that you take what you've read and thought and do something with it.

How'd you do? What have you learned, and what will you do about it? It's not enough to change your thinking—your actions need to change too.

Maya Angelou said, "Do the best you can until you know better. Then when you know better, do better." In other words, we should not beat ourselves up for not doing something as well in the past as we know how to do in the present. Further, we should always implement our new understandings once we gain them, as it is wrong to keep doing what we've always done when we are now wiser and better-equipped. I use Angelou's quote so often that some people have wrongly attributed it to me. Nevertheless, we must hold ourselves accountable for doing better even if the thing that is better is harder to do.

Now What?

One of my other favorite sayings is, "You can't unring that bell," meaning you have heard, seen, or imagined something that you will never forget. You are changed. It was my goal to create change by sharing The Engagement Framework so that you would never again be fuzzy about what engagement is. I also wanted to be sure that you knew what you could do to help yourself and those you work with to increase engagement.

If you recall, also in Chapter 3, I wrote about Jim Knight's invitation to send him a postcard to tell him about how the work changed from those who attended his presentation. With that in mind, I invite you to send me an email at lyonletters@outlook.com. Please tell me about how this book impacted you. What actions have you taken as a result of reading this book?

Do It!

Thomas Jefferson urged us to, "Never put off till tomorrow what you can do today." Arthur Ashe guided us to, "Start where you are. Use what you have. Do what you can." Karen Lamb encouraged us with, "A year from now you may wish you had started today." Winston Churchill cautioned us that, "Perfection is the enemy of progress." Nike simply told us, "Just do it!"

Trust me, I know what it's like to read something for the purpose of making change only to find myself back where I started because life takes over. I also know that when

I make even a small commitment and see it through, that feels like a big win. You can do this.

Trust me, I know what it's like to want to do something that sounds like it might be easy, but it's harder than I thought. That's how I started writing this book. Despite the fact that I love to write, writing this was not always easy. At this point, you know that doing something hard is actually an important feature of engagement. Since I am engaged with engagement, even when it was hard, I persisted. I felt like I had something to say about engagement that hadn't yet been said, and I wanted to get it on paper. Even if no one ever read this book besides my mom and friends, I was truly compelled to write it. And, if I can write this book, you can try to do something you read in it. You will do it not because it is easy, but because you are up for the challenge!

Though it was much harder than I expected it to be, the act of writing *Engagement is Not a Unicorn (It's a Narwhal)* has changed the way I see the world. I find myself sharing The Engagement Framework with more people than I ever imagined because engagement touches nearly everything we do. I hope that you agree.

References

Chapter 1

[1] Walter. (2015, January 28). Schlechty's levels of classroom engagement [INFOGRAPHIC]. Retrieved from https://mrmck.wordpress.com/2015/01/28/schlechtys-levels-of-classroom-engagement-infographic/

Chapter 4

[2] Warren, E. (2016, January 6). Learning specialist and teacher materials - Good sensory learning. Retrieved from https://learningspecialistmaterials.blogspot.com/2016/01/maximize-learning-keeping-students-in.html

[3] Warren, E. (2016, January 6). Learning specialist and teacher materials - Good sensory learning. Retrieved from https://learningspecialistmaterials.blogspot.com/2016/01/maximize-learning-keeping-students-in.html

[4] Schlechty, P. C. (2002). *Working on the work: An action plan for teachers, principals, and superintendents*. San Francisco, CA: Jossey-Bass.

[5] Schlechty, P. C. (2002). *Working on the work: An action plan for teachers, principals, and superintendents* (p. 3). San Francisco, CA: Jossey-Bass.

[6] Lefrançois, G. R. (1997). *Psychology for teaching* (9th ed.). Belmont, CA: Wadsworth Publishing Company.

[7] Heinz dilemma. (2018, October 25). Retrieved from https://en.wikipedia.org/wiki/Heinz_dilemma

[8] King, M. L., Jr. (1963, April 16). Letter from a Birmingham Jail. Retrieved from https://www.africa.upenn.edu/Articles_Gen/Letter_Birmingham.html

Chapter 5

[9] Lipton, L., & Wellman, B. (n.d.). Update article: From obligation to opportunity: Teacher supervision that improves student learning. Retrieved from https://awsa.memberclicks.net/obligation

[10] Blanchard, K., Zigarmi, P., & Zigarmi, D. (2013). *Leadership and the one minute manager updated ed: Increasing effectiveness through situational leadership* (p. 15-16). New York, NY: William Morrow.

Chapter 7

[11] The Franklin Institute. (n.d.). Edison's lightbulb. Retrieved from https://www.fi.edu/history-resources/edisons-lightbulb

[12] Csikszentmihalyi, M. (1990). *Flow: The psychology of optimal experience* (p. 4). New York: Harper & Row.

[13] Csikszentmihalyi, M. (1990). *Flow: The psychology of optimal experience* (pp. 3-4). New York: Harper & Row.

[14] Gerson, K. (2014, June 8). *Benchmarking the change process: Where are we now?* Address presented at July Network Team Institute in New York, Albany.

[15] Duckworth, A. (n.d.). Q&A. Retrieved from https://angeladuckworth.com/qa/#faq-125

[16] Cherry, K. (2018, September 28). Understanding intrinsic motivation. Retrieved from
    https://www.verywellmind.com/what-is-instrinsic-motivation-2795385

[17] Csikszentmihalyi, M. (1990). *Flow: The psychology of optimal experience* (p. 75). New York:
    Harper & Row.

[18] Butler, S. (Trans.). (2013, April 9). *The odyssey*. The odyssey, by Homer.
    http://www.gutenberg.org/files/1727/1727-h/1727-h.htm

Chapter 8

[19] Habit 5: Seek first to understand, then to be understood. (n.d.). Retrieved from
    https://www.franklincovey.com/the-7-habits/habit-5.html

[20] Orwell, G. (1983). *1984* (p. 274). Houghton Mifflin Harcourt.

Chapter 9

[21] Zmuda, A., & Jackson, R. R. (2015). *Real engagement: How do I help my students become
    motivated, confident, and self-directed learners* (p. 15-16). Alexandria, VA: ASCD.

[22] Goldson, E. (n.d.). Speech. Retrieved from http://americaviaerica.blogspot.com/p/speech.html

[23] Goldson, E. (n.d.). Speech. Retrieved from http://americaviaerica.blogspot.com/p/speech.html

[24] Lefrançois, G. R. (1997). *Psychology for teaching* (9th ed.). Belmont, CA: Wadsworth
    Publishing Company.

Chapter 10

[25] Morell, Z. (n.d.). Introduction to the New York State next generation early learning standards.
    Retrieved from http://www.nysed.gov/common/nysed/files/introduction-to-the-nys-early-
    learning-standards.pdf

[26] Marzano, R. J. (2003). *What works in schools:Translating research into action*. Alexandria,
    VA: ASCD.

[27] Appleton, J. J., Christenson, S. L., & Furlong, M. J. (2008). Student engagement with school:
    Critical conceptual and methodological issues of the construct. *Psychology in the
    Schools,45*(5), p. 378. o

[28] Freire, P. (200). *Pedagogy of the oppressed: 30ᵗʰ anniversary edition* (M.B. Ramos, Trans.) (p.
    72). New York, NY: Bloomsbury Academic, an imprint of Bloomsbury Publishing.

[29] Freire, P. (200). *Pedagogy of the oppressed: 30ᵗʰ anniversary edition* (M.B. Ramos, Trans.)
    (pp. 71-72). New York, NY: Bloomsbury Academic, an imprint of Bloomsbury
    Publishing.

[30] Freire, P. (200). *Pedagogy of the oppressed: 30ᵗʰ anniversary edition* (M.B. Ramos, Trans.) (p.
    81). New York, NY: Bloomsbury Academic, an imprint of Bloomsbury Publishing.

[31] Danielson, C. (2016). *Talk about teaching!: Leading professional conversations* (p. 36).
    Thousand Oaks, CA: Corwin.

[32] McKay, C. B. (2013). *You don't have to be bad to get better!: A leader's guide to improving
    teacher quality* (p. 50). Thousand Oaks, CA: Corwin.

[33] Knight, J. (2017, October 4). *The coaching cycle and the partnership principles: Day 1*.
    Lecture, Amherst, NY.

[34] Lencioni, P. (2002). *The five dysfunctions of a team: A leadership fable* (pp. 102-103). San
    Francisco, CA: Jossey-Bass.

[35] Lencioni, P. (2002). *The five dysfunctions of a team: A leadership fable* (pp. 203-204). San
    Francisco, CA: Jossey-Bass.

[36] Knight, J. (n.d.). Accountability and autonomy. Retrieved from
https://www.winginstitute.org/uploads/docs/Accountability and Autonomy.pdf

Chapter 11

[37] First day of school vs second day of school. (2014, August 14). Retrieved from
https://imgur.com/gallery/yDPYa91

[38] Gee, J. P. (2007). *What video games have to teach us about learning and literacy* (p. 2).
Basingstoke, England: Palgrave Macmillan.

[39] Gee, J. P. (2007). *What video games have to teach us about learning and literacy* (p. 222).
Basingstoke, England: Palgrave Macmillan.

[40] Gee, J. P. (2007). *What video games have to teach us about learning and literacy* (p. 58).
Basingstoke, England: Palgrave Macmillan.

[41] Keene, E. O. (2018). *Engaging children: Igniting a drive for deeper learning, K-8* (p. 58).
Portsmouth, NH: Heinemann.

[42] Keene, E. O. (2018). *Engaging children: Igniting a drive for deeper learning, K-8* (p. 61).
Portsmouth, NH: Heinemann.

[43] Keene, E. O. (2018). *Engaging children: Igniting a drive for deeper learning, K-8* (p. 62).
Portsmouth, NH: Heinemann.

[44] Marzano, R. J., Pickering, D. J., & Heflebower, T. (2011). *The highly engaged classroom* (p.
4). Bloomington, IN: Marzano Research Laboratory.

[45] Tips from Dr. Marzano. (n.d.). Retrieved from
https://www.marzanoresearch.com/resources/tips/hec_tips_archive

[46] Jackson, R. R. (2009). *Never work harder than your students & other principles of great
teaching* (p. 80). Alexandria, VA: Association for Supervision and Curriculum
Development.

[47] Goldberg, D. E. (2012, October 12). Student-centered versus student-led education. retrieved
from https://threejoy.com/2012/10/12/student-centered-versus-student-led-education/

[48] Bray, B., & McClaskey, K. (2016, June 19). Personalize learning. Retrieved from
http://www.personalizelearning.com/search?q=stages

Chapter 12

[49] Dueck, Myron. (2014). *Grading smarter not harder: Assessment strategies that motivate kids
and help them learn* (p. 65). Alexandra, VA: ASCD.

[50] Dueck, Myron. (2014). *Grading smarter not harder: Assessment strategies that motivate kids
and help them learn* (pp. 65-66). Alexandra, VA: ASCD.

Chapter 13

[51] Constantino, S. M. (2008). *101 ways to create real family engagement* (p. 128). Galax, VA:
ENGAGE! Press.

[52] Research spotlight on home visits. (n.d.). Retrieved from http://www.nea.org/tools/16935.htm

[53] Couros, G., & Novak, K. (2019). *Innovate inside the box: Empowering learners through Udl
and the innovators mindset* (p. 46). Place of publication not identified: IMPress.

[54] Tuttle, B. (2013, April 09). The 5 big mistakes that led to Ron Johnson's ouster at JC Penney.
Retrieved from http://business.time.com/2013/04/09/the-5-big-mistakes-that-led-to-ron-
johnsons-ouster-at-jc-penney/

[55] Lander, J. (2017, January 28). Can we talk? Retrieved from
https://www.gse.harvard.edu/uk/blog/can-we-talk

56 Bendall, P., Bollhoefer, A., & Koilpillai, V. (2015). *Avid critical thinking and engagement: A schoolwide approach* (p. 253). San Diego, CA: AVID Press.

57 Bendall, P., Bollhoefer, A., & Koilpillai, V. (2015). *Avid critical thinking and engagement: A schoolwide approach* (p. 248). San Diego, CA: AVID Press.

58 Leskin, P. (2019, July 17). American kids want to be famous on YouTube, and kids in China want to go to space: Survey. Retrieved from https://www.businessinsider.com/american-kids-youtube-star-astronauts-survey-2019-7

Chapter 14

59 Hillenbrand, L. (2014). *Unbroken: A World War II story of survival, resilience and redemption* (p. 13). New York: Random House.

60 Couros, G., & Novak, K. (2019). *Innovate inside the box: empowering learners through UDL and the innovators mindset* (pp. xxxii-xxxxii). Place of publication not identified: Impress.

61 Burgess, D. (2012). *Teach like a pirate* (pp. 56-57). San Diego: Dave Burgess Consulting, Inc.

62 Real world learning. (2016, November 27). Retrieved from https://divergentlearning.wordpress.com/2016/11/27/real-world-learning/

63 Authentic learning definition. (2013, September 16). Retrieved from https://www.edglossary.org/authentic-learning/

64 Experiential learning. (n.d.). Retrieved from https://usergeneratededucation.wordpress.com/tag/experiential-learning/

65 Authentic learning. (2018, August 12). Retrieved from https://en.wikipedia.org/wiki/Authentic_learning#Characteristics

66 What is personalized learning? (2018, July 4). Retrieved from https://medium.com/personalizing-the-learning-experience-insights/what-is-personalized-learning-bc874799b6f

67 The value of experiential learning. (2018, February 6). Retrieved from https://www.rhodescollege.ca/infographic-value-experiential-learning/

68 Heick, T. (2018, August 12). A dictionary for 21st century teachers: Learning models. Retrieved from https://www.teachthought.com/learning/learning-models-learning-theories-index/

69 About. (2018). Retrieved from https://www.challengebasedlearning.org/about/

70 Revington, S. (n.d.). Student behaviours when immersed in authentic learning. Retrieved from http://authenticlearning.weebly.com/planning.html

71 Ingram, L. G. (2017, September 14). A classroom full of risk takers. Retrieved from https://www.edutopia.org/article/classroom-full-risk-takers

72 Buoncristiani, P. C. (2018, January 22). Encouraging a culture of responsible risk taking. Retrieved from http://inservice.ascd.org/encouraging-a-culture-of-responsible-risk-taking/

73 Applied educational systems, Inc. (n.d.). What are 21st century skills? Retrieved from https://www.aeseducation.com/careercenter21/what-are-21st-century-skills

74 How competition affects your brain. (2017, October 6). Retrieved from https://heleo.com/conversation-how-competition-affects-your-brain/16689/

75 Kuntz, B. (2012, May). *Focus on learning, not grades*. http://www.ascd.org/publications/newsletters/education-update/may12/vol54/num05/Focus-on-Learning,-Not-Grades.aspx

76 Knight, J. (2018). *The impact cycle: What instructional coaches should do to foster powerful improvements in teaching*. Thousand Oaks, CA: Corwin.

[77] Bradshaw, J. (2014, October). Teaching your students to set their own goals is just a smile away with this freebie! Retrieved from http://www.teacherkarma.com/2014/10/__trashed-12.html

[78] McChesney, C., Covey, S., & Huling, J. (2016). *The 4 disciplines of execution: Achieving your wildly important goals*. New York, NY: Free Press.

[79] Wong, L. R., Aher, G., & Scheffer, J. (2019, May 30). Student-run genius bar: the facilitator's guide. Retrieved from https://www.iste.org/explore/In-the-classroom/Student-run-genius-bar:-The-facilitator

Made in the USA
Middletown, DE
15 September 2021